IN THE FOOTSTEPS OF POPE JOHN PAUL II

IN THE FOOTSTEPS OF POPE JOHN PAUL II

An Intimate Personal Portrait by His American Friend

John M. Szostak
with Frances Spatz Leighton

Prentice-Hall, Inc.
Englewood Cliffs, New Jersey

Art Director: Hal Siegel
Book Designer: Susan J. Kuppler

IN THE FOOTSTEPS OF POPE JOHN PAUL II:
An Intimate Personal Portrait by His American Friend
by John M. Szostak with Frances Spatz Leighton
Copyright © 1980 by John M. Szostak and Frances Spatz Leighton

Printed in the United States of America

Prentice-Hall International, Inc., London
Prentice-Hall of Australia, Pty. Ltd., Sydney
Prentice-Hall of Canada, Ltd., Toronto
Prentice-Hall of India Private Ltd., New Delhi
Prentice-Hall of Japan, Inc., Tokyo
Prentice-Hall of Southeast Asia Pte. Ltd., Singapore
Whitehall Books Limited, Wellington, New Zealand

10 9 8 7 6 5 4 3 2

Library of Congress Cataloging in Publication Data

Szostak, John M
    In the footsteps of Pope John Paul II.

    Includes index.
    1. John Paul II, Pope, 1920–   2. Popes—Biography. 3. Szostak, John
M., date I. Leighton, Frances Spatz, joint author. II. Title.
BX1378.5.S95   282'.092'4 [B]   80-20258
ISBN 0-13-476002-6

This book is dedicated to my mother,
Jennie Szostak,
and to my two sons,
Eric, nine,
and Thomas, seven,
to whom I will leave my most precious possessions—
the gifts and personal letters to me of Pope John Paul II,
both before and after his elevation to the pontificate.
I could not give my sons a
more inspiring start in life.

Contents

Acknowledgments

Many individuals have given their time and knowledge to help make this book possible and come to life before the reader. I give special thanks to those people in Poland and the Vatican who wish to remain anonymous. They and others listed here have been of invaluable assistance in providing the unique material that will make this book interesting reading and serve as a valuable reference to future scholars studying the life of Pope John Paul II.

Rev. Philip S. Majka, northern Virginia
Rev. Stanley F. Milewski, chancellor, St. Mary's College, Orchard Lake, Michigan
Rev. Walter Ziemba, director of the Pope John Paul Center for Research, Orchard Lake, Michigan
Msgr. Valerian Jasinski, Orchard Lake, Michigan
Msgr. Zdzislaw Peszkowski, Orchard Lake, Michigan
Msgr. Alojzy Orszulik, Warsaw, Poland
Bishop Jozef Glemb, Warsaw, Poland
Bishop Bronislaw Dąbrowski, Warsaw, Poland
Bishop Sczepan Wesoly, Vatican
Wladyslaw Cardinal Rubin, Vatican
Rev. Stefan Kośnik, Warsaw, Poland
Rev. Jozef Liczkowski, Warsaw, Poland

Rev. Henry J. Piszkalski, Washington, D.C.
Archbishop Andrzej Maria Deskur, Vatican
Msgr. Janusz Bolonek, Vatican
Msgr. Marian Jakubiec, Krakow, Poland
Msgr. Adam Boniecki, Vatican
Rev. Kazmierz Przydatek, Vatican
Msgr. Jozef Michalik, Vatican
Rev. Pelka Florian, Vatican
Franz Cardinal König, Vienna, Austria
Msgr. Tadeusz Rakoczy, Vatican
Sergio Cardinal Pignedoli, Vatican
Stefan Cardinal Wyszynski, Warsaw, Poland
Franciszek Cardinal Macharski, Krakow, Poland
Silvo Cardinal Oddi, Vatican

Secular
Dr. Anna-Teresa Tymieniecka, Boston, Massachusetts
W. H. Bninski, Washington, D.C.
Hon. Thaddeus Buczko, Boston, Massachusetts
Gordon Peters, Boston, Massachusetts
Stanislaw Glabinski, Polish Press Agency (PAP)
Lucjan Mieczkowski, Press Counselor of the Polish Embassy,
Washington, D.C.
Count Stanislaw Grocholski, Veritas Foundation, London,
England
Jerzy Turowicz, Krakow, Poland
Dr. Jerzy Gatkowski, Academic Assistant of Cardinal Wojtyla
Dr. Jerzy Kloczowski, Professor at Catholic University of
Lublin (KUL)
Franciszek Wicher and Maria Morda, butler
and housekeeper of then Cardinal Wojtyla at the Episcopate
Palace
General Sikorski Institute, London, England

Special Acknowledgments

A special word must be said here to acknowledge the help of a woman who is no longer with us, Ruth Brod, the literary agent for this book. It was she who had the foresight to see the importance and unusual material of this book and who urged me to proceed with all possible speed, while certain events were still fresh in my mind.

It was a great sorrow that this wonderful woman did not live to see the final chapter finished. But I'm sure she somehow knows now.

I also wish to acknowledge the fine editorial help of two other women—Dorothy Berger and Kaye S. Becker. They too shared the emotions of this book as it was in progress and were not ashamed to shed tears at some of the sadder moments and to burst into laughter at some of the humorous moments.

Photo Credits

The photos for this book come from many sources. Snapshots came to me from many clerical friends in Poland and in the United States. Some came from Polish friends of the Pope in the Vatican. Some came from President Carter's very fine personal photographers, including Karl Schumacher. And some came from the Pope's personal photographers, who are among the greatest lensmen of the world and who are called Felici, after the original papal photographers, the Felici brothers, who lived almost a hundred years ago.

Introduction

*T*o claim Pope John Paul II my friend cannot be considered my singular honor alone, but an honor that I share with many people throughout the world. Pope John Paul II has touched thousands, perhaps millions, of lives.

But to be one of the relatively few who walked with him, talked and laughed with him, and absorbed his advice is something I will cherish forever.

Not only did I have adventures with the Pope—both as Pope and as cardinal—but I have talked with many people about him throughout the years, and all of these stories I want to record now to share with those who love him and with history, which will determine, long range, the quality and humanness of the Pole who became Pope.

History will have the final answers, but in 1978 and 1979 and 1980, he was the man who had electrified the world.

People keep asking me how I got so lucky as to meet

a Pope and become friendly with him. I keep explaining that he was a long way from a Pope when I met him, but that he was a very special man for as long as I have known him.

My acquaintance with the man who is now the successor to St. Peter came naturally via my longtime involvement in Eastern European affairs and my correspondence with the Catholic episcopate in Poland going back to the early sixties. This was when I was working at the White House under John F. Kennedy, dealing with ethnic affairs.

As a matter of fact, I wrote various speeches and statements for the president for delivery before Polish and other Slavic-language groups. I was then also a night student, majoring in foreign affairs at Georgetown University.

I have had the good fortune to meet many extraordinary people from all walks of life, but when I met Cardinal Wojtyla and walked with him a while, I began to feel there was something different. It was almost mystical, if that is the proper word to define the strange aura.

Whatever it was, my response to it was a good feeling—almost joyful. October 16, 1978, all my feelings about the man were suddenly understood. Strange things had come to pass, and it was clear that the Lord had singled him out.

Had wanted him to walk in the shoes of the Fisherman.

I am proud to say I knew him when—I mean at a time when he was so obscure by international standards that on his visit to America as a cardinal in 1976 he was snubbed by some of his own brother clergy, who were the innkeepers of the twentieth century.

John M. Szostak

IN THE FOOTSTEPS OF POPE JOHN PAUL II

1

A Man Like Any Other Man— With a Certain Difference

When a great moment of history takes place, people cannot stop talking about it and they look at each other and ask, "Where were you when such and such occurred?"

I remember very well, Monday, October 16, 1978—a dreary day because of rain, a perfect day to stay home. With Congress in recess and the President at Camp David with Israel's Begin and Egypt's Sadat, still trying to hammer out a peace agreement, I did just that, stayed at home and worked. After taking it easy for part of the day, I decided to go into town to take care of a few errands.

I went to Old Town Alexandria rather than Washington, D.C., since it was closer to my home. This was about 2:30 P.M. Along the way I indulged my passion for historic objects and stopped in one antique shop for a quick look around. Suddenly, my ear caught the tail end of a broadcast. ". . . and thus a new Pontiff of the Roman Catholic church

1

was elected today and takes his place in history." But who? The shop looked deserted.

Maybe someone in the street would know. My curiosity was mildly aroused, first because I'm Catholic of Polish descent, and second, because I had a Polish friend among the College of Cardinals selecting the new Pope—Cardinal Wojtyla, Archbishop of Krakow. But, of course, as far as being chosen himself, he hadn't a Chinaman's chance, as we used to say as children.

Out on the street again, I heard music coming from a coffee shop and hurried in, ordering coffee and Danish as an excuse for asking the waitress if she had heard who the new Pope was.

"The news will be on in a half hour," she said.

Two youngsters, standing behind me, nudged me and said, "We saw him on TV—the new Pope giving his blessing."

"Oh, did you get his name?" I asked.

"Naw, we'll hear enough about it at school tomorrow from the nuns. It was some Polish cardinal," they said.

At that moment, my heart started beating wildly, for I knew that it could not be the primary Polish cardinal at the voting, Cardinal Wyszynski, Primate of Poland, because of his advanced age of seventy-seven.

We had just lost an elderly Pope, John Paul, after only thirty-three days as Pontiff. No, it had to mean my friend, Poland's second-ranking cardinal.

"Does the name Wojtyla sound right?" I asked.

Now the boys were catching a bit of my excitement. "Yes, yes," they said excitedly. "It is Cardinal Wojtyla, that's the guy. How do you pronounce it?"

I said, "Voy-TEE-wa. You are sure?"

"I'm sure," said one. "Hey, we're going to be the only ones who can say it right tomorrow. Voy-TEE-wa. Voy-TEE-wa."

"Tell them," I said, "that you met a friend of the Pope and his name is harder—Szostak." I was happy, almost giddy with joy.

They were looking at me with disbelief. "*You* know the Pope? Have you ever touched him?"

"I not only touched him," I said, "but what is more

important, he touched me. In fact, he grabbed me and hugged me when we were saying good-bye after his visit to the United States in 1976."

"Wow," they said.

I realized that I was shaking like a leaf from excitement. Leaving the food I'd paid for untouched, I rushed out and hopped on a bus that would take me to Washington, and to the National Press Building, where my office was when I was not in the Press Room at the White House, covering the President for ethnic newspapers.

Seeing a newsboy from the bus window, I hopped out, grabbed the paper out of his hand, and had to walk a good ten blocks to my office. The startled newsboy was trying to tell me he didn't sell papers on the street, but I gave him a fifty-cent piece, yelling at him to keep the change. The look of fear on his face made me realize that I must be looking wild-eyed and dangerous.

"The Pope," I shouted back at him as I ran toward the office. "The Pope is a Pole!"

He was standing there looking at me as if I had indeed lost use of my senses.

I stumbled along with the newspaper in my hand, gazing at the headline, "POLE ELECTED POPE," all the way to my office, muttering to myself more as a question than a statement, "*I* know a Pope? The Pope is my old shoe friend, the same man I traveled with and ran out to get blueberries for? Now he's a Pope?"

I didn't even stop at my office, but rushed to the National Press Club bar and I was never so grateful to be a member. I only had to buy my first drink and then was treated to several drinks by my colleagues, who were happy to have an excuse to celebrate this joyous occasion—they knew someone who knew a Pope. A few who needed some material on the Pope for stories asked their questions, and I waxed eloquent—I was feeling no pain.

At about 6 P.M. I went over to the White House to see what was going on there, and I was greeted by my colleagues and again was pumped for information about Karol Wojtyla and again I expounded.

Suddenly, I saw the new Pope on TV for the first

time—a replay on the six-o'clock news. I was so moved by his visual presence that I, too, knelt when he gave his first blessing to the people in St. Peter's Square. I could not be there in person, but I was there in spirit. I felt a joy beyond words.

I left the news to hurry to the South Lawn, where President Carter was returning to the White House by helicopter from his weekend at Camp David. With the Middle East crisis not yet resolved, he had been in a sad mood when he left for Camp David on Friday—his face drawn, the famous smile gone from his face.

Now Monday, when he returned with the crisis not yet resolved, the President looked very relaxed and confident, in spite of it. Many questions were called out about the election of the Polish Pope. Carter was beaming with joy, all smiles, saying, "It's great, great, great." Then he went inside. I too was in a state of euphoria, telling the girls in the White House press office, "If Mr. Carter wants to see the Pope, he has to come to me first."

The President was behind me at the moment and laughingly said, "I'll be glad to take you up on the offer." He knew, of course, I was joking. But in the spirit of good citizenship, I did give the White House background material on the new Pope, for which they were very grateful. As a White House correspondent, I was quickly dubbed "the Pope's man in the White House" by my colleagues. This was because any time they wanted to know something about the Pope, they came to me first.

Is it possible to meet someone and realize immediately that this is a great man whom destiny will tap for some tremendous, historic undertaking? I don't know. I've compared notes with many churchmen and laymen who have become close to the man who would be known as John Paul II, and they agree that at first he struck them as a rather shy and retiring person. It was only later that his great strength as well as his charisma became evident.

I, too, had started my association with Karol Wojtyla in a low-key way, through correspondence and messages back and forth, during the years when I was known to the Polish church curia as "our man in Washington."

In 1969, I had almost met him on his first trip to America as a rather new cardinal—he had been appointed by Pope

Paul VI just two years before. It hadn't come about then and now, on July 28, 1976, in Washington, D.C., it was about to happen at Catholic University, where the cardinal was to give a talk on the topic of "The Transcendence of the Person in Act and Man's Auto-Teleology."

Since the title alone was enough to stagger me, I had taken along a college major in the field of philosophy—my own wife, Constance. As a reporter, I decided I could interview her later. I did not dream that before his visit to the United States was over, Wojtyla would give me his own copy of his speech, with his corrections in his own handwriting.

Instead of straining to understand the philosophical treatise, I busied myself taking photographs of the cardinal and others as I had promised to do for the delegation.

After the speech, I hurried over to introduce myself to the cardinal, my cherished pen pal. He seemed not to recognize my name, which I eagerly proffered him, but was a bit reserved. However, after I handed him my business card, everything changed.

He lit up like a Christmas tree, embraced me, and said to a bishop beside him, "So this is the legendary John Szostak."

Now he was talking to me. Now he had much to say. But since everyone was pulling at his sleeve for attention or simply breaking in, I wandered away and continued taking pictures, feeling a bit like the "Phantom of the Opera."

I saw my wife, Connie, hovering on the fringes and I pulled her through the crowd and introduced her to the cardinal. They launched into a nice talk on such an intellectual level that I again became the wandering phantom. I came back in time to see Cardinal Wojtyla jabbing a finger at Connie and exclaiming, "You are a genuine philosopher." It was obvious that he was much impressed with her.

To record Connie's big moment, I snapped the shutter, little realizing that this man would be elevated to the papacy a scant two years later.

Eventually, the crowd thinned down, and he sought me out for more conversation. My first observation of the man reinforced the feeling I had developed about him through our letters. It seemed as if we had met several times before, so close was the feeling between us that we seemed to share.

His first embrace, after he had looked at my card and realized I was the same person he had been corresponding with, was one of a father who has not seen his son for years. It was such a hearty embrace that I felt all my bones would crack—yet it was warm and tender.

As people seemed to be waiting for him, the cardinal said in Polish, "Give me your telephone number so that I may call you at home." I gave it to him and left with Connie, while he prepared to leave with his group. I was sure he'd be much too busy.

At about 10 P.M. that night, Cardinal Wojtyla did phone and did seem genuinely happy to have met me at long last and genuinely impressed with my wife's education. We exchanged many pleasantries in Polish, and I did not hesitate to tell him how moved I had been to finally see him face to face.

Still he did not hang up, and I realized he was getting around to something. Finally, I got the clue—he needed some directions: How could he get to where he was going the next day? I started to explain; then said, "I'll come get you and we can go together, if it will be all right with you."

I seemed to be saying the right thing. Wojtyla replied, "I would like to see you again if this would not be an imposition on your schedule."

"Not at all," I said. "The honor would be all mine. You are, after all, a guest, and how often can we see each other?"

He replied, "You are right." We agreed to meet in the rectory of the Epiphany Church in Georgetown, where he was staying.

When I told him I could get a driver, since I don't drive, he said not to worry, just come. He would have the car and driver.

As I took a bus across the river to Georgetown, I marveled that with all the transportation that had been provided and all the cars at his disposal, he wanted to be with me.

The cardinal chose to sit in the backseat with me, which made it easy for me to point out landmarks and give him my full attention. We talked of many things and I realized that all my barriers were down and I was being completely open with him. Under that penetrating gaze, it was impossible to pad a story or tell him anything but the stark truth.

We talked about my work, my family back in Poland, my family here in the States, the Polish-American community in Washington, and the status of the Catholic church in various parts of America. He gave of himself as well, speaking of the days of his youth, of his life in Krakow, of a few problems of the church.

He thanked me over and over for all the kind deeds I had done through the years for him and for the good of the Catholic church in Poland. At one point, his physical expression of thanks almost choked me up as he took my hands and pressed them between his own as a humble gesture of gratitude.

I tried to tell him that my own contribution was as nothing and that I only wished I could do something really useful for him in his effort to keep the church strong in Poland.

I could not believe my ears as I heard Cardinal Wojtyla ask me to call him by his first name, Karol. I struggled with that thought, but realized that, friend or no friend, this would not be proper. And humble as he was, he did respect my gesture of addressing him as *Ks. Kardynal*, which translates into Reverend Cardinal.

In front of strangers, I used the still more formal address of Your Eminence.

While speeding down Route I-95 South, an idea popped into my mind. Why not ask him to stop by my home, so that he could again meet my wife, perhaps have a cup of tea and sweet rolls—and hopefully have him bless the house, an old Polish custom.

It was instant and impromptu, and so was his reply in Polish, of course, "I would be delighted to again see your wife and children and pay my respects to 'The Little Cardinal.' "

Between close friends, we have a private joke dating back to when my second son was born in 1972, and had reached the mature old age of six months. My wife, Constance, and I had named the baby Thomas More, after one of my favorite churchmen in history—and the cardinal's favorite as well. Little by little I had discovered that Karol Wojtyla had a great sense of humor and was able to laugh at himself.

So, as a gag, I had dubbed six-month-old Thomas More "The Youngest Cardinal" and given him his own mythical country. He even had his own stationery, with coat of arms and address: Thomas Cardinal More, Archbishop of Grand Fenwick.

We dressed him in a red cardinal's outfit, which my mother-in-law had helped sew, and made color photographs taken of him seated on the bishop's throne at St. Matthew's Cathedral in Washington, D.C., one Saturday afternoon when no one was around.

I sent the best color shot to "my other favorite cardinal," Karol Cardinal Wojtyla, Archbishop of Krakow.

Cardinal Wojtyla got a big laugh, especially since it was done in good taste. It reminded him of his own theatrical career. He had a fine appreciation of the humor of the whole thing, in contrast to the local clergy who took this practical joke to be totally out of place.

The cardinal also got a charge out of a funny picture I sent of me in a riding outfit, a World War I military tunic, riding a hobby horse. This was my kind of humor—imitating Erich Von Stroheim. Wojtyla said in a letter, in Polish of course, as all his letters were, that the get-up reminded him of his father's uniform as an officer during World War I.

We pulled up to my garden apartment complex at 3512 Valley Drive, in Alexandria at about 12:30 P.M. I unlocked the door of our first-floor apartment and went inside, yelling for all to hear, "Anybody home?"

No response. I couldn't believe my hard luck—the place was a mess. I muttered something about, "What do you expect when you have two children, ages four and six?" Still, I cringed as I led the way into the disaster area.

Then disaster really struck as the cardinal almost fell over a *Batmobile* car that the children had left in the middle of the floor. I grabbed him just in time to prevent a major ecclesiastic disaster and could just see the headlines, "POLISH CARDINAL BREAKS ANKLE IN AMERICAN NEWSMAN'S HOME."

The cardinal laughed, saying he was unaccustomed to coping with children. He graciously added, "This disarray is a sign of a happy household."

As he sat in my home, talking about my career and the careers of famous men, which I assured him I would never be, he said, "The career of every person on earth began in a diaper, even though today he may be wearing the uniform of a military general or the ribbons of an ambassador. And his career will probably come to an end again in a diaper, except perhaps a slightly larger one."

It was a humbling experience to realize how it would all end and yet a good feeling to know we are all at one level, when it comes down to it.

At that point, I took him on a grand tour of our happy household, pointing out a few items of interest, including an antique mantel which had some American historic significance.

After he blessed the home, Wojtyla asked to use the telephone in the kitchen—a white wall phone. It seemed to be a new experience for him, using a wall phone. He was also very much impressed by the touch dial, remarking that, "This is another outward sign of America being a prosperous nation."

As he wandered around, studying this and that, Wojtyla remarked that the place reminded him of his own flat in Krakow—I was sure he meant the layout and not the disorder.

It was my collection of books that held his attention longest. He sat in a chair in the living room, resting and examining various books, eventually saying, "I see you are a man of many interests. This will become valuable to you in your future career."

A book about Jozsef Cardinal Mindszenty made a special impression on him. He could not let it go from his hands, eagerly leafing through it. I tried to press the book on him, begging him to take it along. I could see how sad he was to leave it behind, explaining that it would not be wise to take it with him. Customs in Poland would confiscate it, he explained, since the book was full of anti-Communist remarks.

However, I did manage to give him another book that had special significance for him, *The Last Measure*, a photo album of JFK's funeral. For this he was most grateful.

In return, he gave me rosaries for my wife and myself and a small wood carving for the house—"The Sorrowful Christ." He also wanted me to have several holy cards, some with his picture.

That evening, when I came home and told my wife

9

about the visit, Connie alternated between sheer joy that this holy man had blessed her home and sheer agony and despair that he had caught her on the one day she had said to heck with everything and taken the children to McDonald's for lunch instead of lifting a finger to straighten the house.

She wanted to know every word he had said. I tried to get through to my little ones that a man from a far-off land had been amazed that children in America have so many toys. He had examined their toy closet and almost refused to believe such a mountain of toys would be used by only two children. "For a whole nursery, yes," he had said. In jest, I had told him that I was of the same opinion.

Jokingly, I had added, "Maybe you can take some back to Poland with you for Christmas, and all you would need to wear with your red robes would be a white beard."

The cardinal laughed and remarked, "You have a good point there. I would be a genuine St. Nicholas, since he was also a bishop."

Before the evening was over, Cardinal Wojtyla called me at home again to thank me for sharing my time with him—I could hardly believe what I was hearing—and also expressing his best wishes to my wife and children. Then he added that he wanted me to be with him at the Eucharistic Congress in Philadelphia as his liaison to the press and that my expenses would be taken care of. He was going to lecture at Harvard and then he would meet me in Philadelphia. I said that I would bring my cameras along so he would have a record.

Between the time we met in Washington and the time when we would again meet in Philadelphia, I proceeded to put together my news stories and pictures for the Catholic press. But it was at that time a limited item of interest. After all, who was Karol Cardinal Wojtyla in 1976? A rather obscure cleric of the Catholic church from the American viewpoint. And one coming from an Iron Curtain country, at that. How could he ever influence their lives?

It was an uphill fight; I was able to get few stories into print.

2

Letters That Changed My Life

While I waited to join the cardinal in Philadelphia, I reread some of the letters I had received from him.

Looking back, it is amusing to see that in one letter the future Pope advised me not to throw away letters and other things I had received from the Kennedy brothers—John F., Robert, and Edward.

"Save the original," he said, "because it could be valuable and useful later on."

The future Pope's letter goes on to say, "In the future, people will not have to know who you are, because when they ask where you worked before, you will be able to show them your letters . . . and this will strengthen your professional standing among them."

I am so glad that I saved his precious letters, and I consider them so valuable that I would never sell them, but hope to leave them as a legacy to my sons, Thomas More—"The

Little Cardinal"—and Eric, with the hope that the words of Karol Wojtyla will be as important in their lives as they were in mine.

What practical advice will Tom and Eric get from these letters, a Pope who once knew their father wrote back in the seventies?

The most practical, I think, is this, written to me two years before I met him, "Always remember, being a person with a good heart and character are the most important virtues in an individual. These qualities will open doors for you and *make life less complicated.*"

I remember that he was not interested in big and expensive gifts, which I could not afford to give anyway, but enjoyed simple, inexpensive gifts. Above all, he valued spiritual gifts, such as one's prayers and friendship.

In one letter, after I had mentioned a prayer I had said for him, he replied. "Your spirit of charity is a comfort to God and to me. To be praying for others is bound to win graces for yourself and your family."

In those days, he would sign his letters, "With cordial sentiments," or simply, "With sentiments, Karol Wojtyla." Frequently, he would say at the end of his letters. "May God bless you and Our Blessed Mother keep you in her care."

From the late 1960s to 1976, I would say that I was in correspondence with Cardinal Wojtyla at least once a month, and not all my letters were of an intense, personal nature. I also kept him informed of what was going on in America, since he did not get our newspapers.

Also from time to time, I sent him items of small personal interest, such as books, photos, and mementos of Washington, D.C. As I remember, Cardinal Wojtyla was very interested in the Watergate scandal, like everyone else at that time. This was back in 1973.

At that time, I was just starting my journalistic career as a freelance photographer and writer. The coverage of Watergate was almost a full-time preoccupation with me. I recall the mementos of this historic event—photos and texts that I sent to Wojtyla.

At one point, I got H. R. Haldeman, President Nixon's top aide, to autograph his hearing text, then went to Attorney

General John Mitchell, and got him to autograph his. When I tried to get Nixon's assistant for domestic affairs, John D. Ehrlichman, to autograph it, he snapped, "Get away, you SOB reporter."

The texts of the Watergate proceedings, even without Ehrlichman's autograph, and my own written accounts of Watergate were greatly appreciated by Cardinal Wojtyla who, as I understood, shared them with his colleagues in the episcopate.

I also remember sending him yearly U.S. Capitol Historical Society calendars. He greatly enjoyed using these. In one of his notes, he said, "The calendar will be a frequent visual reminder of my visits of Washington, D.C., and America."

The man who would be Pope was not the only Polish churchman with whom I had a close association. As a result of my ethnic background, which is German and Polish, and my interest in Eastern European affairs, I became involved with people who have made substantial contributions to the history of Eastern Europe, especially during World War II.

I became close friends with retired diplomats and military people who played a leading role in that part of the globe during World War II. From these contacts, I gradually got to know several members of the Catholic episcopate in Poland. In time, many of them came to America and made a stopover in Washington, D.C. As time went on, I developed lasting friendships with them.

These friendships were further cemented by correspondence. In Washington, I tried to do everything possible to be of assistance to them—making arrangements and obtaining things they needed, including written and verbal information.

Victims of Nazi war crimes—especially Poles—became a major concern of mine, starting with one case.

In 1962, I was asked by the Reverend Joseph Szarek to assist in obtaining restitution for the atrocities that were committed against his family by the Nazi regime in World War II. He was the sole survivor of his family, and I checked and found that the atrocities had been well-documented.

Working in the White House at that time, writing

speeches and taking care of ethnic problems for President Kennedy, helped me bring the case to the attention of the right people—Attorney General Robert Kennedy among them.

It took seven years and the case eventually reached the attention of international authorities in Geneva, who were the final judges. Restitution was made, and I kept on top of this case all the way. In fact, because of this case, I became interested in helping other victims of Nazi atrocities, which I felt was only my duty and moral obligation.

Gradually, I became known to Polish clergymen abroad as their man in Washington, without portfolio. Word would get around among the Catholic episcopate in Poland that to get anything done in Washington "you must see Szostak."

It was a two-way street. During the course of my association with high church personages—in the United States, in Poland, and eventually in Rome—I often used my Polish Vatican contacts to do favors for Americans.

At times, I would obtain letters of congratulations, letters of comfort during moments of sorrow—such as in the case of a death in the family—and Papal blessings for weddings and special anniversaries.

Frequently, these individuals were unaware of my actions in their behalf and probably wondered who was responsible for the kindness.

I have always felt that those blessings I was fortunate enough to receive through my professional and personal contacts, should be shared with others. This has given me great satisfaction, knowing I might be able to be of help to someone at a crucial moment in his life.

I have also done the same with people I knew in the political arena, such as the President, cabinet officers, and prominent members of Congress—getting them to send congratulatory messages or notes of sympathy.

During the period from 1962 to 1976, I met so many church and lay people of importance that I have lost count. Space and time would not permit me to write about all of them. Nor did I have time to correspond with many.

I had to limit my correspondence to only a handful. But among them, one was very special—a relatively obscure bishop named Karol Wojtyla—he was not even a cardinal yet. He would not be made cardinal until 1967.

Even then, I remember his singular humanism, his appreciation for everything, and his sly humor. Above all, I remember that I cared for him and that I was his friend. Wojtyla had heard about me long before I corresponded with him. It is a known fact that the inner circle of the Catholic episcopate in Poland shares all information, especially that coming from abroad.

Having an understanding of the political climate that these people have to live under, I was very sensitive to their special problems and needs. Never would I endanger their position by my actions here in America, contrary to the actions of the many ultra-right-wing groups which hoped to exploit my association with the Polish churchmen.

My response was that it is easy for people in America to be heroes, but those people behind the Iron Curtain cannot afford to rock the boat. They must work with their rulers and make the best of the situation.

As their *man in Washington, without portfolio,* I was in a position to keep them informed about the church and cultural activities of Polish-Americans living abroad, especially those living in the U.S. Also, I was able to report about the status of the Catholic church in America. For this, my Polish church friends were forever grateful. And I was not only able to help them in their professional needs, but also able to develop a personal friendship and exchange valuable advice on matters of mutual interest, including global matters concerning the outlook in Eastern Europe.

By chance—or the hand of God—among those who corresponded with me most frequently was Karol Cardinal Wojtyla. His letters to me grew to be like those of a father writing to his son, giving valuable practical advice. Karol Wojtyla wrote in such a way that one could read a letter several times. Each time there would be a new valuable meaning behind his words. The man had a way with words.

It was born of his personality. Wojtyla could see right into the heart of the matter in a way that very few people could. If I didn't quite tell him something, he knew anyway, and responded.

In 1975, I felt at low ebb. My father had died. My career was going nowhere. Life seemed in a shambles. I will never forget how Wojtyla's letter came as almost a lifesaver, assuring me, "God will never let you down even through times in which for some unknown reason things may be dark. He sees fit to try his faithful servant. But trust him all the more. Don't give up praying."

My dear friend gave an example of suffering that made me feel selfish that I had succumbed to my small personal problems. It was, all in all, the most moving letter I had ever received, and it left me thoroughly ashamed.

He told how, at Auschwitz concentration camp, one man made the ultimate sacrifice of love. That was a Franciscan missionary priest, Maximilian Kolbe, who had founded a mission in Japan.

Eleven men were scheduled to go into the death chamber and he volunteered to take the place of one of them who was the father of a large family. And so, he and the other ten entered the chamber of slow death. "Not a drop of water, not a breath of air, not a piece of bread" did the cruel captors give. And slowly they died.

The cardinal told me to pray to "Blessed Maximilian Kolbe" to "stay in your heart . . . and together with him, renew your courage."

There would be a follow-up 35 years later when Wojtyla returned to Poland as Pope and visited Auschwitz to lay flowers and celebrate mass. The man whom Father Kolbe had replaced—Francis Gajowniczek—in the death chamber was there in the welcoming delegation. He had put on his striped prison uniform to greet the Pope, and it was an emotional meeting.

After the death of my father in 1974, I leaned more and more on Wojtyla as my father figure. He responded in a wonderful way, making me feel that someone of importance did care about what was happening to me every step of the way.

When I told him I was anxious to become a writer and a White House correspondent, he urged me on. And when I achieved my goal, setting up my own news service—the Washington Liaison News Service, supplying stories to various ethnic newspapers around the country and England—he applauded me by mail, even though I bemoaned the fact that I had too few newspapers to earn a decent living.

"I must certainly congratulate you for achieving your

desired goal [as a White House correspondent]," he wrote in Polish. "Please keep this position firm because it will open the road to life for a successful career in its own time.

"Of course, Krakow was not built in a day. This will take time. Your kindness will win the hearts of people that you will be associating with. These noble qualities will earn you respect from others, who will not put obstacles in the way."

How could I help but become kind and helpful to others, even my competitors, with this sort of gentle guidance? I determined not to become a cutthroat reporter and indeed good things have come my way—even the opportunity to write this book.

Of course, there was that other important guideline he threw down and that I tried to follow: "Keep your eyes open for fundamental and important things because you have no time to spend on nonsense. One should not waste time."

Wojtyla, I heard, always took advantage of every opportunity to learn something new, even if he didn't know when he would have need for it.

The way he had learned English is a good case in point. In 1967, his secretary was a nun who knew English, and he humbly asked her to teach him, becoming both her mentor and her student.

And so it was natural for him to encourage me to expand my horizons.

The same letter, dated September 1974, gave another bit of fatherly advice, saying that it was important to "remember that a good diplomat does not say much in order not to betray his plans." Wojtyla said that the wise man strives to find out as best he can what others are planning. He says little but listens much and tries to read between the lines. I was struck by his caution to use "one word less."

He said many things about love and repeated some of them to me in person, writing others in his books as well. I collected these thoughts on love of Cardinal Wojtyla, and I'm glad I did. They give me much to think about when I am out of sorts.

And some of them help me express what I want to say to that special person—my wife.

17

Some of them have even helped me cope with the jealousy that surfaced when it turned out that the man of the hour, the new Pope, happened to be my friend:

> Love alone can cure hatred. If there is
> anything worth doing in the world, it can only
> be one thing—to love.

The cardinal often spoke of love in the larger sense:

> The measure of our own love should be
> the measure of the love we expect from all the
> world. One must try to show more love to
> others than one has received.
> Love alone does all things well.
> Where there is no freedom, there is no
> love. One cannot love as the result of
> compulsion.

On the subject of romantic love:

> Love must be tested like gold in the fire.
> Only small love disintegrates in the fire of
> trials; great love is purified and grows more
> ardent.
> Real purity enables us to love.
> Love can conquer every age. Love can
> overcome the circumstances of every state and
> every situation.

On the subject of selfless love, such as a Catholic priest must have:

> The more love a person wants to give to
> others, the more he must renounce the love
> directed to himself, and the more must he
> forget about his own personal life.

And he also said, "He loves most, who yields most, who overcomes his inner self."

As I have said, Karol Wojtyla had made his first trip to America in 1969. However, as it happened, just at that time I was unavailable. I was employed by the U.S. Conference of Mayors then, and had to travel around the country extensively.

Although sad that our meeting had to be delayed, we said that we would see each other someday, if not in America, then I would come to Poland.

I did not go to Poland. But Wojtyla came again to the U.S. in 1976, and in person he was everything he had been in his letters—and more.

3

The Celestial Bus

*T*he Eucharistic Congress convened in Philadelphia on August 1, 1976. Cardinal Wojtyla led a delegation of nineteen bishops to this week-long world gathering of bishops and cardinals. In addition to the rigorous events of the day that were mandatory for him and his colleagues, he found time to be with his own people—the Poles in America.

Wojtyla attended many receptions held in his honor and the delegation of nineteen Polish bishops—given by the various Polish-American communities in Philadelphia. I had an opportunity to observe some of these firsthand.

As important as he was even at that time—after all he was a cardinal—he was always down-to-earth, never a stuffed shirt. As a matter of fact, he was the one who broke the ice and let everyone unwind. He did it with song and dance.

Cardinal Wojtyla was always the life of the party. The guests would tend to be a bit formal at the outset. But this did not last long, because Wojtyla quickly injected his personality, swinging into a little soft shoe by himself, to the delight of the guests. Soon they would all be grabbing partners and dancing, although the cardinal never danced with a partner.

Once I overheard some guests saying in Polish in a slightly disapproving tone, "How can a man of the cloth do these things?" I told them that their answer lies in the old Polish proverb, *Kto do tanieca ten do rozanca*, which, translated, means "One who can dance, can also say the rosary."

Cardinal Wojtyla would also drink with moderation. He was not only able to have fun, but, in effect, teach others to have fun.

This sort of thing went on all over, everywhere he went. He was indeed a Pied Piper in his own right. This was especially true with youth. The young men swarmed around him. It was quickly apparent that Cardinal Wojtyla understood youth, and youth understood him.

A bus had been chartered so that the Polish church dignitaries would have transportation wherever they went. Cardinal Wojtyla headed the delegation, and there were several priest aides along from Poland to help him and the nineteen Polish bishops in the entourage.

Once, when we all piled out of the bus, someone said, in Polish, "How will we know which one is our bus?"

One of the bishops answered jovially, "Oh, don't worry, you'll recognize it. It's the 'Celestial Bus.' "

The only lay people on the trip were the editor of *Tygodnik Powszechny*, the Polish weekly in Krakow, and I. Jerzy Turowicz, too, had come from Poland with the group, and I found him a brilliant man.

The cardinal was a very complex man. At a moment's notice, he would switch from humor and a bit of frivolity to deep thought and prayer. Sometimes he did several things at once. For example, he would ask me questions and keep reading while I was giving the answers. At first, this disturbed me, and I would stop. But he would explain, "Keep talking, my son, I know everything you are saying even if I don't look at you."

I remember several times when I would be talking to him and the cardinal seemed to be in a world of his own. He would suddenly start reading something or writing in a notebook he kept with him at all times, or simply look off and seem to be studying something in the far distance. If I was slightly flustered, he would sense it, and, without even looking at me, say, "Go on, son, I am listening. Do not pay attention to what I am doing."

It was uncanny the way he did not have to look at a person to know what was going on inside of him.

It would flatter me that sometimes he considered what I was saying important enough to take notes on, also. Wojtyla was a great note-taker. Wherever the cardinal went, he would have two things with him—a book he was studying and his notebook in which he was writing. I rarely saw him without these two.

The more I talked with others, the more I learned about how precious Wojtyla viewed every minute to be. And naturally, I felt much better about the fact that he had been talking with me while writing and doing other things.

I was told by Bishop Sczepan Wesoly, who knew the cardinal in Poland and later in Rome, that many times when Wojtyla attended meetings he would listen to what was being said and at the same time write letters and other correspondence, but still be aware of what was going on.

At one Vatican Council meeting, Cardinal Wojtyla actually was writing a book, *The Acting Person.*

Still, people did not feel hurt by the cardinal's strange way of doing two things at the same time. When he spoke to people, he gave the impression that each of them was the most important person in the world. Just a moment or two of those steady eyes gazing penetratingly into yours was enough to do the trick, I found. It was a heady feeling.

When he was suddenly remote, no one would dare to disturb him. Yet the bishops continued with their own discussions. I remember this was very much the case when we left Philadephia in our bus en route to Washington, D.C. All the bishops were in good humor, laughing, joking, and singing.

They reminded me of a group of school kids on their way to a picnic. Karol Wojtyla, among them, was in a different world. The expression on his face—especially in his eyes—showed that he was not a part of it. Then, suddenly, he came out of his reverie and walked down the aisle, talking and joking with everyone and distributing chocolate candy. I was amused to see him breaking off chunks of huge Hershey bars for everyone.

By the time our bus ride was over, we had consumed enough sweets to last us a long time. In everything he did during the trip, he was most generous and persuasive—you could not say no. Since I could not eat all the candy he was forcing on me, I took some home to give my children. Now their little friends know that they once ate candy touched by a future Pope.

During our stay in Philadelphia, while attending the Eucharistic Congress, we were lodged at St. Charles Borromeo Seminary, located in the suburbs in a remote park-like atmosphere. Since this was summer and the students were on vacation, we had the entire place to ourselves, ensuring a certain degree of privacy for the cardinal and the delegation of Polish bishops.

My room was located on the second floor of the seminary, in a corner, with a window overlooking a garden shed. Cardinal Wojtyla was several doors down from me, across the hall. Since there was only one washroom on the floor, we shared it.

At one time, I was using the wash basin next to him and noticed he was shaving with an old-fashioned shaving brush. I showed him my shaving cream. He was interested in trying it out, and when he liked it, I gave it to him. The cardinal remarked that he could not get good shaving cream in Poland and the better kinds had to come from abroad. Wherever we went, Wojtyla was very much interested in the ingenuity of American manufacturers in producing their best items en masse for Americans. In Poland, he explained, the best products are made for export or can be purchased with hard currency in special stores.

The cardinal was a very sentimental person. I could not believe that he was wearing only a stainless steel watch—he who could have gold watches. But that was just the thing. This watch had been given to him by someone dear to him, and he was very fond of it.

When he became Pope, there he was, still wearing his steel digital watch.

I took it upon myself to do little things that would

make the cardinal feel more at home in America. For example, I discovered he had a passion for blueberries—and in fact, all kinds of berries in general. I would go and get him extra blueberries—in addition to coffee, or whatever.

It was after breakfast that the future Pope and I really got to know each other.

During breakfast, the cardinal and I would sit at a round table talking about everything under the sun. Several bishops would join us, and the conversation would go on and on. After eating, we would shove the plates to the middle of the table and continue talking and drinking coffee.

The cardinal would question in depth. A great listener as well, he would absorb information like a sponge. He was interested in everything about the West—the attitudes of the people; the American way of life, economically and politically; the special problems of the Polish-American community and other minorities; the problems of the Catholic church in America; the problems of religion in general and the directions it was taking in the modern world—marriage and divorce, birth control, and abortion. All human problems and their solutions concerned him.

In a solicitous way, Wojtyla asked about my home life and the problem of raising children in America. I found myself telling him straight stuff—the good and the bad, the ups and downs. I remember the advice he gave, saying that he always advised couples never to broach touchy subjects in the evening or engage in criticism of self or one's mate. "It is best to put off all difficult matters till morning."

Once, when I was crabbing about how much work I had to do to support a family and keep my editors happy, the cardinal stopped me and gave me a different slant on work. "Labor," he said, "is not a curse or a punishment, but confidence placed in man by God who is calling on man to cooperate with Him." And so, he said, man should view labor as an honor.

He deplored the idle rich who had no specific work to do. "Man specializes and grows more perfect through concrete work," he said, adding that "People who do not fulfill a concrete task become distorted and decrease their gifts."

When I talked of the difficulty of concentrating on

work sometimes, he understood, commenting that "Inner tranquility is the indispensable condition of fruitful work."

Strangely enough, that simple observation has helped me a great deal in getting much more work done. I simply take a few minutes to get my mind at peace and tackle the writing with serenity, knowing it will be my best.

Even in letters, before he was Pope, Wojtyla would give me valuable advice on not overworking and learning to relax and care about my health—getting plenty of exercise.

"The problem of lack of time," he once commented to me, "is not solved by hurrying, but by calmness." He himself did not hurry, but seemed to get a job done in record time with easy serenity.

During our long breakfast talks in Philadelphia and the bus ride to Washington, D.C., that followed, we also discussed at great length the present church-state situation in Poland.

I was told of the difficulties the church has in Poland in coping with the competition of the state. Since I was a journalist, all sorts of things were related to me in vivid detail. It was the cardinal's desire that these matters come to the attention of the American people—especially of the Catholic community in America—via the media.

While giving me a shopping list of violations by the state against the church, the group in no way made a blanket condemnation of the state. As a matter of fact, they praised the effort of the Polish government in helping to do good "for the benefit of the nation"—*dla dobru narodu*—in such areas as housing, education, health care, employment, and telephone and telegraphic communication.

What they were fighting for was to get the Polish government to live up to promises of letting the church have freedom without government impingement or harassment. Things like freedom to build as many churches as were needed.

Some of the problems involved the government's placing obstacles in the way of religious instruction for children. Local authorities seemed to stay awake thinking up ways to lure children from going to church and church activities, scheduling movies and outings for exactly the same time.

It amounted to a subtle and sometimes not so subtle

game of tug-of-war, a game which had been going on since 1945.

Cardinal Wojtyla quoted a piece to me from his annual Corpus Christi celebration speech, noting that "The church, being a vast community, a community almost as large as the Polish nation itself, we cannot be outside the law.

"Definition of the church's legal status is at the same time the definition of our place and of our rights, everything which originates in the concept of freedom of religion which is recognized in the whole world and declared in international documents."

He was speaking, of course, in Polish, and he added, "The church does not want to meddle in politics. However, it represents universal moral values and that is what the church must assert against any government."

On the road and during the trip, when others were concerned about locking up possessions and making sure nothing would be stolen, Wojtyla laughed and said he was not worried. Once he said, "Where everything is guarded, things get stolen, but where everything is in the open, something will always be left."

We talked of our childhoods and the significance of Poland to both of us. It was something that brought us closer together. And strangely enough, we had Krakow in common.

We even had the cardinal's beloved Czestochowa in common. In fact, my grandparents, who were of some wealth, were married in that famous town of the Black Madonna by Adam Stefan Cardinal Sapieha, who saved Karol Wojtyla's life during World War II, and whom Wojtyla eventually succeeded as Archbishop of Krakow.

My mother's parents came from a town near Krakow, and my grandmother studied home economics there and became a high-school teacher in nearby Katowice. My mother's father was an electrical engineer, who had studied at the University of Krakow.

The cardinal listened with interest as I told him how, on my mother's side, we had the titles of baron and baroness, which dated back to the reign of King Ludwig the Great in the late 1700s, and how my title disappeared along with the family wealth, as a result of the many wars that were fought in Europe.

I quoted my mother's comment about the days of the Depression that followed World War I—"In those days you needed one suitcase of money to buy a loaf of bread in the morning and two suitcases to buy that same loaf in the afternoon."

We both agreed that I was better off as plain John Szostak in the United States, busy with my work as White House correspondent to various newspapers, than an idle baron in Europe trying to find amusements to make the time go by.

Over and over, the cardinal commented on how each man has only an allotted amount of time and must make the most of it.

But, going back to our growing closeness, we discovered that a second cousin of mine, my mother's first cousin, Zygmunt, had studied for the priesthood with Karol Wojtyla. He had not been as lucky as Wojtyla in escaping the rigors of Poland in World War II, but he had died of pneumonia.

My mother's own brother—whose name was also Zygmunt—had studied for the priesthood at the start of the war, but was drafted into the Polish army before the German invasion. He escaped being captured by the Germans, fleeing first to Rumania and then to England, where he fought with the Polish Free Army.

The cardinal wanted to know half facetiously, how a nice Polish boy like me happened to be born in Germany, but of course he guessed right—my father had been part of the army of strong young men forced by the Germans to leave Poland and perform mandatory labor in the fields of Germany.

It was backbreaking work, and the greatest thing that could happen after the American liberation was to come to the United States, which my parents did in 1949, when I was about seven years old.

The cardinal was also interested in my father's background and I was able to tell him that one of his forefathers had been a palace guard to Czar Nicholas I. But what pleased Wojtyla most was learning that one of my father's cousins

27

was the Reverend Andrzej Szostek, the youngest academic assistant under Professor Karol Wojtyla when they both taught at the Catholic University of Lublin, Poland, in 1956.

Cardinal Wojtyla enjoyed telling jokes. He liked to hear Polish jokes as long as they were in good taste. He said that in Poland they tell jokes about the Russians.

In one of them, the cardinal told how during the Stalin era the Soviets proudly built a monstrous structure to house the University of Warsaw. Not daring to call a spade a spade, the Poles explained that to appreciate its true architectural beauty, one must first get to the top of the building and then look down.

The humor of Cardinal Wojtyla was evident during the trip when he decided to take advantage of the opportunity to ski in Montana. He knew exactly one person there—Father Joseph Gluzek.

Wojtyla told the townspeople, "You probably wonder what I am doing here, since there are no Polish communities or Polish centers. I am here in Montana because I have my priest here, and I am his bishop. That is why I am here."

The cardinal paused and added in an off-hand manner, "And while I'm here, I might as well see your ski slopes." With a twinkle in his eye, he added, "Several of my Polish friends in Philadelphia told me, 'Don't go to Montana, because there is nothing to see.' I told them I don't care if there is anything to see or not, I have my priest there and I want to see him."

The cardinal quickly became a part of his friend's Great Falls parish, whose members had never met a cardinal before and were trying to cater to him.

He would have none of it, and would not even let himself be served first at an outdoor barbeque in his honor. He insisted on standing in line with his plastic plate and fork, waiting his turn, joking and entertaining the children.

When Father Gluzek took Cardinal Wojtyla for a grand tour of the mountains, he warned the cardinal that there were spots that were very steep and dangerous, and that the place was full of bears. Cardinal Wojtyla laughed and said, "Only bears?"

One evening, Cardinal Wojtyla said he was doing everything the American way and called for the standard American bedtime snack. He got milk and cookies, and was amazed.

Cardinal Wojtyla hated to say no, and when he did, he tried to make it at least an amusing experience rather than a rejection. In 1976, when some priests from Vancouver, Canada, were very disappointed that they could not get him to deviate from his schedule on the east coast of Canada to visit them on the west coast, the cardinal made them a promise.

He would come another time, he said. Then he added, laughing, "Next time, I will hijack the plane, if necessary."

Many things were accomplished on the bus from Philadelphia. Part of the time, the cardinal and I sat composing an article we had been talking about covering human rights as they pertain to Poland and the Communistic regime. Cardinal Wojtyla explained that his name could not be on it, and so only my name appeared on the by-line.

I worked very hard on the article to explain the problems of the church in the captive world and was elated at the results. It was an important story, one that needed to be told. Yet editors turned it down. Too controversial, they said, in light of then Secretary of State Kissinger's détente policy.

It was not until July of 1977 that I was able to get the significant message across, and then it was as if I had hit the jackpot because I not only was able to present the article as testimony before the congressional hearings of the Helsinki Commission, but the complete text was placed in the *Congressional Record*.

Not because I helped on it, but because it gives the Pope's views and message in anecdotal, easy-to-understand terms, I feel it is imperative to reproduce our joint article as it appeared in the *Record*. After rereading that testimony today, I find it almost as relevant now as it was when printed in 1977, or when the future Pope and I collaborated in 1976.

The joint effort was introduced on the floor of the House on July 15, 1977, by Congressman Douglas Walgren of Pennsylvania, under the title of "Freedom of Religion in Poland." Let me share it with you exactly as it appeared so that you can get a true picture of the atmosphere from which Karol Wojtyla emerged victorious—and, in spite of which, he became Pope.

Mr. Walgren: Mr. Speaker, as a member of the Delegation from the United States Congress to the Parliament of Europe meeting prior to the review of the Helsinki Accords, I want to recommend to my colleagues the testimony of Mr. John M. Szostak on the failure of the Communist regime in Poland and to allow full expression of the basic human right of freedom of religion.

For over 1,000 years, the Roman Catholic Church in Poland has exercised a very important role, not only in religion but also in social, moral and educational matters. The social and educational work of the church has been greatly hampered in the past 30 years by the closing down of schools and the liquidation of its religious centers and organizations.

Religious instruction has been banned from the school curriculum and it is also being obstructed even outside the schools. The construction of new churches is met with enormous obstacles, and social activities of the parish are greatly impeded.

Poland's record of religious freedom in those past 30 years is a dismal one due to violations of the basic human rights that its citizens cannot fully enjoy and practice openly. The Polish Constitution guarantees the freedom of religion in theory only, however.

Active participation impedes one's success in the professions and career advancement. It is a known fact that a practicing Catholic cannot hold high office or head a department or any other executive position in the state or the economic sector.

The so-called guarantee of religious freedom under the Polish Constitution is systematically violated. The people of Poland, especially its youth, are constantly persecuted and harassed for having exercised this basic human right.

Only the old people are left alone to practice their faith with very little opposition. The present regime feels that it would be counterproductive and next to impossible to stamp out religion in Poland overnight without bloodshed. Therefore, time is their only weapon. The strategy is to indoctrinate the youth by stepping up their campaign of atheism via materialism to create a new generation of nonbelievers as an answer to the Marxist dream of creating a perfect Communist state society.

Poland, and other Eastern European nations, including the Soviet Union, are today witnessing a great spiritual renewal among their youth, as well as the older generation. Much of this is going on underground for fear of social and economic repression. The movement of religious renewal is there and growing.

This movement has become a great concern to the Polish Government officials. They do not know what to do or how to cope with the new problem as they consider it to be.

A card-carrying party member who wants to protect his career must send his children for religious instruction in secret and practice his faith in the same manner—oftentimes traveling to a distant town where he will not be recognized and in disguise.

Although religious instruction is allowed in Poland, obstacles are put in the way to discourage this kind of practice via the school curriculum that has made it extremely difficult for the students to attend.

The Polish Catholic Episcopate has sharply criticized this tactic as a direct and open violation of the constitution that guarantees religious freedom—in theory—to the people of Poland.

The Communist regime here again systematically obstructed the construction of new churches and religious facilities, blaming it on the lack of material and skilled labor.

The overflow of faithful attending religious services is not only an example of religious devotion, but most of all, the lack of new churches that are desperately needed by the Polish faithful.

Catholic publications are restricted on the pretext of paper shortage, so are publication of books that are only permitted to be printed in very small quantities so as to avoid mass circulation.

Pastoral letters are confiscated, and recently attempts have been made by the regime to forge the pastoral letter of Cardinal Wyszynski in hopes of creating confusion within the Catholic Church in Poland—this has failed. For the average Polish citizen, the pulpit and foreign broadcasts are the only avenues of truth and information from the west.

The Polish Government considers religious holidays—such as Christmas and Easter—as nothing more than social affairs at which to eat and drink, rather than meaningful religious experiences.

The same is considered of weddings and baptisms. Every effort is being made by the regime to promote atheism especially among its youth during these solemn occasions, proclaiming that God is dead and that religion is a novelty for the old people.

Foreign publications, especially of a religious nature, are strictly prohibited and are confiscated if brought into the country by a foreign visitor or by a Polish national returning.

The chairman of the Central Committee for Customs in Poland stated on January 31, 1976, that "such material be forbidden since it leads public opinion into error by giving information not in agreement with reality or information otherwise potentially damaging to the welfare or interests of the Polish Peoples Republic."

Forty years ago, Pope Pius XI issued the encyclical Divini Redemptoris in which Communism was condemned in that organized religion cannot collaborate with Communism because Marx condemned all religion as the opium of the people. Atheism is the very core of Communist doctrine. To deny this fact is indeed living in a fool's paradise.

The history of Communism in Poland and in other parts of the captive world is an uninterrupted chain of violations of the fundamental human rights—especially the right to worship.

The ultimate goal of the present Communist regime is to stamp out religion in Poland altogether because Communism can only survive by total elimination of the rights and dignity of man.

This is what the Catholic Church in Poland stands for and preaches. The basic principles on which Catholic social teaching is built is the dignity and freedom of the individual. Communism in Poland and elsewhere is totally opposed to any system which defends the dignity of man as an individual.

Pope Pius XI, in his encyclical Divini Redemptoris, stated that, "The problem of communism lies in the cultural revolution which aims at producing a new type of man without faith, without hope, without love and also without personal freedom and responsibility."

The present Communist regime in Poland feels that the Roman Catholic Church poses a threat in that it is an elaborate international organization undermining the authority of the Communist state. Because of the prospect of outside influence which is considered to be in conflict with their Marxist doctrine, it is therefore considered to be a very serious threat.

Kazimierz Kokal, head of the Office for Religious Denominations, in May of 1976, flatly stated that, "The Church is the enemy which should be annihilated. Religion has, in the long run, been extricated from human consciences and thought."

Furthermore, Kokal stated, "We shall yield nothing to the Church." Therefore, after 30 years of Communist rule in Poland, very little has changed in regard to the government's policy of church and state relationship. It can be compared to nothing more than a cat and mouse existence.

Today the regime continues to strive through a sophisticated campaign of atheism and social harassment in its goal to stamp out religion in Poland altogether.

The west often asks why do the Polish people enjoy more freedom than the rest of the Soviet bloc?

The answer is quite simple. After 1,000 years of Christianity and survival of the Nazi barbarism during World War II, the Communist regime in Poland has been unsuccessful in their efforts to stamp out religion without creating additional problems and obstacles for the regime.

The Polish Catholic Episcopate knows and understands that as long as there is a Communist Government in Poland, this struggle will continue.

Another reason for this so-called Polish freedom is that the Communist regime knows that the true power in Poland is the Roman Catholic Church, under the pastoral guidance of Stefan Cardinal Wyszynski, the Primate of Poland. This tradition of the church being supreme in Poland has been around for over 1,000 years.

The Polish nation would have gone through many devastating revolts against the present regime if it were not for the plea for peaceful cooperation by the Polish Catholic Episcopate. The Communist regime knows this and so does the Polish nation.

The Roman Catholic Church in Poland is prepared to uphold the virtues of the gospel that is committed to her, regardless of what obstacles are put in the way by the present Communist regime.

The Polish Catholic Episcopate believes that the God-given dignity invested in man should be restored to the human individual if there is to be genuine peace and harmony in Poland.

The basic virtues of the gospel are the right to maintain and develop one's corporal, intellectual, and moral life—especially the right to worship—and education in private and public.

Pope Paul VI stated that, "The Church is concerned, above all, with the right of God and can never dissociate herself from the rights of man created in the image and likeness of his creator."

Therefore, man can only foster and penetrate these rights through the guidance of the Holy Spirit.

The Catholic Episcopate in Poland believes that the responsibility of evolution in the area of Human Rights and genuine religious freedom in Poland rests not upon a single international organization but upon everyone without exception.

The Roman Catholic Church in Poland feels that the Helsinki Commission can be instrumental in strengthening the international juridical mechanisms for the purpose of making effective the full operation of human rights for the people of Poland and other captive nations in the Soviet block a possible reality. This can only be achieved through evolution not by revolution.

The Catholic Episcopate believes that the suppression of the right to worship and other basic human rights in Poland have become institutionalized and this violates the most fundamental rights of life, liberty and the pursuit of happiness.

The Catholic Church's mission of evolution is to create or reactualize world opinion by an auto-critical conscience in the hopes that with the cooperation of the various international human rights organizations, an effective mechanism may be achieved and thus assure the realization of genuine religious freedom and human rights to the people of Poland.

Incidentally, I lost track of how many times I heard Cardinal Wojtyla use the phrase "evolution, not revolution." It was his credo.

Eventually the future Pope did seem to bring about a little easing of the Polish government's hard-line attitude toward the Church. For one thing, Polish churchmen now are permitted to participate in Social Security benefits. Also, a Polish-language edition of the Vatican newspaper, *L'Osservatore Romano*, is allowed to be imported into Poland without restriction on the number of copies.

After we had been serious for a long stretch, on the bus the cardinal would break into song—mostly Polish folk songs and some religious hymns. One song that I will never forget is "Jak Szybko Mijaja Chwile." Translated, the song says, "How quickly time passes. In a year, in a day, in a moment, we will part. All that will be left will be sadness and longing."

This sad song always brings tears to my eyes. Every time I hear it, I think of Cardinal Wojtyla and that bus ride. It was almost our theme song—*Jak szybko mijaja chwile, Jak szybko Mija Czas, Za rok za dzien, Za chwile Razem nie bedzie nas.*

4

A Future Pope's Eye View of Washington

I often think of how lucky it was that Pope John Paul II saw Washington when he was just a cardinal. Not just because I had the pleasure of walking beside him and seeing it through his eyes, but because he saw it *his* way.

He would never be able to see it with such freedom again and with such naturalness. When he returned in 1979 as Pope, there was hardly a moment's privacy, even for studying something at leisure—whatever he looked at, everyone else looked at, curiously.

And when he looked away from what he was studying, all eyes were turned toward him. Ah, no, there was no more time, in 1979, for savoring such things as the art of Constantini Brumidi as he wandered up and down the halls of Congress, studying the powerful work of the Italian whose murals cover the walls and ceilings as well as the inside of the Capitol dome.

So I did not realize how important it was in 1976, as I

tried to be the guide and keep everyone more or less together and moving along. Wojtyla watched my endeavors to herd him and the nineteen Polish bishops with amusement, and now and then would give me a little fake salute as if he were taking army orders.

As our "Celestial Bus" left Philadelphia, I was already thinking of Washington—but first there would be a few adventures in Baltimore.

It was party time in Baltimore, and we were a happy group when the bus rolled to a stop at the Polish parish of the Holy Rosary located near the waterfront, in an area called "Little Poland."

We had been welcomed to Baltimore by the local clergy, who included retired Lawrence Cardinal Shehan and present Archbishop William D. Borders. That had been at the Roman Catholic cathedral, Mary Our Queen Basilica, which Cardinal Wojtyla had also visited on his first trip to the U.S. in 1969.

Now the cardinal was in great good spirits, spreading cheer among everyone—some fifty people—as drinks were downed with the traditional toast of *Na zdrowie*—"To your health." Then the cardinal burst into song, singing the familiar "Sto Lat," with everyone joining in with gusto—"May you live to be a hundred and more." To Poles, this song is the equivalent of singing "For He's a Jolly Good Fellow."

I was getting used to the cardinal, so I was not at all surprised to see him climb on top of a chair to make a little speech about how he felt to be among his own people who were also his brothers and sisters in Christ. "The ocean, which is only a geographic boundary of separation, has never separated our hearts and souls with those living in Poland."

Then he climbed down, after calling out, "Let us drink and be merry."

I, too, had done a little climbing and was taking pictures from the top of an upright piano, clinging to a nearby lamp fixture for balance.

The cardinal certainly knew how to keep a party going. These guests were having as much fun as a bunch of kids at a birthday party. All that was needed were the hats and balloons to make it complete.

Then the party was over, and it was time for Cardinal

Wojtyla and the delegation to join the people waiting in the church hall in another building. Now the reception was formal. The cardinal was greeted by the mayor of the city, and everyone found a place at a sit-down luncheon, where the cardinal was treated to Polish-style cooking as prepared by the ladies of the parish.

The menu included ham, kielbasa (Polish sausage), potato salad, tossed salad, hot rolls, coffee, and Polish sweets. There were coffee *babka* and poppyseed torte. But no wine or spirits of any kind were served. That surprised me. I had also been surprised that there was no sauerkraut or other Polish traditional vegetable to go with the kielbasa. But the meal was a success, anyway, and the cardinal especially enjoyed the poppyseed torte.

Years later, at the Vatican, I found out why, as you will too.

Before eating, the assemblage was treated to a rare experience that they would be able to tell their grandchildren about. They were led in prayer by a future Pope. Later, he also rose and blessed everyone—creating a moment of elation in the room.

After the meal and a short expression of thanks from the cardinal for the warm welcome, he was treated to a surprise when a huge, colorful sheet cake was rolled out in his honor, decorated with the inscription: *Witam Niech Zyje Nam Sto Lat*—"Welcome, may you live to be a hundred."

At that moment, everyone broke into the familiar Polish "Sto Lat" song.

There was only one sour note. Governor Marvin Mandel, of Maryland, who was at the banquet, refused to come over to shake hands with the cardinal. I wanted to be sure to get a photograph of the two men together, and so I sent a note to the governor requesting him to please come over, but he ignored it.

Then the master of ceremonies, one of Baltimore's clergy, went over to ask the governor personally to come and be introduced to the honored guest from Poland, but again without results. I will never forget seeing Governor Mandel sitting there, puffing on his pipe, stone-faced, as others around him laughed and sang and had a good time—especially the cardinal.

After the public reception in the parish hall, Cardinal Wojtyla and the Polish bishops took a tour of Holy Rosary Church, and again I saw the cardinal's mood change before my eyes. He now sat engaged in silent prayer while all the others walked around and talked.

I had wanted to take just such a photo of the cardinal, lost in prayer, but somehow it seemed so private a moment, that he should be left alone. I simply sat near him, thinking of what an extraordinary person this man was. So deep was his communion with God that faith seemed to radiate from within him.

After the cardinal left the church, we went out into weather which had also changed mood. It was drizzling and I followed the cardinal with my umbrella, which was in need of repair and left us both rain streaked. No matter. Once we were rolling down the highway again, happy songs emanated from the bus, the cardinal conducting.

Now there was a new voice among us. Father Philip Majka, a Washington-area priest, acted as the liaison between the Baltimore and Washington, D.C., clergy, when they met with the cardinal and bishops. An outstanding young priest, Father Majka joined our happy bus gang in Baltimore and accompanied us during a tour of Washington the next day.

Together, he and I had worked out the itinerary for sightseeing in the capital city.

We arrived at the office of the U.S. Catholic Conference of Bishops at 1312 Massachusetts Avenue, NW, running late as usual. But when I pointed out the lobby murals of Jan Henryk de Rosen, the cardinal did not mind being considerably later as he examined them very closely, enjoying their beauty.

There were three huge panels—the central one showing the Savior seated on a throne with one foot resting on a globe showing the Western Hemisphere, and the side panels depicting the struggle between the forces of good and evil.

To show the sheer size of the display, the central mural alone measured thirty-five feet long and was ten feet high.

Cardinal Wojtyla was very impressed and held forth on de Rosen's contributions to religious art, mentioning that the artist was represented at the Vatican.

Our host this time was Bishop James Rausch, General

Secretary of the U.S. Episcopate, whose office, unfortunately, was on the sixth floor. Since there were two antiquated elevators in the building, the party was almost over before everyone made the scene.

Fortunately, I arrived in time to see Cardinal Wojtyla in a playful mood, plopping himself down at the bishop's desk and pretending to be boss. "Pay attention before I replace you all," he said with mock sternness.

Eventually, they did get down to serious business and hold a small conference. I took the opportunity to hurry to the National Catholic News Service, several flights down. I told them there was a story and picture opportunity upstairs because Cardinal Wojtyla was in the building with a delegation of nineteen Polish bishops meeting with Bishop Rausch at that very moment.

I said that if they had no one to send, I would supply the pictures and story myself. Their response was completely negative. They already had pictures of the cardinal in their files, they said, and he was not important enough for a story.

I climbed the stairs with leaden feet. It was snub number two. Mandel had been first, and now this.

The tables turned, and I had the last laugh in 1978 when this obscure cardinal became Pope. The News Service suddenly remembered me and hounded me for those photos which I had once promised to give them. I must admit to some pettiness in first refusing to give them any of my now-precious photographs, but when the editors prevailed on some clergy to use their good offices with me, I did part grudgingly with some of the desperately needed pictures.

Nursing my wounds, I returned to the meeting in Bishop Rausch's office and started taking photos by myself, ending up having a very good time.

It was back on the bus at five, and this time we were on our way to "Little Rome," which was the popular name for the Catholic University area, because of its many religious houses and colleges. The cardinal and his group were the guests of St. Joseph's Priory, near the campus, and as the cardinal rested I helped unpack his luggage.

That evening, August 9, 1976, the cardinal and the bishops concelebrated a well-attended mass at the National

Shrine of the Immaculate Conception—the same place where President Lyndon Johnson's daughter Luci was married during his administration.

The most important moment for Cardinal Wojtyla came immediately after the mass, when he went down the aisle to one of the Marian Chapels honoring Our Lady of Czestochowa, the venerated patroness of Poland. At a reception that followed, there was talk of how, in 1656, King Jan Casimir had crowned the original icon painting in Poland "Queen of Poland."

I took a group photo of this historic event. And when Cardinal Wojtyla returned to America as Pope in October of '79, he again came to the same church and chapel to pay his respects to his favorite patron saint, Our Lady of Czestochowa.

After the cardinal had paused at the chapel, a reception followed. And after that, the delegation went back to St. Joseph's Priory for a private dinner reception hosted by the U.S. Catholic Conference of Bishops.

There followed an evening's schedule of banquet and more talk and more talk. I did not know how the cardinal could survive it all, but he did and seemed to thrive.

I, also, was invited to the dinner, and it was a spectacular event, catered by Ridgewell Caterers, famous for their embassy parties and for those of society in Washington.

They brought the finest of table linen, candles, crystal, and china. It was like the White House state dinners that I had covered and, on a few occasions, at which I had been a guest.

The meal was typical American party fare—fruit cup, tossed salad, filet mignon, green beans almondine, special whipped potatoes with cheese-filled topping—made into pretty individual servings—various wines, parfait, and coffee.

The dinner lasted until about 10:30 P.M. or so. Many toasts were exchanged and again there was the traditional singing of "Sto Lat."

Then everyone adjourned to their rooms—but not for long. They opened their suitcases, pulled out bottles of cognac and vodka, and reassembled to have a real Polish-style celebration.

Gone were the clerical collars. Since this was strictly a stag party, the churchmen were dressed in T-shirts and slacks, like suburbanites on a summer's night. Much teasing and jokes abounded, as they sipped drinks that had been poured into water glasses filled with ice.

The jokes flew as the men unwound. Since I couldn't keep up with them, I frequently retired to the hall to dump my cognac into the potted plant that stood in front of a statue of the Madonna—may heaven forgive me.

That night, I suffered my first withdrawal pains. I realized the party was almost over. In just a few days, I had gotten so used to the humorous, the playful, the serious, and the inspiring moments with the cardinal that I could not bear to accept that this visit was almost over, and perhaps would never come again.

In the morning, when I arrived at St. Joseph's Priory at 7:30 after about five hours sleep, the cardinal kiddingly asked me what took me so long. I just gave him a dirty look.

During breakfast, we outlined the agenda for the day. I was going to give them the deluxe guided tour—the U.S. Capitol, Library of Congress, Air and Space Museum, John F. Kennedy Center for the Performing Arts, mass at St. Matthew's Cathedral, lunch at the historic Gadsby's Tavern in Old Town Alexandria, a visit to Arlington National Cemetery—and, gasp, on to the National Airport for departure to Detroit.

The gasp was the cardinal's as he snapped to and saluted me, saying, "Yes, Mr. Director, we are at your command." One of the bishops added, "Szostak is a very influential man in Washington. The whole city will be under control until they've gotten us safely on the plane."

But even with our massive schedule of places, at the last minute we could not get started because a reporter was finally showing up to interview Cardinal Wojtyla about his trip to America and get his reflections and observations.

Unfortunately, the interview would not be shown in the United States, because the reporter was from the Voice of America and Radio Free Europe.

After breakfast, while the cardinal was busy with his interview, I helped with the baggage. I remember Wojtyla's bags were extra heavy. His were loaded down with books—what else? One bag was bursting at the seams and had to be tied with a belt to hold it together.

Finally, we departed St. Joseph's Priory about 9 A.M., en route to the Capitol. Everyone was most impressed by the breathtaking view of Constantino Brumidi's paintings under the dome and the view of the city from the west side of the Capitol steps.

I took them down into the bowels of the Capitol building to the underground trolley for a subway ride to the Dirksen Senate Office building. They were startled to learn that congressmen and senators use subway cars for such short distances. Wojtyla remarked with amusement that this was just "another outward sign of American know-how and wealth."

They were also impressed to see the *Congressional Record*. They could not believe that such a huge and perfect magazine format is printed every day. Coming from a nation that is always short of paper, they were also dumbstruck when I showed them the trash room of the Capitol basement, with all the trucks lined up in convoy formation, full of paper and printed matter to be discarded.

They had to take pictures to believe it. One bishop remarked with awe that people in America have so much they do not even know what to do with it.

There was just one office they particularly wanted to see—that of Senator Edward Kennedy. Since I used to work there, I knew many of the staffers, and they were happy to assist. I took my group around as though the place were mine. Naturally, they were amazed at such easy access, and I hadn't the heart to tell them it was just because of my Kennedy connection.

As we passed the Supreme Court building en route to the Library of Congress, there was an unhappy moment as one of the bishops remarked that this was "American Auschwitz." He was referring to the Supreme Court decision of 1973 legalizing abortion, saying the decision would cause the death of millions of unborn babies. He shuddered when I asked whether the group would be interested in touring the place.

We hurried on to the Library of Congress.

There, Wojtyla looked with amazement at the fine organization and efficiency that assured easy access by anyone to information on books. He set to work immediately, testing out the system by looking up a particular book of philosophy by a Polish scholar, and he smiled with pleasure when he found it. Yes, the Americans were keeping up with literary works from abroad as well as their own.

But the highlight of the visit to the Library of Congress was the discovery of an exhibit of Polish publications as prepared by the library's Slavic division. "And they did not even know we were coming," he said with a chuckle.

After the tour of the Capitol and Library of Congress, we boarded the bus again and buzzed over to the Air and Space Museum.

Now the fun began. Cardinal Wojtyla and the Polish bishops were like kids, scattering all over the building.

Their eyes were as big as saucers. They wanted to see everything, which was impossible for the time allotted. However, we compromised by agreeing to concentrate on the space exhibits only.

Cardinal Wojtyla was captivated with the Moon Buggy, which had been invented by a Polish immigrant, an engineer at NASA. The cardinal and the bishops bought out the complete supply of postcards of the Moon Buggy from the card rack. Money ran out, so I paid for the remainder of the Moon Buggy wonders—about a $10 subsidy.

Getting them away from the Space Age exhibits was almost impossible. I chased after them like a harassed teacher with children on a field trip. They were going everywhere and scattering in every direction. I had to remind them of the time.

At one point, I had to take some of them by the hand. They were a bit shook up when I said that they must be on time for mass at St. Matthew's Cathedral. They were certainly not going to be late for that. So they hurried to the bus. It took a few other travelling priests as well as myself to round up this happy, boisterous gang, among them a future Pope. Not for a minute did I dream that I was acting as a guide to a future Pontiff on a tour of a museum.

Once we got back on the bus en route to the John F. Kennedy Center for the Performing Arts, I gave them the lowdown on how it had been built and the important gifts from various nations that it housed.

As an added treat, I had the bus stop at the Watergate Hotel, which is just next door to the Kennedy Center, and I ran in to pick up a few souvenirs. I met them on the bus after their tour. The mementos that I grabbed from Watergate were postcards, pencils, matchbooks, and a spoon lifted from the Watergate Coffee Shop. On the bus, I was distributing these treats like candy to kids. All the mementos went like hotcakes. They were delighted to have them. I gave Cardinal Wojtyla the spoon. He looked at me and said, "I hope you will confess this to a priest the next time you go to confession." He gave me a wry smile and added, "What else did you get?"

I said, "The deed to the Watergate. However, they are mailing it."

Wojtyla answered, "Knowing you, even that is possible."

While en route to St. Matthew's, I pointed to sights outside their windows.

One of the happiest things I was able to do was arrange a visit between the cardinal and the great Polish-born church artist, Jan Henryk de Rosen, whose work we had seen just the day before and who lives not too far from me in Virginia.

De Rosen, a senior citizen of eighty-five at the time, had been involved in designing murals and mosaics for cathedrals and churches for some fifty years.

The Polish community was invited to participate in the mass that Cardinal Wojtyla celebrated at St. Matthew's Cathedral. I drew attention to the fact that we had a renowned artist in our midst—Jan de Rosen.

I knew him from Polish circles and had even gone to watch him work at his studio near my office in Washington. I had brought Polish churchmen from abroad to see him designing religious mosaics.

The Polish bishops invited de Rosen to join them on the bus to Gadsby's Tavern in Old Town Alexandria, for the luncheon in honor of the cardinal.

Short, white-haired, and stooped, de Rosen looked

like anything but the artist who was credited with creating the largest mosaic in the world. This masterpiece is in the United States and covers 13,000 square feet in the main dome of the St. Louis Cathedral.

Listening to the cardinal and artist talk, I learned details about how the famed creator of mosaics and murals works—laying out the design and the exact colors in tempera for the tile setters and painters to execute on walls and ceilings.

But the most important thing that was revealed in the conversation was the artist's experience with papal art. In 1933, he had been commissioned by Pope Pius XI to do two battle scenes for the walls of the Pope's private chapel at the summer papal palace at Castel Gandolfo, near Rome. Pius XI happened to like battle scenes.

The Polish artist, who did not immigrate to the U.S. until 1937, and who fought with the French forces in World War I, worked two years on these battle scenes, only to have Pope Paul VI order them covered over. "Paul VI did not like battle scenes," De Rosen observed sadly, and so his work now lay hidden under thick draperies.

The story has a happy ending, however. As soon as Wojtyla became Pope, he ordered the draperies removed.

Later on, after Wojtyla was back in Poland, several individuals asked me why Cardinal Wojtyla and the bishops did not try to see the White House, even on a regular public tour. Hadn't they wanted to?

The answer was simple. Cardinal Wojtyla, as a representative of the Polish church, did not want to make this trip to Washington, D.C., a political one. It was a private visit to the people and the Polish-American community of Washington.

However, several Polish-American ethnic leaders almost caused an incident through kind-heartedly trying to arrange for Cardinal Wojtyla to visit the White House and meet with President Gerald Ford. There was no problem in making this possible—as a matter of fact, the appointment was already made by these overzealous ethnic leaders.

But they had made arrangements without checking the personal wishes and feelings of the cardinal. So, I became the liaison, making the desires for the privacy of Cardinal Wojtyla quietly known to the White House. The White House respected this wish, and no meeting was held between President Ford and Cardinal Wojtyla. The ethnic leaders were outraged, and now I had to be a liaison between the cardinal and them.

"Cardinal Wojtyla and the bishops have to go back to Poland," I explained, "while you are still in a free nation and can afford to be a political hero. However, this must not be achieved at Cardinal Wojtyla's expense." Wojtyla just smiled, but did not say anything.

So now, with no stop at the White House, we were on our way to St. Matthew's Cathedral, where the bishops and Cardinal Wojtyla concelebrated a pontifical high mass in Polish before a congregation of Polish-American worshippers at high noon.

The sermon was preached by then Archbishop Wladyslaw Rubin of Rome, who was destined in 1979 to become Cardinal Rubin in the first consistory of John Paul II.

The mass took about an hour. I kept busy taking pictures of the mass in progress. I had hoped that the Catholic press in Washington would use some of these pictures to write a story. Here we encountered snub number three. Again they were not interested in the story because the event and man were too obscure. These pictures did not see the light of day until later, when the little-known man became Pope John Paul II. Then everyone was suddenly after all of my pictures—and I released only part of them, being very selective about where they went.

After mass, the cardinal went outside the door to greet all the people who had attended, hugging and kissing the children and having a few words with each. He was extremely fond of children, especially babies.

When I saw pictures of his warmth with little ones after he became Pope, I was not amazed or view this as unusual behavior. I kind of expected it. I would have been amazed if he did not continue along these lines as Pope.

Now, in Washington, with all the handshaking and embracing of parents and children alike, Cardinal Wojtyla was about to miss his own bus. He was bending over and listening intently to a little elderly lady who was talking into his ear. I stood behind her, waving my hands at him and pointing to my watch.

I managed finally to get him on the bus and off to Alexandria's Gadsby's Tavern. George Washington was supposed not only to have eaten there many times, but he also held his birthday ball there and among those invited was the famous Polish revolutionary war hero, Tadeusz Kosciusko.

There was a little stir. The cardinal and his bishops were delighted that they were going to dine in the same place Tadeusz Kosciusko had dined.

We were twenty minutes late, and all the guests were waiting at Gadsby's Tavern. Even so, the irrepressible cardinal could not resist making a quick dash across the street to take a closer look at a Polish arts and crafts gallery whose street sign proclaimed, "Old Warsaw Galleries."

Wouldn't you know it, with his luck the owner turned out to be an old and dear friend from the cardinal's home in Krakow, Mrs. Barbara Lazo. Even in the scant few minutes he spent with her, he left his old friend and neighbor glowing with happiness.

And no harm was done. When Cardinal Wojtyla made his grand entrance into the tavern, everyone gave him a standing ovation. Again, a woman played an important role at the banquet, Vice-Mayor Nora Lamborne of Alexandria presented him with a key to the city.

The menu was very filling, and it was said that it could have come right off the table of the Father of His Country, George Washington—plenty of red wine, plenty of roast beef, potato dumplings, green peas, salad, and pastries and coffee.

But there was a little shadow of unhappiness hovering over the table because one man was missing, Bishop Thomas J. Welsh of Arlington, Virginia, the highest ranking prelate of the area.

The word that buzzed around the table was that two invitations had been tendered the American bishop. The Polish bishops at the table kept watching the door. The feeling was that someone from the diocese office should have been on hand to greet them. Instead, it seemed, there was no response, written or oral, not even a phone call to the assemblage at Gadsby's Tavern explaining what had happened.

It was taken as snub number four.

Later, I learned from reliable sources that the bishop had even been in the area, but it turned out he was innocent. *Others* at the chancery office had thought that the occasion was too *obscure—a Polish* cardinal and bishops were too *obscure* to interrupt his schedule.

All these ecclesiastical snubs reminded me of the old and familiar Christmas Story in which Mary and Joseph are told by the innkeeper that there is no room for them in the inn. Little did the innkeeper realize that Christ the Redeemer was about to be born unto Mary and Joseph. And little did these clergymen know at that time that this obscure Polish cardinal would some day become the 263rd successor to St. Peter.

And before I leave the subject, let me mention that when the group went on to Detroit, after Washington, a similar fate again awaited Cardinal Wojtyla. His fellow cardinal, John F. Dearden of Detroit, also ignored a reception for him.

But Cardinal Wojtyla and the delegation of nineteen Polish bishops had learned to accept infinitely worse treatment under the Nazi occupation of Poland and later under the Communists during Stalin's time. So they accepted their lot with humility.

But to return to the elegant luncheon party at Gadsby's which many people had cared enough to pay $17.50 to attend, a problem developed. Since it was an election year, a sprinkling of politicians had turned up.

They were warmly welcomed by the cardinal, but then they announced they wanted their pictures taken with the Polish prelate to use in their political campaigns back home among ethnic voters. It was the one thing Wojtyla had tried to avoid during his visit, even to the extent of avoiding a meeting with the President of the United States, Gerald Ford.

I looked at the cardinal, and he looked a little grim, though he tried to be gracious. Before I took the pictures, I slipped a note to Wojtyla telling him to pose and that my lens would be set for overexposure.

He smiled and murmured so only I could hear, "Dante has a place for people like you." The politicians posed, and I just clicked away as each one asked to be next to pose with Wojtyla.

Eventually, I simply sent them the overexposed slides with a note of regret that the pictures just did not come out. I know it must seem like much ado about nothing to American ears, but, as my friend Cardinal Wojtyla remarked more than once, few Americans had any idea of what life was like behind the Iron Curtain.

Even these pictures could have made life harder for the Polish church leaders after their return to Poland had they been used with propaganda pieces against the Polish government—which was the avowed intention of some of those politicians in seeking ethnic support.

By the end of the luncheon, we were running about an hour late. The officials at Arlington National Cemetery were prepared for our visit, and they gave us a VIP tour once we arrived.

Cardinal Wojtyla requested that his first stop be to pay his respects to the famous pianist, Ignace Jan Paderewski, who is temporarily interred in the Maine Memorial that was erected to honor those who lost their lives aboard the USS MAINE during the Spanish-American war.

Paderewski died in New York in 1941 during a concert tour of the U.S. His last request was that he be returned to Poland when it is once again a free and independent nation. President Franklin D. Roosevelt honored his request by letting his remains be interred in Arlington.

Inside the Maine Memorial, Ignace Jan Paderewski's remains are in a coffin that is sealed in a wooden packing crate for shipment, and resting on a metal stand. On top, a brass plate reads "PADEREWSKI." This was a moving moment. A dead silence befell all. The bishops and Cardinal Wojtyla kissed the box holding the remains and then recited in unison in Latin: *Requiem aeternam dona eis Domine. Et Lux Perpetua luceat eis.* ("Eternal rest, give him, O Lord. And let perpetual light shine upon him. Amen.")

The cardinal also saw the marker in honor of Ignace Paderewski that was dedicated by President John F. Kennedy in 1963. It was just twenty-five feet from the Maine Memorial.

Before we left the interior of the crypt, I managed to give Cardinal Wojtyla a small sliver from the crate that holds the remains. I put it in a paper napkin for him.

Cardinal Wojtyla was so touched by this gesture that he embraced me and kissed my hand in gratitude. I could see how moved he was and, in turn, *I* was immensely moved.

At one point during the tour of the Maine Memorial crypt, one of the bishops picked up a handful of soil and put it in his pocket. He said to me, in Polish of course, that he was doing this because of his age—that he might never come back again. He wanted to take with him this genuine symbol of freedom and wanted this soil to be on his grave. It was a very touching moment for us all.

After I had taken photos of the group at the memorial crypt, we walked to the JFK and RFK grave sites, where again the cardinal and bishops prayed in silence.

Referring to the dead president, Wojtyla said sadly, "America and the world lost a great leader who wanted to do so much but was prevented by certain sinister forces." Similar comments were made about Robert Kennedy.

Now we were back on the bus with no margin of time, heading for nearby National Airport. After Detroit, the group would split up for individual tours of Polish communities in the U.S. and Canada.

For security reasons, the cardinal and bishops were split up into two flights, one hour apart, en route to Detroit. Cardinal Wojtyla left on the first flight. I helped to check in his luggage as well as that of the bishops.

Feeling the heaviness of the cardinal's suitcase, I suddenly remembered how, in Philadelphia, someone had given him an armful of anti-Communist material to read, with a warning not to take it back with him.

The cardinal looked up from the table at which we were sitting at the time in Philadelphia, and said, "*We* [the Church] are not afraid of *them*. They are afraid of *us*." When it was time to leave, he carefully sifted through the literature to see what it was wiser and more politic to leave behind.

The last ten minutes were very emotional. It was a final farewell. It could be a very long time before we would see each other—perhaps in Poland, perhaps in America, perhaps never. Again, not realizing that a future Pope walked among us.

That familiar song was sung, "Jak Szybko Mijaja Chwile" ("How quickly time passes. . . . All that will be left will be sadness and longing").

All of us were misty-eyed. Cardinal Wojtyla thanked me for all that I had done for him, not only in America but also for the favors of the past in Poland via small gifts. And, above all, he thanked me for my friendship.

When Cardinal Wojtyla embraced me, my cheek felt his tears. He said to me and to the others who had gathered to see him off, "We look to America and its church for inspiration to the people of Poland. We will never forget the generosity of the American people."

He again embraced me and said, "My son, be thankful that you are an American and for the freedom you enjoy in this great land of yours, and never forget Poland." He added that he was certain he would see me again "perhaps in Poland next time, and I hope that I can reciprocate your kindness in Krakow." My own eyes misted as he said, "I will remember you all in my daily prayers."

I escorted him to the steps of the plane. Before he went inside, he smiled a sad smile. One could tell that it was a sad departure. I waited until Northwest Airlines Flight 367 left the ground. This was August 10, 1976, at 5:30 P.M. Little did I, or anyone for that matter, suspect that the next time we would meet in America this unknown Polish cardinal of the four snubs would already be the 263rd successor to St. Peter.

───────────── ◄══❯► ─────────────

The letter that I received from him upon his arrival back in Poland was dated "Krakow, October 26, 1976," and brought a wonderful feeling that helped ease the loneliness I still felt after having walked in the shadow of this great and warm human being for even a short time.

His first words were, "It was for me a great joy and a personal pleasure that I could meet with you in Philadelphia and Washington, and to spend several days with you.

"It would be for me a greater joy if I could see you again. However, we have not given up hope." We had been talking of my coming to Poland to visit him and to see the home of my ancestors. I was glad to see he still maintained, "I am certain that . . . you will be our guest in Krakow someday."

It was a fairly long letter about the American trip, but what gave me special satisfaction was learning that I had been of some service in making the trip easier for all my Polish churchmen friends. "The fact that the bishops felt so good and relaxed during their visit," he wrote, "is because you have created for them a family atmosphere."

I was always eager to see what new way he ended his letters to me. This time, he signed off with, "I send to you my brotherly best wishes and blessings for the New Year in your work. I place you under the protection of Our Lady of Perpetual Help. With sentiments, Karol Wojtyla." Again, before his name, he drew a cross.

We exchanged Christmas cards.

After Christmas, he wrote again, saying, "I am grateful for the warm welcome I experienced in Philadelphia and Washington, and for the help of my friends there, but most of all for the union of thought and heart which your words witness and which reaches over the ocean.

"May God bless you and send a happy New Year to all your family!"

The cardinal signed the letter with a cross and his name, Karol Wojtyla.

5

"The Child Is Father of the Man..."

Strangely enough Karol Wojtyla grew up with the prophecy that there would someday be a Polish Pope. While a student in Krakow, Karol would explore old churches, monuments, and castles around the city—some of which were in ruins.

Of all the monuments, the one he revered most was the crypt of Wawel Castle, because it contained the tomb of Juliusz Slowacki, the nineteenth-century Romantic poet who dreamed of impossible things—and predicted the election of a Slavic Pope.

In Philadelphia, we had compared religious upbringings. My parents had stressed in me a deep sense of religious, moral, and academic values, as was the case with young Karol Wojtyla.

We had both been altar boys, I in upstate New York, where my mother still lives. Wojtyla had been born right across from the church in his hometown of Wadowice.

My childhood had been easy compared to his. He had to get up at a very early hour every morning in order to help with the seven o'clock mass. On top of that, he had to fix his own breakfast, because his mother had died when he was nine.

The loss of his mother had been the greatest tragedy of his life. He made me realize how very lucky I was to still have my mother, even though I was an adult with my own family started. Because of him, I showed my appreciation by phoning her more often and flying to visit her in Schenectady, New York.

From others, I learned that by the time Karol was ten or eleven he was acknowledged to be the brightest student in all of Wadowice. I was far from the brightest in Schenectady, but as I told him, I did achieve a certain notoriety in the local newspapers when I built my own early color television set and applied for and received a patent for a certain TV improvement—but no money.

We did not share hobbies—Karol had collected and later written poetry. I had collected archeological relics such as animal skulls and stones with fossilized deposits, and had, with a slightly younger friend of ten, set up a museum in my own home—open to the public. And that too had caused a certain local notoriety.

We did share soccer.

Karol had turned into a tough little boy and even acquired the title of "daredevil" for taking chances with his life in swimming in the flooded Skawa River.

And as a little rascal, that wasn't the only way he made his mark in school. He developed a talent for impersonating his teachers, which was much appreciated by his classmates.

He also played at parish priest, offering the mass and making his playmates serve as altar boys—a game not too well received by the priests.

But though he had his pranks, he was known for his good heart and was quickly singled out as the favorite. For example, he served as president of his school sodality.

The Pope's early memories of Christmas are much different from those of an American child. His Christmas tree, called the *choinka*, was decorated with ornaments made of eggshells, paper, straw, and pine cones. The paper was cut into shapes of snowflakes, and straw was woven into shapes of angels. Instead of strings of popcorn, he had strings of nuts and dry mushrooms.

The big meal came on Christmas Eve and was called *wigilja*, meaning vigil dinner. Sauerkraut was always served, and at the end of the meal traditional gingerbread cookies cut in the shapes of shepherds and stars were passed around.

The nicest Christmas Eve custom, however, concerns a special bread baked in a mold of the Infant Jesus. The special bread, called the *oplatek*, is traditionally brought to the homes of the families of the parish by the organist of the church, who is then given a little gift of money.

The bread is then ceremoniously served by the father of the family at the Christmas Eve dinner. First, he breaks the bread, with the mother holding the one end, and then, with each child in turn.

Religion was a part of Karol Wojtyla's life from his earliest memory, as were the nicknames of "Lolek" and "Lolo." The sound of church bells was part of the sound of childhood. So was the odor of incense and getting up in the cold to be on time to help serve the 7 A.M. mass.

Even then, Karol showed signs of being an administrator. He organized his fellow altar boys and made sure each did his job to keep the services running smoothly.

He also showed early signs of a feeling for theater.

As a young lad, Karol Wojtyla had two favorite books. He liked to read aloud from *The Teutonic Knights* and *Quo Vadis?* both by Henryk Sienkiewicz, and he also loved to recite the poetry of Adam Mickiewicz. This was his first introduction to the theater as an amateur actor.

His father was a stern man and that may have helped Lolek develop into a thoughtful boy who read much, but who also grasped at school friendships for any humor and youthful joyfulness that he could bring into his life.

The house is still there—7 Koscielna Street, in Wadowice, Poland. The street name, incidentally, means "church." It is fitting that the man who lives in Wojtyla's old apartment at this writing, Zbigniew Putyra, is an old school chum, who is now a teacher of physics at the high school which both he and Wojtyla once attended.

From the window of the apartment, you can still see the sundial that Karol Wojtyla looked down upon. Inscribed on it is a motto, "Time passes. Eternity remains."

Little Lolek used the same leadership he displayed at church, as the number one altar boy, when it came to school-work. He never denied help to any of his little friends who needed it. And, since he read and studied more than they did—as if to honor his mother's memory—he was a popular boy, indeed.

Not that Lolek would not compete in sports. He was a fierce competitor in soccer, playing the position of goal-keeper. But education was a different matter. In *gymnasium*, which is what high school was called, Lolek became a student of the philosophers Kant, Hegel, and Schopenhauer.

It was in high school that his interest turned to the theater. He could feel a role and express it in a very convincing way. And, it was in high school where he met his friend and history teacher, Mieczyslaw Kotlarczyk, with whom he would form an underground theater during World War II. It was considered to be one of the best amateur theatrical companies in Poland.

How strange that we cannot see who will influence our lives. The unknown quantity in Karol's life was Prince Adam Sapieha. It was just a little thing that happened in high school that much later would bear fruit in Karol's becoming a priest and start him on the road to the Eternal City.

This long association began in 1938 when Krakow's Archbishop Adam Sapieha, who had been a prince, came to Wojtyla's high school graduation ceremony. As top student, Wojtyla was chosen to give the welcoming speech to the great churchman who was honoring their school.

Sapieha was so impressed by the quality of the speech and the style of the speaker that he immediately wanted to know if the young scholar was interested in becoming a priest. Through a teacher, Wojtyla informed the high church-man that he was planning to study Polish literature and semantics at the ancient Jagiellonian University where the famous astronomer, Nicolaus Copernicus also studied.

But life had other plans. And one day, he would be the successor to this very prince, and this prince would save his life.

Lolek could not have had a more complete religious education. Both his parents were pious and kept an atmosphere of religious piety around their two children—Karol, who was actually Karol Joseph, Jr., and his older brother, Edmund.

Karol, Sr., an administrative officer in the Polish army, believed in strict discipline, and it seemed rather cruel at the time that he sometimes made his sons study in bitterly cold rooms to toughen them up.

As it turned out, he was right, and the resistance to cold that little Lolek developed made him grow up to enjoy hiking and skiing in freezing weather.

The gentle one in the family was Lolek's mother, Emilia Kaczorowska, who treated her sons with tenderness and love, and who was a former schoolteacher. But even as a little boy, Karol Wojtyla knew something was wrong. His mother was frequently ill, and some of her nieces would come to help take care of the house and children.

In spite of her poor health, she was known as a woman who was always smiling and cheerful. Religion was her strength.

In 1929, when Karol, Jr., was only nine, his mother died during childbirth, delivering a stillborn girl. It was the first, and perhaps, greatest tragedy of the future Pope's life.

As a result of this close association with ill health, his brother, Edmund, determined to grow up to be a doctor. He did, becoming an intern at Bielsko.

Tragedy struck again in 1932, when Edmund caught scarlet fever from a patient and died.

But, before that, in the early years after their mother's death, the two boys were close to one another and to their father, and often went on outings together—hiking and swimming.

I soon realized, as I got to know him, that one of the

greatest influences on Karol Wojtyla's life had been the loss of his mother, Emilia—which would be Emily in English.

Mrs. Zofia Berchard, who was one of Karol Wojtyla's teachers in elementary school, remembers that when he was eight years old just before his mother died, he was a very friendly child who displayed rare talents as a happy leader. Death made him withdraw into books.

Helping him cope with death, Karol's father and twenty-four-year-old brother, Edmund, would take Karol on spiritual retreats to the Marian shrine at Kalwaria Zebrzydowska.

It was there that Karol would later go by himself during important periods of his life, in moments of sorrow and joy.

After Emilia died, father and sons were more dependent than ever on each other's company. During their long walks Wojtyla Sr., taught Lolek some of the World War I military songs that he had sung in the Polish army. I have four samples that I want to share with you:

> Wojenko Wojenko cozes ty za pani
> ze za toba ida ze za toba ida chlopcy malowani
> Kto ciebie po kocha, kto ciebie po kocha
> w krotcew grobie lezy

Translation

> *War, oh war, what sort of woman are you*
> *That you are pursued by the handsomest of men?*
> *If one falls in love with you,*
> *He will soon lie in his grave.*

> Choc Buza huczy w kolo nas
> do gory wzniesmy skron
> choc burza huczy wkolo nas
> nie placzie dzieci nie placzie
> Nie zginie Polska nie

Translation

> *Although a storm rages around us, we are not afraid.*
> *The wind tears through us, but we struggle courageously*

And look forward to a brighter future
As a white eagle soars into the sky and cries
"Do not weep my children, Poland will never be lost,
never."

Jak to na wojence Ladnie
kiedy ulam z konia spadnie
koledzy go nie ratuja
jescze konmi go po trautuja
Spij kolego w ciemnym grobie
niech sie Polska przysni tobie

Translation

When a lancer falls from his horse,
His friends show no pity,
But trample him with their horses
"Sleep dear friend in the dark grave
And dream of Poland."

Uzywajmy puki czas
bo za sto lat nie bedzie nas

Translation

Let us be merry while we still have time,
For in a hundred years there will be no more of us.

Karol's father never remarried. Since Wadowice was a small town, all the people shared the family's sadness and took little Lolek under their wing. It was especially hard on Lolek because his brother, Edmund, was fifteen years older than he. It was almost as if he had two fathers rather than one father and a playmate.

A teacher who still remembers Lolek from the time he was nine years old recalls his melancholy air lasting for several years, during which he stayed by himself much of the time, thinking and reading. Then he seemed to go completely the other way, becoming very social with children of his age and jumping back into living with intensity.

By the time Lolek graduated from high school, his father had retired and was hard-pressed to support them both. When he saw how great a student his son was and how desperately the boy wanted to go to Jagiellonian University, Wojtyla, Sr., made the sacrifice of moving to Krakow, the site of the university.

Probably the whole direction of Karol's life, which led by a winding path to the door of the Vatican, can be attributed to this move. Now Karol met and came under the influence of a mystic, a religious man who was to be the greatest influence on his life decision.

The man was, at first glance, only a simple tailor. But, Karol felt a strange affinity and learned that the tailor, who was twenty years older than he, Jan Tyranowski, had started out as an accountant but had become a tailor in order to have time to meditate and pray, as well as to study Christian mysticism—especially the life of St. John of the Cross.

I had heard so much about this wonderful man of God from Wojtyla and others that I almost could see young Karol climbing the narrow stairs to the second-floor flat at 11 Rozana Street in Krakow to visit him.

Once a week, Karol and some of his young friends would meet at Jan's flat in a group they called "The Living Rosary." When World War II came, the meetings were held at great risk of being noticed by the Gestapo. People were killed for such unauthorized gatherings.

A few times, they did have to disband until it was safe to start the meetings again. Tyranowski's flat was not that of the ordinary tradesman. It was filled with fine Victorian furniture and family portraits, as well as with religious paintings. The walls were lined with books, many on religion and theology.

At this stage, it was not the tailor who looked out of place in these surroundings, but the future Pope who was dressed in shabby old overalls and clogs and often showed signs that he worked in a limestone quarry.

Both men looked past the trappings of clothing, position, or work titles to achieve heights of spirituality in striving to become closer to God by following the way of St. John of the Cross.

At eighteen, Karol Wojtyla's life was fast becoming a tug-of-war for his soul. Should he follow his dream of becoming an actor? Or should he follow the guidance of the devout tailor who pulled him in the direction of the priesthood?

Karol Wojtyla's first theatrical performance had been in high school, when he played the juvenile lead in *Maiden's Vows*, a classic comedy written by Aleksander Fredro in 1832.

As his acting improved, so did his enthusiasm for the theater. By 1937, Karol starred in and helped direct his high-school drama club's production of *Sigismund Augustus*, a play by Stanislaw Wyspianski. He and his group did so well that they toured other towns in the area to put on their show.

As a young freshman just starting university life, Karol would spend most of his time studying or engaging in intellectual discussions. He had no regular girl friends.

He went to cafes because he hungered for friendship and camaraderie. He could even be a bit of a prankster, hiding someone's drink or poking gentle fun.

It was at this time that young Karol was introduced to the newly formed Krakow theater fraternity, later known as Studio 39, for the year it was founded. And his strong speaking and singing voice, as well as his pleasant good looks, marked him for leading male roles.

The theater seemed the most exciting place in the world to young Karol. An important theatrical experience that Karol Wojtyla would speak of in later years was playing the lead role in a musical drama called *The Knight of the Moon*.

This was a Faustian legend about a nobleman who sold his soul to the devil. At the end of the play, he is being carried off to hell, but fights back with prayer, even in midair. His prayers work and he is let go, only to land on the moon.

Even stranger things were happening on earth, however, in the real world. A madman was on the rampage. He threatened Poland from the West, and his name was Hitler.

6

Of War and Peace

Where was Karol when the bombs fell?

Only a man like Karol Wojtyla would calmly face the first day of a war, ignoring air-raid sirens and the burst of shells as he helped serve at the altar. Almost everyone else was heading for the bomb shelters.

The *blitzkrieg* started on Friday morning, September 1, 1939. It was young Karol's routine always to go to confession on the first Friday of every month. Though bombs screamed, starting Germany's hit-and-miss destruction of Krakow, nineteen-year-old Wojtyla showed up as usual for mass, only to find there was no one to help the priest in the Wawel Cathedral.

Wojtyla, having been an altar boy for years as a child, proceeded to help the vicar, as only a few faithful huddled in prayer. He would always remember how the sound of sirens and bombs almost blotted out the words of the mass.

It took only one month for Poland to fall under the devastating Nazi war machine. Life would never be the same, and Karol would know only life under occupation—from that day forward—Fascism followed by Communism.

At nineteen,. Karol was forced to mature quickly as war and enslavement came to Poland, and his way of life crumbled in ruins around him almost overnight. Now began a Nazi reign of terror. All high schools and colleges were ordered closed. The use of the Polish language was forbidden in schools, and youth were ordered to learn German.

Books were burned, libraries were destroyed, and the nation's treasures were destroyed or hauled off to Germany. The Polish press was closed down, as editors were liquidated.

Many churches were closed. Some were burned, some made into storage rooms for the German conquerers. Cemeteries were plowed under. Polish churchmen were being arrested and put into concentration camps.

At one point, Karol Wojtyla was almost a part of a group of intellectuals who were being rounded up to be sent to a concentration camp for extermination. It happened in November 1939 when many professors and theatrical people were lured to the university by the Gestapo, supposedly for a cultural meeting.

A promise had been thrown out to them of new cooperation to improve the cultural life of the area. When the professors and others showed up, they were herded together and shipped off. At the last minute, Wojtyla, who had intended to go to this meeting to see about the reopening of theaters, had been warned by a friend, who knew from underground connections that the meeting was a trap.

Many died horrible deaths of starvation and in gas chambers. This was only one incident. The underground heard of many more throughout Poland, including the murder of many clergy. Before the nightmare was over, 3,647 priests and 1,117 nuns were put into concentration camps. Of these, 1,996 priests and 238 nuns were put to death—many at Auschwitz concentration camp.

As the plot thickened and the Gestapo tried to infiltrate the underground, Wojtyla and the loyal underground army fought back by means of counterintelligence directed against the infiltrators and the Gestapo brains who were directing the infiltration.

Assassinations of Gestapo took place, as well as general confusion. Those in Wojtyla's theater group not only assumed disguises themselves, but trained others in the underground to impersonate German officials and forge permits and passes.

Though I talked with Cardinal Wojtyla at length about these days, he played down his own part and never told exactly what he did. It was from others that I learned how important his work had been in the resistance movement, even though after a relatively short time he had to spend most of his days hidden deep under the Episcopate Palace in Krakow.

Silence was something Karol Wojtyla learned well in the underground. To keep mum was the first commandment of this netherworld. Those who talked endangered other lives. Many underground soldiers died, tortured by the Nazis, during interrogations. Some took their own lives rather than betray their fellow patriots.

When the theater became a part of the underground operation, the members set about saving the lives of those on the Nazi extermination lists, which included the names of the total Jewish population of Krakow. The Jews were being rounded up and shipped off in what was to be called "the final solution" by the Nazis.

In Karol's hometown of Wadowice, a good portion of the townspeople had been Jewish, and he played with Jewish children everyday.

Karol Wojtyla and other members of Studio 39 would try to help the Jews of Krakow by hiding them in private homes, churches, and barns until they could be given safe passage out of the country.

Very important in the work was the securing of new I.D. cards for Jews and helping with disguises of clothing, wigs, and makeup. There was a Polish underground railway, with Romania being the first stop for the refugees in the early days of the war.

It was not a perfect operation of which Karol Wojtyla

found himself a part. There was always some betrayal, even among the Poles, who were part of the fifth column, as the traitors who helped the Nazis were called.

Often Wojtyla would hear of the torture of underground agents who were caught, or even suspected of being part of the underground. Gallows were erected in public places, and bodies hung for all to see and take warning.

Everyone had to have a work permit. Karol Wojtyla and I would have conversations about this time in his life, and I told him how my father had not been so lucky as to get a work permit to remain in Poland. He had been impressed into a work force that was shipped to a farm in Germany to provide food for the Nazi conquerers.

One of my earliest memories is of a Nazi officer who kept coming to the farm on which my father worked. He would place me, then only a toddler, on his lap and get a kick out of teaching me to yell out, "Heil, Hitler," with the accompanying stiff-armed salute.

My parents didn't think it was funny, but there was nothing they could do. At least they were eating.

Wojtyla did not fare as well. He was often hungry after the dark days of 1939, and what was worse, he had to find bits of food and wood to take home to his father, who was in poor health.

At first, Karol, through the help of underground friends, managed to get a work permit that he could flash when asked for it. Without it, he would have been quickly deported or imprisoned.

By day, he hewed stone—backbreaking labor—in a quarry. And by night, he attended some classes that professors risked their lives to hold in their living rooms. He also was soon using his theater work to help cover up the fact that he was busy smuggling Jews out of Poland.

After he became Pope, one of his first meetings was with the leading survivor of the Jewish community of Krakow.

Wojtyla once sat after breakfast talking to a group of us about how fearful German soldiers became as they patrolled the streets of Krakow. They took to stopping people by shouting, "Hands up," instead of saying "Stop," because so many German soldiers had been shot by the underground.

Wojtyla would always carry along a false identity and smiled now as he told us how at one time he had carried the papers of a Gestapo inspector.

Before he was so hunted that it became dangerous to go out at all, he had learned his way through every alley in the vicinity of Krakow.

From the widow of one of Wojtyla's fellow underground theater group, who told it to a priest friend of mine, I learned of the future Pope's greatest exploit. The wife of his schoolteacher and cofounder of Studio 39, Mieczyslaw Kotlarczyk, told how Karol Wojtyla was able to save a trainload of Poles and Jews who were destined for the concentration camp. The theater group, acting as Nazi officials, diverted the train elsewhere. They waited till night.

Then, in darkness, the box-car doors were pulled open, and Wojtyla and his group hid the prisoners in various places in Krakow until they could be smuggled out of the country a few at a time.

But Wojtyla wouldn't talk of his own exploits. Instead, he preferred to talk of how he and the other underground actors and seminarians would scrounge to survive. The Nazi plan, he explained, had been to starve the Poles into submission.

"To survive," he said, "we had go to the countryside to get food. Sometimes we would barter articles of clothing, small valuables. I had to sell an extra pair of pants that I had.

"To bring it back was even more difficult due to the German patrols inspecting. Here, again, we had to disguise ourselves as German officials to get back into town."

Meat was so scarce that they were happy to get a supply of lard as a substitute. They lived on dry black bread, lard, onions, a few potatoes, and if they were lucky, a little tea.

In the winter, the young actor would stalk about at night, stealing coal and wood from the Germans. For a time, he discovered a bonanza, stealing the chairs in the building where the Nazis showed their propaganda films, breaking the chairs into fire wood.

I could identify with what he was saying. Even in Germany, I had the same diet of bread smeared with lard and over it, for flavor, was placed a slab of onion. And my mother had been forced to make soup out of clover leaves. I remembered how my father and I went scrounging in the darkness for half-rotten apples left under the trees and told the cardinal of those precious apples.

But to return to those grueling days in the stone quarry, since he was not as strong as he would eventually be, he was switched to an easier but much more dangerous job—placing the explosives that would break up the rock.

Karol Wojtyla's coworkers at the stone quarry recalled years later how he would search for or barter for cabbage, potatoes, or coal—anything to keep himself and his aging father alive.

His father, Karol Wojtyla, Sr., had developed heart trouble, and a family of friends—the Kydrynskis—were helping to look after him and feed him. One day, early in spring 1941, Karol returned with medicine for his father and found his father dead of a stroke. He spent that night on his knees beside his father's bed, not rising until morning. The Kydrynskis insisted that he stay with them for a while.

After Karol's father died, his friend, Mieczyslaw Kotlarczyk, and his wife, Sophia, were suddenly homeless and needed a place to live. Karol insisted they live with him. Even then, Karol Wojtyla was so humble that he turned the whole flat over to the couple, staying in the tiniest room himself.

Like Karol, Kotlarcyzk lived a life of danger. He died an early death. His widow was deeply touched when Wojtyla published poems and articles in tribute to her husband, using the pen name of Andrzej Jawien.

Years later, in 1956, Karol wrote a poem about those days called "The Quarry." It was about his memory of the work there, and the tragic death of a fellow worker, who was his friend.

Written during the Poznan uprising when the workers took to the streets and demanded more freedom from the Soviet Polish puppets, this was one of Wojtyla's first open manifestations of his unending fight for human rights.

But again, returning to World War II days, by the time

the U.S. entered the war on the side of the Allies, Karol was working for the Solvay Chemical Company, unloading bags of lime and tending boilers.

Wojtyla did not think that what he was doing in the underground was half enough, and he acted so rashly that each time he left on a mission his friends said final farewells, expecting never to see him again.

Though young Wojtyla felt moments of sheer terror as the Gestapo would appear on the scene, his youthfulness also helped make it a game in which there was excitement and even a thrill in being such a good actor that they thought he was one of them.

His ability to imitate and mimic his teachers back in grade school came in handy when he imitated German officers, or a delivery boy, or whatever disguise he had chosen.

Wojtyla's theater group was responsible for forgeries of German documents, orders, and ordinances, which created much confusion among the Germans, who were accustomed to following orders and pronouncements.

In Krakow, for instance, an announcement was posted in the streets and mailed to all German officials, proclaiming that the Reich ordered the registration of cats in the German army.

Another time, the daring theatrical rascals invented new passes that were supposedly ordered to take the place of old passes. Thus, they were able to obtain many authentic passes in exchange. Other times, they fouled up delivery schedules.

The Allies recognized the Polish underground as being the leading underground movement of World War II, and Poland was hailed as an inspiration to the Free World. The highest recognition of Poland's underground came from the Nazis themselves. Toward the end of the war, and near the time of their downfall, Nazi leaders were quoted as saying that if they had an organization as dedicated as the Polish "Underground State," Germany would never face humiliating defeat.

The Nazis had given several directives to the occupation overlords on the treatment of Poles—"Work or die," and, "Extinguish all vestiges of cultural life."

Karol and his defiant Studio 39 players considered it

their obligation and an integral part of the resistance to the enemy to continue their secret readings and performances.

It's touching to look back now and imagine Karol Wojtyla defying the Nazis in one of those secret productions, when he played the astrological sign of Taurus, wearing a bull's head in the play *The Moonlight Cavalier*.

It is a minor miracle that Studio 39, which name was changed to Rhapsodic Theater, continued to put on Polish patriotic and classical works—all during the Nazi occupation. And even though they were busy with underground work, in all they put on twenty-two performances of eight different plays.

One day, Karol went to his old schoolteacher and theater friend, Mieczyslaw Kotlarczyk, and told him, "Please don't cast me any more. I am going to be a priest."

Wojtyla's mystic friend, Jan Tyranowski, had nudged Wojtyla in the direction of the priesthood, but it was two near-fatal accidents that shocked Karol into embracing the church. It was almost as if a higher power were flinging him into it.

First, it was a streetcar accident, a senseless episode from which he awoke in a hospital. He had time to think, and his thoughts were strangely religious. He felt a sudden interest in becoming a Carmelite, but persuaded himself that his God-given talents made acting his life's mission.

He left the hospital only to be struck, almost immediately, by a German army truck. This time he got the message, and this time he knew that with the limited number of days that man is granted on earth, he must use those days in service to the church and to God.

Wojtyla gave this account to some of his friends: "I do not know what happened. I was walking to work along Konapnicka Street, and when I woke up, it was the next day, and I was in bed with my head bandaged." But that was not the worst of it. Wojtyla suddenly remembered that his seminary notes from his secret studies for possible priesthood had been in his pocket. He was still trying to make up his mind. If the Germans found them it would be the end of Wojtyla—he would be summarily shot or sent to a labor or concentration camp. Even worse, they might torture him to find out who he was studying with.

His mind was eventually set at rest when the mysterious woman who had found him came and whispered that she had also found the notes and destroyed them. "Do not fear arrest from me," she said. That fear over, Wojtyla proceeded to get a friend to join him in studying for the priesthood and spent his recuperating time—doctors who treated him had given him a certificate of exemption from work—coaching the friend in the required subjects he would need to be admitted for seminary study.

Now Karol was leading a double and triple life—working at the chemical plant, studying for the priesthood, and engaging in his underground activities with his theater friends.

For over a year, seminarian Karol Wojtyla was lucky. Then he learned that he was on the Nazi blacklist and that they were actively searching for him. Prince Adam Sapieha, the archbishop of Krakow at that time, also heard of the price on Wojtyla's head and sent scouts to find him and bring him to the sanctuary of the church.

Now Wojtyla began an even more dangerous life, hiding in the basement of the Episcopate Palace and surfacing at odd moments to do some daring deed, then slipping back into the bowels of the palace again. He came and went, through a window, slipping in and out wearing a theatrical disguise.

But eventually discretion became the better part of valor, and Wojtyla disappeared from sight and lived, like a male Anne Frank, in the underground passageways of the palace. He was joined by other seminarians.

Since he did not show up for work any more, the underground started a rumor to protect him—he had been killed or shipped to a concentration camp.

When the Nazis were routed, Karol Wojtyla came out of hiding and welcomed the Soviet army of liberation. There were great reunions among friends.

Karol saw agony and hardship greater than his own among his former classmates. He responded with sympathy and generosity. Among his fellow students, many were half-starved and in need of medical aid. Some were escapees from extermination camps. Since many of his friends had been Jewish, many of their parents had been killed by the Nazis in gas chambers.

United Nations relief work was instrumental in providing rapid physical recovery of seminarians and other friends.

There were so many repairs needed. The palace that had been their sanctuary and salvation was in shambles, even without windowpanes, and Wojtyla and his fellow seminarians set about finding and fitting new ones and retiling the roof.

Then they tackled the seminary across the street that had been occupied by the Nazi storm troopers during the war years. The next job Karol and his friends tackled was the reorganization of the seminary library, which was in shambles.

They were anxious to have everything restored and in at least semifunctional order so that formal schooling could resume openly with top professors to guide them. At this point, Karol Wojtyla was in his third year of seminary training, or its equivalent, thanks to his underground studies.

It was a sad time for Archbishop Adam Sapieha when the repairs were completed and the students left his palace to return to their former homes now that they no longer had to hide. Prince Sapieha admitted that he felt lonely because Karol and the other seminarians had been like children to him.

When, that same year, Archbishop Sapieha was elevated to cardinal, Karol Wojtyla led his friends in preparing a party and program of entertainment to celebrate.

For his part, Karol chose to recite the passage from Henryk Sienkiewicz's *Quo Vadis?* dealing with the persecution of St. Peter in Rome. In 1978—thirty-two years later—Karol repeated these same words in his own inaugural address, not as Karol Cardinal Wojtyla, but as Pope John Paul II:

> Peter wanted to leave Rome during
> Nero's persecution. But the Lord intervened.
> He went to meet him. Peter spoke to Him and
> asked, "Quo Vadis Domine?"—"Where are
> you going, Lord?" and the Lord answered him

at once, "I am going to Rome to be crucified again." Peter went back to Rome and stayed here until his own crucifixion.

When the Russians "liberated" Poland, they promised that the university could operate freely and the church would be normalized, but Wojtyla found his country had traded one set of masters for another.

However, the seminarians' studies were resumed under more conventional conditions, and Karol Wojtyla was ordained a priest on November 1, 1946.

The years in the quarry left a mark on Karol Wojtyla and, even as Pope he would single out men who had worked with a pick and axe in quarries. In March 1980, when I was visiting him in Rome, he greeted a group of quarrymen from the marble mines of Carrara as if they were long-lost brothers.

Telling them how much joy they were bringing him by letting him remember his own career, the Pope said, "Please take my greeting to your friends who share the toil, the difficulties, and the risks of your exhausting work.

"Providence willed that I, too, at a certain period of my life, had the hard experience of quarry work. I have therefore been able to realize personally what difficulties it involves. Strength is not enough—skill, control of one's nerves, rapidity of reflexes, and courage are also necessary.

"It is not enough to be able to operate the machines. You must be familiar with the mountains, know their secret, and also their hidden dangers. Above all, solid moral gifts are necessary to support the fatigue of a day spent at grips with pneumatic drills, chisels and mallets.

"There are, furthermore, unexpected occurrences and accidents which can change the environment of work in a few seconds into the setting of a tragedy. I have experienced this too and these events remain marked on one's soul for the whole of one's life."

He could have added the physical body as well.

Even today, the Pope bears the mark of these accidents

that so influenced his life, a shoulder that is different from the other. Some people remark that he seems slightly stooped, but it is the effect of the early injuries.

I consider the Pope's experience with Jews to be one of the things closest to his heart, even today. I remember that tears came to Wojtyla's eyes when we talked about World War II and the Nazi terror that his countrymen and mine experienced.

He had to dry his eyes when he mentioned the needless death of the Jewish people at Auschwitz and Treblinka, and how sad it had been to hear of new deaths of friends in the underground.

After the war, Karol Wojtyla continued to try to help the remaining Jews and alleviate their new sufferings under the Russian occupation and the Polish Communist party.

As soon as he had enough power, Wojtyla, as Archbishop of Krakow, organized Catholic seminarians at the University of Krakow to restore the Jewish cemeteries.

Tombstones that had been defiled were tenderly cleaned and repaired. Wojtyla dared speak out against anti-Semitic actions inspired by the local Communists who were now in charge of the government, demanding that they cease and desist their hostility.

Hoping to change the climate of the country, Archbishop Wojtyla helped get articles published on Jewish history and culture. In a church journal under his direction, called *Common Weekly—Wspolny Tygodnik*—he personally ordered the printing of a series of stories commemorating the Jewish victims of the Nazi holocaust.

And it wasn't just a remote and theoretical concern. As documented by a Polish Jewish leader, Maciej Jakubowicz, Wojtyla throughout his years as Bishop of Krakow always kept his door open to Jews, who could come to discuss the problems of the Jewish community.

When they had difficulty in securing kosher meat, for example, they appealed to him to intercede with the authorities. Nor did he always wait for Jewish spokesmen to come to him. After he was made cardinal, he showed up one Friday night at the Krakow Synagogue during religious services.

He had heard that the Jewish congregation was having

trouble maintaining its synagogue, he said, and wanted to know how he could help. It was a problem shared by Catholics and Jews alike in the supposedly atheistic land. When Cardinal Wojtyla returned to Poland in June 1979 as Pope John Paul II, one of the most important things he scheduled was a trip to Auschwitz concentration camp to honor those who had been sacrificed to the barbaric Nazi would-be conquerers of the world.

And there he spoke words that showed his surviving Jewish friends that he had not forgotten them and still shared their agonizing memories:

> In particular, I pause with you, dear participants in this encounter before the inscription in Hebrew. This inscription awakens the memory of the people whose sons and daughters were intended for total extermination.
>
> This people draws its origins from Abraham, our Father in faith. The very people that received from God the commandment, "Thou Shalt Not Kill," itself experienced in a special measure what is meant by killing. It is not permissible for anyone to pass by this inscription with indifference.

I have the tape of this speech at Auschwitz, given to me by some Vatican friends. I was impressed with how his voice was so choked with emotion at this point that he slurred some words, which he then repeated. Mixed with the tears was an underlying note of anger.

The following month, John Paul II held an unprecedented audience with a group of Polish-Jewish-Americans to discuss the proposed Janusz Korczak Literary Prize with the members of the Anti-Defamation League of B'nai-B'rith.

Korczak was a brilliant Polish Jew, an educator, physician, and pioneer in child welfare, who had chosen to go along to the gas chambers of Treblinka rather than abandon the orphans in his charge to save himself.

One of the men who attended the meeting at the Vatican was Abraham H. Foxman, who told the Pope, "Your Holiness, I was born in Baranovicze, Poland. I am a survivor of the holocaust." He went on to say, "I am alive today because of the compassion and humanity of a Polish-Catholic woman, who risked her life to save me from the Nazis. I want again to express my thanks to her through you. I ask that you bless her soul."

The Pope leaned forward and seemed moved.

After the meeting was over, the Jewish leaders said, "We are delighted with your courage and your forthright statement on human rights." The Pope reflected a moment and replied, "Don't thank me yet. I have only begun."

As they started to leave, John Paul II took the hand of Abraham Foxman and squeezed it, saying, "Thank you for your precious words."

There has already been another incident.

The Pope was able to bring about the dramatic release of a Jewish child from Great Britain who had been kidnapped and held in Sardinia.

After the Pope's broadcast appeal to the kidnappers of Annabel Schild, arranged for the father by Basil Cardinal Hume, little Annabel was taken from the cave where she had been imprisoned and turned over to her father.

The kidnappers might not fear the long arm of the law, but they did not dare defy the longer arm of a Higher Power—and His spokesman on earth.

Rolf Schild, the ecstatic father, immediately cabled his thanks to the Pope, saying, "AS A JEW ORIGINALLY FROM GERMANY WHO LOST HIS PARENTS IN A GERMAN CONCENTRATION CAMP IN POLAND, AND ON BEHALF OF HIS ENGLISH FAMILY, I THANK YOU . . ."

7

A Small Vatican Connection

*J*ohn Paul II had a small Vatican connection long before he was made Pope. Paul VI, the Pope who made him cardinal, leaned on him as a theological consultant and chose him to conduct his personal Lenten retreat for 1976. The meditations from that retreat have been published in book form as *Sign of Contradiction* (The Seabury Press Inc., New York, 1979).

And before that, at forty-seven, he was the youngest member of the College of Cardinals meeting at the Vatican in 1967.

And long before that, at twenty-six, he was sent to Rome as a fledgling priest by Prince Adam Sapieha, who recognized something in him that set him apart and who wanted Karol Wojtyla to prepare himself to fulfill his destiny.

In order to understand the personal, intellectual, and spiritual life of Karol Wojtyla as priest, bishop, cardinal, and now Pope, one must know something about St. John of the

Cross, who lived in sixteenth century Spain. One of the first things I learned in becoming Cardinal Wojtyla's friend was that he had tried to mold his entire life in the image of this humble monk, son of a Spanish weaver.

John of the Cross was saintly in his holiness and extraordinary sweetness of disposition in spite of the abuse he suffered at various times in his life, especially from unreformed friars, who kidnapped him and kept him prisoner for almost nine months.

Even then, he used the time celebrating the glory of God and writing poetry that would live after him. He is considered to be one of the three greatest poets in Spanish literature.

His most famous work is in prose, however. It is *The Ascent of Mount Carmel*, and its theme is that, to seek union with God, man must always do "not the thing which is easiest but that which is hardest, not the most pleasant but that which is least pleasant . . . desiring to be stripped and emptied of everything the world can offer and to be poor. . . ."

Tyranowski, who fanned Karol's curiosity about religious mysticism, once told someone that Karol was one of the few persons he knew who had the same mysticism as St. John of the Cross.

Karol did follow in the saint's footsteps, even to the extent of becoming a poet, just as the Spanish saint had.

Few realize how difficult it was for Karol Wojtyla to follow the path that would lead to priesthood—and, eventually, the Vatican.

When Cardinal Sapieha accepted young Karol for study for the priesthood, he put him under the close guidance of professors and seminary lecturers, who risked their lives to come to the palace and give the lessons to future priests.

In all of Poland, there were only seven such underground seminaries. Since textbooks were rare, mostly destroyed by the Nazis, Karol Wojtyla had to learn from mimeographed notes, which he had to memorize, and then destroy, for fear of the Germans finding them, especially in a street search.

When Karol Wojtyla started his seminary studies, he was still working in the factory as well as carrying on his theatrical group's underground work. One friend remembers Karol sitting beside a boiler at the plant, struggling to understand deep theology. At times, young Wojtyla, would be discouraged by the difficult subject matter and the almost unbearable pressure of his total existence—but not for long.

Somehow, his deep faith sent a will to live and fight surging through him again. God had to have a plan.

While a seminary student, Karol Wojtyla would initial all his notes with the letters OAMDG (*omnia ad majorem Dei gloriam*—"*all to the greater glory of God*").

The prince, Cardinal Sapieha, continued to look after Wojtyla as if he were his son and immediately assigned him to continue his studies in Rome at the pontifical university, St. Thomas Aquinas, which is popularly referred to as the Angelicum.

No one was happier than Jan Tyranowski when Karol Wojtyla was to be sent to Rome for further studies. Tyranowski, the scholar and humble tailor, came often to visit young Wojtyla at the seminary. Since it was he who first introduced Karol to the writings of St. John of the Cross, they had much to talk about. Karol planned to make the life of the saint and his divine writings the basis of his doctorate thesis.

The ordination of Karol took place in the private chapel of Prince Sapieha. Even as cardinal, Wojtyla remembered that scene well and spoke of it with emotion. It had been a rainy, cold, gloomy day—November 1, 1946.

There was a shadow over his heart as he offered his first mass for those still mourned, who had passed away long before their time—his mother and his brother, Edmund.

Everything about the occasion was emotional, including a reception for him at the home of his godmother, Mrs. Wiadrowska. It was held in the same room where he had lain, immobilized, recovering from his wartime accident on the street. Without that accident, he might not be Father Wojtyla this day, hugging his godmother and making little jokes with his friends.

It was a bittersweet occasion. His friends were sad that he would be leaving them, even though he assured them it would only be for two years. Still, Rome was far away and no one knew when they would meet again. And ah, yes, there was a tinge of envy that the scholarly Karol was leaving the grimness of Poland for a much happier place.

Karol had never been far from home and certainly not out of the country, and it was both exciting and frightening to set out into the world, going where he knew no one and where no one knew him.

Father Wojtyla's first impression of Rome caused him to feel like that of a child in a fairytale world, full of joy and amazement. It was both a physical and spiritual uplift.

But not everything was sweetness and light in Rome. The studies were hard, and he was lonely for his friends.

Adding to his distress and isolation, there was no room for him at the Polish seminarians' dormitory, where he would at least have known the language, and he was forced to live at the Belgian College, where the language was French.

When he would write back to his friends in Poland, many times Wojtyla would say, "Please pray for me that I may to the best of my ability become an imitator of Christ and of those who reflect Him so perfectly."

He was referring, in part, to Jan Tyranowski, who was dying, and whom he considered a saintly man.

When Tyranowski died, Wojtyla was deeply grieved. Again, it was like losing a member of his family. Hadn't the humble tailor molded Wojtyla's spiritual career, nudging him until he surrendered his being to the church? It was as if Tyranowski had seen his protégé safely onto the path of destiny before quietly slipping away.

Wojtyla set about studying French intensely. He also struggled with Spanish in order that he might better understand the writings of St. John of the Cross in Spanish. And he cram-studied Italian. Every waking minute was consumed with his effort to understand and be understood in three languages.

So well did he do with his studies of French that in summer 1947 he took his vacation in Belgium and France, making it a most worthwhile experience by ministering to displaced Polish World War II workers who now found themselves unwelcome refugees in those countries.

In 1948, Wojtyla received his Ph.D. in philosophy at the Angelicum writing his dissertation on the subject his mystical friend had introduced him to. The title of his treatise was "The Virtue of Faith in the Works of St. John of the Cross."

Eventually the two years were up and Father Karol Wojtyla, rich in experience and linguistic skills, returned to Krakow, an older, wiser man. His first assignment might have been a humiliating experience to a lesser man. Archbishop Sapieha assigned him to a small parish in Niegowic as deacon.

To call the place simply rural is not enough. There was no electricity. There was no St. Peter's or Dome of Michelangelo, no statuary. There was an outhouse, a cowshed, and some chicken coops.

Gone were the amenities he had grown accustomed to in Rome—but there was something to take their place. A multitude of children's faces looking up, and the faces of the elderly and the hungry looking down at the earth with sadness. Father Wojtyla developed a great fondness for children and a great anger against want.

Wojtyla had not set himself above his flock and, indeed, he was a bit of a puzzlement to them.

The villagers had expected their new priest to come in an automobile, or at least a taxi, piled high with clothing and the comforts of life. Instead, he hove into view in a horse-drawn cart, his only possessions a suitcase and a few books.

One person from whom I learned a little about John Paul II's early days is Father Stanislaw Substehny of Poland, who recalls, "Wojtyla tended his parish on foot, wearing shabby trousers, a waistcoat, worn-out shoes, and carrying a briefcase that I would be ashamed to take with me to the market," he said. Niegowic was a tiny parish and a poor one but the young parish priest accomplished a lot, even starting the building of a new church.

He quickly showed that he did not place himself above the townspeople and drew very close to the peasant faithful. He would do anything to be of help. If a neighborhood farmer was ill, he would pitch in and take his place in the fields.

Father Substehny told how Wojtyla would often visit the very poorest people on the other side of the "tracks"—in this case, the river.

One time there was a woman who came to see him to complain that she had been robbed. Father Wojtyla gave her what money he had—and even a feather pillow.

The gift of the pillow greatly distressed some of his flock, for they had gone to a lot of trouble to get that pillow for him. They had discovered that he was sleeping on bare boards.

Wojtyla never changed. He continued to give away any little luxury that was given to him if he saw someone who needed it more.

Never ceasing in his drive for a higher education, Father Wojtyla was again leading a double, triple, or quadruple life—priest, builder of churches, writer, and student—commuting to the Jagiellonian University, twenty-five miles away, by bicycle, to complete the academic work he had started in Rome.

For his extended doctoral dissertation, "The Problem of Faith in the Works of St. John of the Cross," in 1949 he was awarded a degree in Sacred Theology (S.T.D.) maxima cum laude.

The people of Niegowic had never known a man like the Reverend Wojtyla, with such an approach to religion and the celebration of life. They worried that he was too good to stay long, and that they would lose him.

They were right. Too soon he was ordered to come to Krakow.

He was sad to be leaving them, but happy to be going back to the place that was closest to his heart—Krakow—and to begin his new position as full pastor at St. Florian's. He left, too, with the knowledge that a new church was rising heavenward. It would take ten years to complete what he had started.

In Krakow, Father Wojtyla refused to be hemmed in by one career and joyfully branched out as chaplain to the university students. He became a professor of theology at Jagiellonian in 1952, only to have the Communist government swoop down in 1954 and close the theology division.

It was fortunate that Wojtyla managed to earn a third doctorate in ethics before the Communist authorities, under Russian influence, abolished the department of religion at the Jagiellonian University.

This time, his thesis was "Evaluation as to the Possibility of Founding a Catholic Ethics on the Basis of the System of Max Scheler." Armed with the title of "docent," Father Wojtyla endured much hardship to become a lecturer on ethics at the Catholic University of Lublin, the only Catholic college still in existence in Poland.

Again, this was in addition to his pastoral duties in Krakow. Loving the university life and the give and take of bright young minds, Father Wojtyla would travel to Lublin in an all-night train ride for his three-day-a-week stint.

He would be so tired that it was difficult for him to control his fatigue, and often he fell asleep as students recited. But he was much loved, and as far as his students were concerned, could do no wrong.

His classes were overcrowded as his fame spread throughout the campus. His students listened closely as he talked to them, though they wondered at his poverty—they could see the threadbare sleeves of his cassock, his worn-out shoes, and always that same, dark-green shabby coat, worn with the collar turned up.

Very few students ever knew that he would devote more than half of his salary, then and later on as bishop, in assisting needy students who never knew where aid came from. Students of Wojtyla remember him not only for his intellect and kindness, but as a great listener, because they knew he was there to help them anytime, day or night.

"Uncle" Karol would always arrive fifteen minutes late, and it was a half hour before he started the lecture. He would comment jokingly, "My dear students, you know that my life is governed by Krakow time."

By then, Father Wojtyla was made head of the department of ethics at the university. He introduced a novel teaching technique—taking school to nature and God by holding seminars along the lakes and rivers, forests and mountains.

The seminar outings would end with a bonfire, games, and singing. "Uncle Wojtyla", as he loved to be called, soon got to be the most famous uncle in the countryside. It was on one of those outdoor seminars that Uncle Wojtyla learned of his elevation to bishop. His students were so excited that they carried him on their shoulders to the bus—much to his embarrassment.

Uncle Wojtyla was installed as bishop in the splendor of the Wawel Cathedral in Krakow on September 28, 1958. Friends from every phase of his career came to celebrate.

But he still lived in his two-room flat and refused to even think of moving to something a little more in keeping with his new title.

As bishop, Karol Wojtyla had to limit his academic duties by going less to Lublin. As a result, his lectures became longer and fewer. But the students, in protest, travelled to Krakow to have extra time with him, and there, Bishop Wojtyla would spend hours with them on hikes along mountain paths.

One time, he even performed a wedding in a little country church in the mountains at 7 A.M. on a Monday morning. The couple would be married by no one else, and that was the only time he had available.

One of my favorite stories about the Pope concerns the time after he had been elevated to archbishop and was on a skiing trip in the Tatra mountains on the Czech border. Somehow, he got carried away and found himself in Czechoslovakia.

The Czech border guards, who detained him, insisted on seeing his I.D., which he did not have in his possession. After telling him what a serious offense he had committed, they finally asked roughly, "Who are you?"

He replied, "Karol Wojtyla, Archbishop of Krakow."

A guard laughed heartily and replied, "Sure, and I am the Pope."

Eventually, someone did come along and identify him to the shock of the border guards, and Bishop Wojtyla was released. Their shock was understandable, considering how he was dressed—in old tattered sweaters, old-fashioned skis, and stocking cap. And of course, wearing his usual air of humility.

Father Wojtyla had been the despair of his friends. Instead of spending his Christmas gift money from his parishoners on himself, he gave it to poor students to buy books and supplies.

Once when he went on sick calls, he noticed a woman had only rags to cover her in bed. On his next visit, he brought his own covering.

He was just the same after he put on his bishop's

robes, wearing one mended garment to death and using his funds to buy clothes for those who were even poorer. His staff took to hiding his old robe and bringing out a suitable one for him to wear for special occasions, so that he would not embarrass them by looking poorer than they.

One time, friends recall, he was walking around in such a threadbare cassock that they collected money and bought him a new one. He didn't wear it. And after they had waited long enough, they checked with his housekeeper and learned that he had given it away to someone who needed it more than he.

He also ignored an automobile at his disposal. Instead, he wheeled around town on his bicycle, robes flying behind him.

Then there was the matter of the palace. In 1964, some thirteen years after Archbishop and then Cardinal Sapieha died, the Polish authorities had finally permitted the post of archbishop to be reactivated and Bishop Wojtyla was immediately elevated to succeed his old protector and mentor.

But he refused to move into the Episcopate Palace, the same building in the basement of which he had spent years hiding during the Nazi occupation. It wasn't the memories. It was just that his taste was too Spartan for palaces.

One day, he returned home from his rounds to learn that all his possessions were gone from his flat. His friends had simply scooped up everything and taken it to his proper home, the archbishop's palace.

Archbishop Wojtyla could not carry the stuff back, but he could be stubborn, too. He refused to sleep in the large ornate bedroom of the palace with all the priceless antique furniture, but instead chose to use only a tiny suite of two small rooms, as he had in his old flat.

He designated the remainder of the palace as meeting rooms and centers of various social and church activities.

When Archbishop Wojtyla went walking through his grand new home carrying skis one morning following the move, the poor, confused housekeeper thought he was carrying some new kind of bishop's crozier—the tall staff carried by high churchmen. That a bishop could go flying down hills on skis was unthinkable!

Even in those days, Wojtyla showed signs of being

quite different from those around him. Sometimes, though he tried to hide it, he was known to show his humility and union with the poor people around him by sleeping on the hard floor instead of his soft bed. And sometimes he would fast for the same reason.

When Wojtyla became archbishop and was, against his protests, moved to the fancy and remote Episcopate Palace, the palace came alive overnight with people from all walks of life. The archbishop seldom had meals by himself. He ordered that the palace be open to the public and not be a lifeless place.

One servant remembers his routine well. Wojtyla would get up about 5 A.M., celebrate mass, eat breakfast with his staff, and then go off to work in the chapel until 11 A.M. Following that, he would talk with anyone who came in off the streets until late afternoon, when he would have lunch with the last visitor.

Now came his time to be alone. He would take long walks in the park, meditating and praying, and then at 7 P.M. or later have supper with more guests, finally retiring at midnight.

One of the greatest struggles of Karol Wojtyla was to try to force the Marxist government of Poland to issue a permit to the Catholics of Nowa Huta to build a church.

The name of the place means New Foundry, and it was built by the regime as a model socialist town—actually a showplace—with not a church in sight but only nice wide streets, neat apartment houses, and a huge steel works named for Lenin.

In protest, the Catholics of the area had erected a simple wooden cross on a field where they gathered every Sunday to hold twelve masses, kneeling on the ground, in rain, shine, snow, and even winds so high that the words of the priest were drowned out.

In 1960, the authorities had attempted to stop this worship as against government policy, and a little battle had ensued with the worshippers throwing stones and police firing tear gas.

When Karol Wojtyla became Archbishop of Krakow in 1964, one of the first things he did was to pepper the authorities with petitions and requests for appeals for a construction permit for the church. Since the whole idea of the town had been to impress Moscow with a model city that was to be totally atheistic, he made no progress.

One morning, October 14, 1967, at 7 A.M., Karol Wojtyla, the new cardinal, arrived in town, and after a quick mass, seized a pick axe and started breaking the ground himself for the foundation. Others followed suit, and soon everyone was digging with a pick or shovel.

The cardinal mustered architects to contribute their services in designing a thoroughly modern church and was involved in every aspect of the building. Granite was brought from a riverbed and hand-polished by the young people of the area.

Slowly, the house of God took shape, and when it was time for the dedication, May 15, 1977, Wojtyla had a great present for the church—a cornerstone which had come from the tomb of St. Peter in the Vatican. It had been given to Wojtyla by Pope Paul VI.

On that May morning, ten years after he had first swung that pick axe, Karol Wojtyla, with tears in his eyes, put the cornerstone in place with his own hands. It seemed appropriate that the heavens too were crying and more than fifty-thousand Poles stood in the rain to witness and to receive his blessing.

On May 29, 1967, when he had just turned forty-seven, Archbishop Wojtyla became at that time the youngest member of the College of Cardinals. As to be expected of him, this elevation did not change him much—only his duties increased by more travel, especially to Rome for council meetings.

When Cardinal Wojtyla returned from Rome after receiving his red hat from Pope Paul VI, there was a reception held in his honor by his friends. In the receiving line, one of his old-time friends congratulated him, addressing him as "Your Eminence."

Wojtyla stopped him short by asking, "Jurek, have you taken leave of your senses?" Wojtyla still wanted to be called "Uncle," the nickname he had taken for himself.

But "Uncle" was no patsy. As a professor, he gave a

lot of himself and demanded perfection. Writing a master's or a doctoral thesis under his supervision was regarded as an extremely difficult task.

Time and again, Professor Wojtyla would shake his head sadly and tell a student, "It's not good enough yet. Carry on. Work at it some more." It became a special mark of distinction to have a thesis that Cardinal Wojtyla had labeled "good."

It was a little joke spread by the seminarians that in order to qualify for becoming one of Cardinal Wojtyla's academic assistants, there were three requirements: writing a good Ph.D. thesis, learning German, and the ability to ski.

The cardinal had not spent his own time merely teaching and skiing. He had over forty academic publications and three books to his credit.

As I have mentioned, one of my own relatives was a student of the cardinal. In July 1978, this cousin, Father Andrzej Szostek, sent his typed thesis to Cardinal Wojtyla for review and grading. However, Pope Paul VI died before this could be finished. Knowing how important such a thing would be in the career of the young scholar, before departing for Rome Cardinal Wojtyla paused long enough to write a one-page letter praising Szostek's work and suggesting an examination date of November 11, 1978.

The rest is history—the event that took place as a result of the voting in the Sistine Chapel changed the picture completely. Now there really was no time for a Pope to review a doctoral thesis. But still, my relative's old professor did not desert him.

Pope John Paul II, as one of his early bits of work, found time to send a letter to the dean of the faculty at the Catholic University of Lublin, asking that his private letter to Father Szostek of July 1978 be regarded as a review of the Ph.D.

Thus, for the first time in the history of the Catholic University of Lublin, a private letter became an official academic review. When their professor was elevated to Pope, the students hung out a big banner reading, "Our Professor, the Pope."

8

A Puff of Smoke

The year 1978 will go down in history as "The Year of the Three Popes"—Pope Paul VI, Pope John Paul I, and Pope John Paul II. Pope Paul VI had died suddenly at the age of eighty-one while at his summer palace, Castel Gandolfo, on August 6. John Paul I, who succeeded him, lived only thirty-three days as Pope.

All of us have a story to tell as to how we learned of the sudden and unexpected death of Pope John Paul I.

Naturally, the thing that I was most interested in when the funeral and the voting for the new Pope was all over was finding out exactly how my good friend behind the Iron Curtain in Poland, Karol Wojtyla, found out about this untimely death.

Franciszek Wicher, a lay staff member at Cardinal Wojtyla's Episcopate Palace, brought the news to him at about 8 A.M. on September 29. Franciszek entered the dining room where Cardinal Wojtyla was having breakfast and said, "Excuse me, Your Eminence, I have an urgent message."

Wojtyla asked, "What is it, Franciszek? You look shaken." Franciszek replied, "His Holiness Pope John Paul is dead. He was found dead this morning in bed while reading a book."

At that moment, Cardinal Wojtyla got up, pushing aside the scrambled eggs that he was eating, his face pale, his hands beginning to tremble.

Without saying a word, he walked to his private chapel and prayed there for several hours. Later, when he came out, Cardinal Wojtyla summoned his staff, and in an emotional tone said, "Please pray for me, as I need God's help in these coming days. For my future is very uncertain."

Later, Wojtyla went up to his room and packed once more for his second journey to Rome, never to come back as cardinal. During my visit with Franz Cardinal Koenig, who lobbied in Wojtyla's behalf, I learned that this time the lobbying effort would be even stronger.

This possibility, a matter of grave concern, was on the mind of Cardinal Wojtyla. The papacy was not what he wanted. Not at all. Before he left Krakow to go to the airport, he turned to one of his assistants and said, "Stanley, let's pause for a moment and enjoy our beloved Krakow, as I might not be back again."

The day that Karol Cardinal Wojtyla was to leave for the airport to take a flight to Rome and elect a new Pope, an old lady came to his office, all shaken, as though some great tragedy had occurred. Since the cardinal's office was always open for visitors off the street, occasionally he did hear some unusual problems.

The elderly lady, her face streaked with tears, touched his heart as she said, "Your Eminence, someone stole my cat. Will you help me find it?" Her voice choked.

The cardinal calmed her down, then summoned his driver, and escorted the grieving woman to the car. Off they rode, the three—driver, cardinal and distressed woman—up and down the streets of Krakow looking for the cat.

Unbelievably, the lady spotted her cat on the doorstep of someone's house, just sitting and waiting. The old lady was joyously reunited with her beloved pet and the happy woman was driven to her home. Soon after, the cardinal was driven to the airport to fly to Rome.

This was one of his final deeds of kindness as Cardinal Archbishop of Krakow.

There were tears in his eyes as he embraced his staff and then departed in the black Polish Fiat for Warsaw to join his colleague, Stefan Cardinal Wyszynski, the Primate of Poland, for the trip.

At the airport in Warsaw, someone asked Cardinal Wyszynski about his intended successor as Primate of Poland—would it be Cardinal Wojtyla? Wojtyla was not present to hear. Wyszynski replied, "Cardinal Wojtyla will never wear the robes of a primate. The Lord has a special role for him to fulfill—as yet unknown to man."

In Rome, before the conclave, a Polish journalist from Krakow had lunch with Cardinal Wojtyla at the Polish Pontifical College, where, incidentally, I have also been a guest on several occasions.

This particular incident occurred right after the funeral service of John Paul. The Polish journalist noticed that Cardinal Wojtyla was not himself, appeared very remote, his mind distracted. It was a feeling of those close to Wojtyla that he would be the next Pope, but no one said anything—they just kept this in their hearts, as did Cardinal Wojtyla. After all, such a thing was unthinkable. Italian Popes were a long tradition.

A few days later at the Vatican, a news photographer was taking several pictures of Cardinal Wojtyla, as he did of all 111 Cardinals who were in the running. Cardinal Wojtyla asked the photographer in a joking way, "Why are you taking so many pictures of me, you certainly do not believe I might be the next Pope?"

The photographer indicated he was just doing his duty, but that who it would be was in the hands of the Lord.

The job of Pope almost boggles the mind. The position makes him all-powerful and infallible. He is the supreme judge and the lawgiver.

He derives his power from the *Dictatus Papae* of 1075, proclaimed by Pope *(Hildebrand)* Saint Gregory VII:

> The pope can be judged by no one; the
> Roman church has never erred and never will
> err till the end of time; the Roman church was
> founded by Christ alone; the pope alone can
> depose and restore bishops; he alone can make
> new laws, set up new bishoprics and divide
> old ones; he alone can call general councils
> and authorize canon law; he alone can revise
> his judgments; his legates even in inferior
> orders, have precedence over all bishops, an
> appeal to the papal courts inhibits judgments
> by all inferior courts; a duly ordained pope is
> undoubtedly made a saint by the merits of St.
> Peter.

It is felt by Catholics that the Almighty acts to influence the College of Cardinals in guiding their selection of a new Pope upon the death of the previous one.

So now, each of the men who were being weighed in the balance remained in a tiny makeshift room as the will of the Lord was slowly unfolding.

From the description I heard of it, Wojtyla was also still carrying the same beat-up suitcase which I had helped him pack and check through at the airport when he was in the United States in 1976. Now at the conclave, that same familiar, tired suitcase was parked in the Room No. 91, which was his little cubicle in the Vatican among all the other cardinals who were stuck there, forbidden to leave until that little billow of white smoke proclaimed from the improvised chimney the triumphal entry of a new Pope—*Habemus Papam!*

When the cardinals went to vote in the Sistine Chapel, each would bring something along to occupy their free time. Some brought candy, books to read such as novels, but Cardinal Wojtyla brought a copy of a quarterly review of Marxist theory, much to the amazement of all the other cardinals.

One chided him, saying "Isn't it a bit sacrilegious to bring Marxist literature into the Sistine Chapel?"

The offbeat cardinal smiled and said, "My conscience is clear."

Wojtyla was said to know more about Marxism than

the Communist leaders of Poland, and this, it was rumored, made them very uncomfortable, especially upon his elevation to Pope.

Why Wojtyla? Why was he chosen? Who was behind the scenes of his election?

Several months after the election of Karol Cardinal Wojtyla to the throne of St. Peter, I learned from an inside Vatican source that it was Franz Cardinal Koenig of Vienna who played a key role in selling Cardinal Wojtyla to the conclave.

Cardinal Koenig of Austria is the foremost Vatican authority on relations with Eastern Europe.

When I met with Cardinal Koenig in Washington, D.C., in the spring of 1979, I talked in private with him about this matter. Knowing that I was a close personal friend of Wojtyla, he was more open with me in talking about the election of Pope John Paul II without breaking the vow of secrecy about what goes on in that very private enclave.

I also spoke with others and believe that I have pieced together what really happened. In the first place, this was not the first time Cardinal Koenig pushed for Wojtyla to be elevated to the papacy. He had first brought forth Wojtyla's name in August at the conclave that elected Albino Luciani as Pope John Paul I.

At that time, the very thought of a non-Italian Pope came as a thunderbolt. The Italian cardinals were stunned that anyone would even think of breaking away from the 456-year-old tradition of an Italian on St. Peter's throne.

When the second conclave started, the idea of a Polish Pope no longer had the shock of a clap of thunder during an electrical storm, but merely a thoughtful sound of rain falling, rain that fell on fertile soil.

Again, it was Cardinal Koenig, planting a little seed of thought here and a seed there. The way some described it, it was a simple matter of divide and conquer.

The climax came during the luncheon break on October 16, 1978, between the morning and afternoon sessions of the second day, when Koenig stepped up his lobbying. Without his effective arguments, Cardinal Wojtyla could not have been elected in the scant two days of voting.

Supporting Koenig's candidate were the German cardinals and the U.S. cardinals. As someone picturesquely put it, the Holy Spirit, speaking through these groups, put Cardinal Wojtyla over the top to get the necessary majority to be elected Pope. The 111 cardinals sealed in the Sistine Chapel took eight ballots spread over 32 hours and 48 minutes to elevate one man above all others.

Many things had gone together to make Cardinal Wojtyla stand out from the rest. His knowledge of languages, for one thing, would enable him to deal with many nations of the world and talk with people of those nations on more intimate terms. Also, he had written many books.

My longtime friend Bishop Sczepan Wesoly of Rome told me that one of the main reasons why Cardinal Wojtyla was elected Pope was because of his extensive travel abroad. No Pope before this one had traveled so much. Though he had not wanted or sought the mantle of the papacy, he had gotten to know cardinals in their own environment, and this had cemented their relationships.

At first, it had looked as if tradition would be followed with the election of an Italian, Giuseppe Cardinal Siri. Then, from what I have learned, when Siri did not rally the proper strength, the support seemed to drift toward another Italian, Giovanni Cardinal Benelli, Archbishop of Florence. Then again, support shifted, as it was clear that, even in high church circles, politics is played and old scores are settled by withholding support.

Cardinal Wojtyla was a compromise candidate in spite of himself. It was almost as if he saw the handwriting on the wall and tried, feebly, to erase it.

Since the days of Pope Pius IX—1846 to 1878—the Pope had been referred to consistently as the prisoner of the Vatican, because after King Victor Emmanuel II of Italy expropriated the papal states in 1871 popes no longer left the Vatican once they had been made pontiff.

Besides this, one of Wojtyla's best friends, Bishop Andrzej Deskur, who lay at death's door as the voting was taking place and who knew the Vatican life thoroughly, always described the job of Pope with one word—"Impossible!"

On the fateful day, as a coalition worked to build on

the reasons why the stranger from Poland was the proper man, already, even before the vote was taken, his colleagues were starting to treat him as a man set apart when they adjourned for lunch.

Some even congratulated Wojtyla, but he reacted as if he had been struck, rather than honored, and his mouth was set in a grim line.

And, when, after lunch, the ballot showed that he had ninety votes—fifteen over what was required—he did not respond to the applause as anticipated, but buried his face in his hands and wept.

Maybe one reason Karol Wojtyla seemed so shaken at the turn the voting had taken was a prediction that had been made by a mystic. The mystic was the Franciscan Padre Pio, who was revered for having bleeding nail prints—the mark of Jesus suffering—on his palms, and for the smell of roses about him.

The way the story goes, Cardinal Wojtyla had visited the stigmatic a few years before the mystical holy man had died, and the monk had told him, "You will be Pope one day, but your pontificate will be short and will end in bloodshed."

In Rome, some say that is the reason the Pope works at such top speed to accomplish as much as he can in whatever time has been allotted him. The more cheerful say that the reason the Pope seems so unconcerned about security while everyone around him is worrying about it for him is that he feels whatever is to be will be and has already been ordained.

Teetering on the brink of being elevated to the highest office in the Catholic church, that of Christ's vicar on earth, Karol Wojtyla was a picture of despair as he sat in tears under Michelangelo's painting, *The Last Judgment*, contemplating the question he had been asked—whether he would accept the office.

When he finally answered, it was not in any of the modern languages he knew, but in Latin. "Knowing the seriousness of these times," he said, with measured words, "realizing the responsibility of this election, placing my faith in God, I accept."

Then Jean Cardinal Villot, the Vatican secretary of

state who had asked the first question, spoke again, asking by what name Wojtyla wished to be known.

This time, the pause was not so long as he again answered in Latin. "Because of my reverence, love, and devotion to John Paul and also to Paul VI, who has been my inspiration, my strength, I will take the name of John Paul."

Later, I learned, Wojtyla, my friend, had waited so long after the first question that some of the cardinals fully expected him to reject the papacy, so that they would have to go on to still another night vote.

The easy part was over. Then came the need of breaking the news to the Italian populace, who had been waiting night and day in the square below—a few even hanging from lightposts for a better view.

Some of my sources told me that certain cardinals had feared that the excited crowd might respond with anger and even turn their backs on a foreign Pope.

After all, he was the first non-Italian Pope elected in over four hundred years—the first elected since the year 1522. That had been Hadrian VI (Adrian) of Holland, whose days had been numbered.

But returning to John Paul II, at first the crowd did seem a little shocked and sullen when Pericle Cardinal Felici appeared to announce the new name. The people were very quiet and some asked aloud if this man was from Africa or Asia. Some pounded their foreheads in consternation, and there were even a few boos.

Maybe that was part of Wojtyla's reluctance—his feeling of apprehension about acceptance, as well as the unknown quantity of the Communist government of Poland and the unknown factor of how the Russian sister government would react to the selection of a Polish Pope. Would this make it harder for his countrymen—eighty percent of whom were Catholic?

After the white smoke, about an hour had elapsed before Wojtyla stepped onto the balcony waving at the one hundred thousand faces below in St. Peter's Square.

"Now the most reverend cardinals have called a new bishop to Rome. They have called him from a distant country," he said in words that had only a slight Polish accent.

He might be a Pole, but he was speaking to the crowd in Italian—beautiful Italian—calling the multitude "dearest brothers and sisters." He went on to explain step-by-step, in a way that took them into his confidence, just what had happened, and starting with the acknowledgment that, "We are still grieving over the death of our beloved Pope John Paul I."

They listened silently as he continued, "And now the most reverend cardinals have called a new bishop of Rome. They have called me from a distant country—distant, but always so close because of the communion in the Christian faith and tradition. I was afraid to receive this nomination, but I did it in the spirit of obedience to Our Lord, and in the total confidence in his mother, the most holy Madonna."

Now the crowd was starting to stir and respond to him. The Italians shared his feeling of closeness with Mary, mother of Christ.

"Even if I cannot explain myself well in your—" he paused, and said the magic word, "*our*—Italian language, if I make a mistake, you will correct me."

Now there was a union. He had made himself one of them and had shown his humility, and there was happiness in the square at last.

Did anyone outside of Europe really feel or predict that one Karol Wojtyla was destined for the papacy? Just one person that I know of—Dr. Jude Dougherty, dean of the School of Philosophy of Catholic University of Washington, D. C.

The morning Wojtyla was elected, Dr. Dougherty told his sons at breakfast, "Today we will have a new Pope. He will call himself John Paul II, and he will be our friend, Karol Wojtyla."

Dr. Dougherty had met the Polish cardinal in 1976, the same time I did, and had a special feeling about him from the first. "I felt we were in the presence of a great man," he said, mentioning the fact that "there was no ecclesiastical aloofness about the man," in spite of his great intellect, his "courage of his convictions" and his "tremendous piety toward his traditions and roots. He acknowledges his debt to God, to his country, and to his people."

Word of this uncanny prediction had reached John

Paul II, and when the Pope arrived at Catholic University and spoke there during his 1979 visit, he stepped off the stage, turned to Dr. Edmund Pellegrino, who was his host, and said, "Where is my friend, Jude Dougherty?"

In another moment, the psychic man was being hugged and received a papal kiss.

People kept asking me why this humble Pole had been chosen. Then, suddenly I remembered what Wojtyla himself had said about how there is always the man who is right for the times. He had said, "God so acts in the world that the prouder, more arrogant, more conceited and more self-assured the times, the humbler the servant He sends into the world."

9

A Pope Called
John Paul II

On the night that he was elected Pope, and after he had
made his speech from the balcony, John Paul II excitedly tele-
phoned his friends in Krakow from his Vatican office. He said
that he had a special request. He wanted the bishop's office
in Krakow to send several important guests to his investiture.

These were his cleaning lady, his driver, his gardener,
his handyman, and the receptionist who announced his visitors. Right from the start, John Paul II seemed to belong to a
new breed of Pope.

His actions showed it in every way.

During the first day or so of his pontificate, John Paul
II kept getting lost in the long corridors and courtyards that
make up the Vatican. One time he had to go to his car, which
was waiting for him, but made a wrong turn and found himself waiting outside the Vatican bank.

The chauffeur, realizing something must be wrong,

was rushing through the narrow streets around the Vatican hunting for the lost Pontiff. He found him, waiting patiently outside the bank, enjoying the air and the surroundings.

But, the next day, John Paul II determined not to get lost again. Therefore, he asked a Swiss guard the way to the elevators, speaking in the guard's native German.

"Over there and to the left around the corner, Your Holiness," answered the guard, waving his hand in the right direction.

"Show me," said the Pope. "I'm still confused."

"I can't leave my post," the guard said stiffly.

Grabbing the astonished guard by the elbow and pulling him along, the Pope said, "Your job is to protect me, no? So, show me the way and protect me."

In those first days, whenever he was lonely, John Paul II would make a swing around the offices, popping in unexpectedly to talk to various staffs, hoping to get into conversations about interesting problems.

And in those days, he would also call up his friends in Krakow. When they would pick up the telephone, he would say, "It's me, Karol." The people on the other end would almost fall out of their chairs. Then he would draw them into conversation to hear what was going on and explain to more than one, "It is not easy for me to be Pope and leave my beloved countryside."

One of the first acts of John Paul II after his election to the throne of St. Peter was to visit a mutual Polish friend, Bishop Andrzej Deskur, who was in the hospital and was said to be on his death bed. He was head of the Vatican Press and Communications Office, and I had known him for about eight years, but the Pope had known him for many more.

It was Deskur who first introduced Wojtyla into Vatican circles many years before. So now it was an emotional visit. Deskur could not believe that a Pope would take time for hospitals when he had so many other things to do. But John Paul II did not rush. He stayed for more than fifteen minutes, acting as if that *was* all he had to do.

A small miracle took place and soon after the Pope's visit, his dear friend was on the mend. When I was in Rome in 1980, Deskur was well and back in his office, where I saw him for a quick hello. I also congratulated him because he had just been elevated to the rank of archbishop by John Paul II.

Then there was the unprecedented, happy madhouse of a press conference. Hundreds of reporters were there from all over the world, expecting a cut and dry formal statement read by the new Pope. Instead, they were treated to a rare battle of wits.

The fact that the new Pope was holding an impromptu press conference came as a shock to the Vatican protocol experts, who had not planned it that way. Pope John Paul II, without warning, had turned a formal audience for journalists into an easy give-and-take, question-and-answer session, following his scheduled fifteen-minute speech on press and ethics.

Here he was, the first "Papa" actually fielding questions like those crazy Americans—and seeming to enjoy every minute of it.

> *Reporter:* Do you feel a prisoner of the
> Vatican?
> *John Paul II:* Not yet in four days.
> *Reporter:* Will you go to Russia?
> *John Paul II:* If they let me.
> *Reporter:* Will you hold regular press
> conferences?
> *John Paul II:* As soon as I am allowed to.
> *Reporter:* Will you return to Poland?
> *John Paul II:* I'm too young not to return
> home.
> *Reporter:* Do you agree with the name you
> have been given, "The Pope of hope?"
> *John Paul II: (With a little smile.)* I—*hope*—
> so.

It had been a jolly interview, with the Pope switching easily from one to another of five languages in which reporters called out the questions.

When he realized that one of the reporters was an Italian TV news director who had been shot by terrorists, the Pope opened his arms and embraced him warmly. Even tough and case-hardened journalists responded to the special warmth of the new Pope, and seemed to want to touch him as he walked along the cordon of outstretched hands.

Incidentally, this was the first time in history that a Pope had held a regular open-question press conference, and I wondered in a little corner of my mind whether his association with me hadn't helped him feel at ease with the press and realize that we're just plain people no matter how tough we try to sound.

I got a kick out of the fact that, even with the press, the warm-hearted Pontiff did not neglect to give the same blessing that a Pope gives at the end of a papal audience. The reporters were starting to leave and were chatting noisily, but he cupped his hands to be heard above the clatter and shouted the Latin benediction over the din.

John Paul II was certainly proving to be a most unique Pope for his very humility. Just because Popes before him had done something in a certain way for hundreds of years did not mean that he had to do the same.

For example, as Pope he would frown on having his ring kissed. He preferred a handshake or an embrace.

On the day after his inauguration, October 23, 1978, the Pope held a special audience for his countrymen. The crowd sang to him the traditional "Sto Lat"—May you live to be a hundred—followed by a brief talk by Stefan Cardinal Wyszynski, the Primate of Poland.

After saying he knew what a costly decision it had been for the Holy Father to give up "your city of Krakow, the Tatra mountains, the forests and valleys and the solitary walks that gave you joy and renewed your strength," the primate knelt to kiss the Pope's ring in homage.

Then, to the amazement of all present, the Pope got up from his throne, embraced the primate, and kissed *his* ring.

This brought tears to the eyes of both men and to those witnessing this great act of humility.

Cardinal Wyszynski was lost for words. To have had the Pope kneel before him! No one had ever witnessed such a spectacle of humility in a pope.

He had not changed. He had been the same as cardinal. For example, there is the case of Father Bernard Witkowski of Philadelphia, who arrived at the cardinal's residence in Krakow in 1976 as part of a group who were briefing the cardinal in anticipation of his trip to Philadelphia to participate in the Eucharistic Congress later that year.

Father Witkowski, quite naturally, took the cardinal's hand to kiss his ring, upon their meeting. To the priest's astonishment, the cardinal did not let him kiss the ring, but instead embraced the priest warmly.

But to return a moment to the emotional scene between John Paul II and Stefan Cardinal Wyszynski, the Pope's voice choked as he said, "Most reverend and beloved Cardinal Primate, allow me to speak my mind in simple terms. There would not be a Polish Pope in the See of St. Peter today if it were not for your faith—which did not shrink from prison—and your hope."

Few people, outside of Poland, know that Wyszynski had been held as virtually a prisoner for three years by Communist authorities, who were seeking to stamp out religion. He had actually been under house arrest in a monastery. All the time he was gone, his cardinal's throne in Warsaw had been laden with flowers while his congregation waited for him—and that is the way he found it when he was released.

Most people remember how other Popes appeared in public only in the most dramatic way—carried aloft in a sedan by retainers. Pope John Paul II not only marches along on his own two feet, but he has inaugurated outdoor audiences in St. Peter's Square, rain or shine. He arrives, not borne aloft on a throne, but standing in a little white jeep.

Again, this is no different from how he has always been. As a further illustration of his sense of humility, on one occasion Wojtyla attended a reception in Krakow being held for a priest who had spent thirteen grueling years in a Soviet labor camp in Siberia.

As guest-of-honor, Cardinal Wojtyla was led to a special ornate chair at the head table. However, he refused to sit in it, saying, "There is nothing special in being a cardinal in Poland. Here is our special man," and he asked that the priest from Siberia sit in the ornate chair, while he got himself an ordinary straight-back chair.

Monsignor Nikolaj Kuczkowski of Krakow, who told me about this, tried to explain how hard the cardinal worked at achieving a perfect feeling of communion with the people who served him.

Monsignor Kuczkowski also described the kind of listener the cardinal was in dealing with problems of the archdiocese of Krakow. "Wojtyla would talk about big and small problems, always listening intensely. From time to time, he would interrupt and ask additional questions in order to get a fuller picture or to bring out additional details.

"He would listen to everything, but we knew that first of all he was interested in a detailed and accurate account of the matter and not just a commentary. He left the judgments to himself and was not prone to revealing whether he shared anyone's opinion or not."

Monsignor Kuczkowski said that the cardinal did not reduce his contacts with his assistants to only the matters of curia business, but that there were many occasions for free and informal talks. "We, the clerks of the curia, were as free as anyone else to tell him of problems big and small."

He marveled, "We felt a part of him, and yet there was something in his person that set him apart and somehow above all others. There was a distance, though it was not a physical distance, caused by some high ecclesiastical aura or power. It was a mystical distance, if I may use this expression."

I thought Monsignor Kuczkowski put it very well. It was exactly what I had experienced travelling in the United States dealing with the cardinal and future Pope. Wojtyla was able to communicate on my level and everyone else's level—and yet there was something always there that left you feeling this man was somehow set apart.

Part of it had to do with the wise and philosophical comments he was always making in conversations—some were analytical to help us understand ourselves, some were spoken as guidelines for future behavior. Many comments that he did not make in my hearing were told to me by his Polish colleagues, who were very dedicated to the cardinal, their superior, and who gained strength from his wise words.

Naturally, I was especially interested in hearing everything this hallowed man said on the subject of the Almighty.

I envied him the completeness of his feeling. "It isn't enough just to believe in God," he once said. "One must trust God completely." I realized that most of us believe in God, but we trust our own judgment.

Another time, he said, "Man is not called merely to admire God, but also to cooperate with Him."

I had never known anyone with greater humility than Cardinal Wojtyla, and at first it was hard to understand how so powerful a man in his world of the church—the number two churchman of a whole nation—could be this way. Then I read something of his that suddenly made it clear to me. Translated from Polish, it goes something like this: "Man is fully happy only when he is serving and not when he must make commands. A really great man, even when he exercises authority, is a servant."

In his working relationships, Cardinal Wojtyla would not permit others to shield his feelings. More than once, he demanded that his assistants advise him on what to do and not tell him what they *thought* he wanted to hear.

Cardinal Wojtyla believed in preciseness and the efficient use of time. He was not rude, but considerate of other people's feelings—what he wanted out of them was cooperation, a team effort.

The cardinal was not one to scold others. He merely made sure he didn't waste time, even when others did. Once, his driver forgot to fill the gas tank before taking the cardinal to the funeral of a friend. The cardinal said not a word as the driver rushed off and returned with gasoline, but walked serenely up and down, saying his rosary.

From the people around him, I learned of the cardinal's work habits in Krakow. As Monsignor Kuczkowski put it, "Cardinal Wojtyla was able to share all his problems with God by praying alone and working in his chapel."

It was hard, he said, to reconcile this workaholic with the man who would go out to ski dressed in old woolen rags, laced up boots, and old-fashioned skis made of Polish hickory wood. "Some called him the ski daredevil of Krakow," Kuczkowski laughed. "They said he had to have a guardian angel. That we all have, but the cardinal must have had a platoon with him."

There are many true stories about the Pope's humor. When he was a cardinal, someone once remarked, by way of voicing disapproval of Wojtyla's unseemly sport of skiing, that no *Italian* cardinals were skiers.

"That's strange," the Polish cardinal said innocently, "in Poland, forty percent of our cardinals are skiers." His detractor pointedly commented that there were only two Polish cardinals. Still the height of innocence, Wojtyla remarked, "Oh yes, but in Poland, Cardinal Wyszynski counts for sixty percent."

In this way, my friend, himself, was guilty of telling a Polish joke. And in his usual way, humor and humility went hand-in-hand.

And speaking of humor, some of us who had known the Pope "when" laughed when we read in the newspapers that elevation to the papacy had gotten him included in the list of best-dressed men. As a young priest, bishop, and cardinal, Karol Wojtyla was what one would call the poorest dressed clergyman in all of Poland.

He was also probably the worst-dressed among the 111 cardinals who had come to cast their votes. When Wojtyla came to Rome in October 1978, he arrived in a threadbare cassock, a battered hat, and a tattered overcoat that had been mended over and over.

Clothes meant absolutely nothing to him. Only souls.

Wojtyla believed that what is torn or worn can be mended. He would use the money intended for clothes in one-to-one acts of charity which were handled with strict anonymity.

It was not unusual to see Karol Wojtyla walking around in worn clothing, shirts with worn-out collars, and socks with holes in them. The condition of his shoes was often alarming. He used to put cardboard in his soles to make them last a bit longer.

After he had acquired the rank and position to have a housekeeper, nothing changed. His housekeeper would remark that his undershirts looked like work rags, with all the holes in them.

When he was a cardinal, his housekeeper, confirmed

that she had never known him to have a closet full of clothes. It was a sparse collection of exactly what was needed.

During the U.S. visit as a cardinal in 1969, he saw American clergy spruced up in fine-fitting silk suits of the best material money could buy. He could not believe his eyes. The remark he made to one priest quickly made the rounds: "I doubt that the Polish president has the same quality of a suit as you do."

Only when Karol Wojtyla started travelling and was increasingly involved in the council affairs of Vatican II, did he spruce up a bit by having at least one good outfit that would not embarrass his colleagues.

Even as a sportsman, he did not go in for fancy outfits. Cardinal Wojtyla would wear anything that he could find and some of the combinations came out looking a bit outrageous. It had to happen. One man, meeting the cardinal on one of his hiking trips, mistook him for a beggar and offered him assistance.

The cardinal was not at all distressed but was, in fact, happy at the show of kindness. He was such a man as would do some of his own mending so as not to bother the help.

Only when he became Pope was there a revolutionary change in his dress style. Much of this change was forced on him by the nature of his position and the Vatican staff who hovered around him to make sure all was dignity and perfection.

But I had to smile as I clipped out the newspaper story telling that the 1979 Fashion Foundation of America had named Pope John Paul II the man of the year because he was "impeccable in his appearance, always striking, adding a light touch of fashion when he donned a Mexican hat."

The Fashion Foundation went on to say that John Paul II wore his robes "far better than most recent Pontiffs had."

Beggar, indeed!

People ask me what impresses me about the Pope's philosophy.

One of the greatest things I heard the cardinal say was on the subject of forgiveness and I believe if unhappy people could respond to his words, it would put half the psychiatrists out of business. "Forgiveness," he commented, "is the restoration of freedom to oneself. It is the key held in our own hand to our prison cell." How many people I know are under counseling because of the guilt feelings they cannot live with.

On the subject of guilt, Wojtyla made another wise statement. "When we seek forgiveness, *we* must be ready to forgive."

Another thing that impressed me was his philosophy of silence. The cardinal loved silence in which to meditate, and seemed to deplore verbosity. "The more deeply people develop within themselves in their interior life, the more prone they are to silence," he said. But the greatest thing I heard him say on silence was "Every great work, all holiness, is born in silence and recollection."

And commenting on a person who talks too much, he said, "Only falsehood wraps itself in a flood of words. Truth is brief."

Cursing was another thing that he did not like. "A curse," he said, "distresses the ears of its target, but it dishonors more the man from whose heart it spews forth."

Karol Wojtyla was not ashamed to cry and recommended tears, even as a release from anger and frustration. "It is better to cry than to be angry," he said, "because anger hurts others while tears flow silently through the soul and cleanse the heart."

The cardinal was not concerned about physical beauty. "Someone may have an ugly face," he said, "but when it is illuminated by love and grace, then it becomes dear."

During our travels in 1976, the cardinal would be talking to a group of bishops and me, and he would frequently quote what he had once told his students in Lublin or what he had written or said on a certain occasion. His recall was amazing, but so memorable were the things he said and wrote that sometimes a bishop would break in and correctly add to his quote.

Incidentally, the Pope has no objection to the so-called Polish jokes, and said so. They were fine, as long as they were not cruel.

Before I went to visit him in Rome in 1980, I made a

note of a few Polish jokes that were being told about him so I could show them to him later. One was about the first thing the new Polish Pope had done on moving into the Vatican—order wallpaper for the Sistine Chapel.

One of the Polish jokes the Pope laughed at as cardinal, but with sympathy, was told by one of his party—something about how the modern Pole earns 4,500 zlotys salary, spends 6,500 of it, and keeps the rest for savings.

Along the line of money, I was interested to see that when the Pope left Poland for good, to take on his new job as Pope, he obeyed the law of the land by taking with him only 1,000 zlotys, the legal amount any Pole is permitted to take out of the country.

There are also all kinds of stories about the Pope's attitude about material things.

It wasn't just little things that the future Pope gave away—a pillow, a featherbed, a warm coat.

When Wojtyla came to the United States the first time in 1969, a prominent Dearborn, Michigan, Catholic layman, Edward Arcy, wanted to do something special for the humble Polish cardinal he had met at Orchard Lake Seminary.

Arcy decided that the cardinal could get much more work done if he just had a big car. In record time, a 1970 Ford LTD arrived in Krakow complete with power steering, air conditioning, and radio. Not only that, but Arcy arranged for any needed parts to be shipped on request.

The cardinal used the car but he was not quite comfortable. It just wasn't he to have such a car when there was so much need around him.

The way Arcy told the story, the cardinal gave the car to a village that raffled it off, and the proceeds enabled the village to build its own little church.

When Wojtyla returned to the United States in 1976, he asked to meet his benefactor and thanked him in person for what he had made possible.

There is a postscript to the story worth noting. In 1979, Father Walter Ziemba, the head of the seminary at Orchard Lake, raised money from school alumni, and this time the former cardinal—now turned Pope—received a stranger surprise. A $25,000 gleaming white Cadillac arrived. The Pope was still not ready for personal pomp, and again it was auctioned off for charity.

I have heard so many priceless stories about Wojtyla through the years.

Bishop Sczepan Wesoly of Rome could not get over Cardinal Wojtyla's endless acts of humility. Once, when his car got a flat tire and the chauffeur got out to fix it, Wojtyla wanted to share the work and help change the tire. A cardinal changing a tire, indeed!

At any and all times of the day, my friend, the bishop recalled, he would see Cardinal Wojtyla walking along with a rosary in his hand, saying his prayers as inconspicuously as possible.

He also went on austerity fasts. The fasting was harder to hide, and it sometimes upset other priests who liked to eat well and indulge themselves in such fine foods as pâtés, smoked sausages, and such game as rabbit and wild geese.

Nor, when he had become a cardinal, had he grown more interested in food or punctuality. While others were waiting to have lunch with him, he would be somewhere en route engaged in a conversation in a corridor.

It was known that Cardinal Wojtyla never refused to talk to anyone. So priests and parishioners alike trapped him in halls and wherever to discuss their problems. The soup would get cold by the time he arrived at 2 P.M., or even later.

At first glance, there seemed to be a contradiction. He, who insisted on making good use of time, even while traveling in a car, might take an hour to walk down a corridor because he was engaged in talking to some townsperson with a problem.

It was true.

The people he met along the way had never seen anyone with such work habits, and he made local history in Krakow. He had transformed the back seat of his car into a miniature office, even installing a table and reading lamp.

How could one reconcile this seeming discrepancy?

The answer is that the cardinal considered people and their problems of much greater importance than a time clock.

And he considered his *work* to be ministering to the needs of people.

But getting back to the car office, people who rode with him were stunned but tried to be nonchalant as he would chat with them for a while and then say, "Let's do some work, since time is running short."

They could read something or look out the window. What most of them didn't know is that they were perfectly free to talk because he has the gift of being able to concentrate on two things at one time.

It was only when he lapsed into meditation or prayer that, by his expression, you knew he wanted all conversation to cease.

One night in Poland, when the cardinal was on a fairly long journey from one city to another, his lamp went out and he could no longer work. It was probably the only time he ever was awake without working for four whole hours. He was most unhappy about it and ordered his driver to find the nearest filling station, sternly requesting that the lamp always be tested before a trip so that no such thing would occur again.

Americans could not understand the cardinal's attitude toward time and how he was always behind schedule because he refused to hurt the feelings of whomever he was talking to, no matter how humble.

I myself was impressed with how gentle he was in disagreeing with someone, how he did not condemn but only tried to explain what he called a better viewpoint. Nor did he have contempt for anyone. He said, "We must always look on the man and not look at what he does. Though he does much or not well, or even badly, he is a man."

Yet, though he didn't look down or condemn, he still advised me and others to try to be strong and do the right thing, no matter how difficult. "It isn't enough to be born a man," he said. "One must also *be a man*."

Then there is his feeling about animals.

The Pope, all of his life, has loved animals. As a great outdoorsman, he would speak of how he admired nature and all its creations, including the animals. He would study them and try to find out as much about them as possible.

Some likened John Paul II, when a young man, to St. Francis of Assisi, who was also a lover of animals and an outdoorsman. Wojtyla would take frequent trips to a zoo. The animals came to know him and would come to him and he would feed them.

I have a candid shot of him with a puppy, and his face shows his tenderness.

There is also a famous picture of him feeding a kangaroo in Australia. It was hard for Karol to have pets, but for a time he did own a dog and a few birds, I believe canaries.

And what about this business of sports, some have asked me. Is he a showman? Is he a skier for the effect?

Far from it!

Cardinal Wojtyla, when skiing, preferred going up the mountains to going down. Sometimes it would take him six hours to get to the top. Yet, he did not like ski trails, because they had too many people.

He relaxed best alone on the trail—just he and his thoughts of the mightiness of the Almighty.

Sometimes, when he wanted company, he would say to just a few good friends, "The weather is very bad, I hear. There won't be anyone on the mountains today. Let's go and try it." Then they would brave the bad weather and ski against the winds and all the elements. The cardinal would return somewhat tired but relaxed.

Some have asked me what, if any, innovations the cardinal came up with to help the people right around him in Krakow.

In his Krakow office, Cardinal Wojtyla formed the Center for Family Pastoral. The project was based on his book, *Love and Responsibility*. The center concerned itself with the spiritual and material well-being of married couples, regardless of religious belief. They were also given medical assistance, and it was a place single mothers could turn to for help.

One of Cardinal Wojtyla's concerns was a growing lack of sensitivity in people. He felt it was something we need to think about and question ourselves about. He said, "The whole world today demands an even greater sensitivity toward Man, maybe because sensitivity is disappearing."

Maybe that's why, no matter how little he had through the years, he still gave to the more needy anything that he himself did not absolutely need.

The Pope has many articles, papers, and books to his credit, and I am sure they will be studied for content long after he is gone. One woman, whom I met while following the footsteps of the Pope for this book, spent over a year compiling and organizing his body of work, which involved translating from Polish to English.

She is Harvard professor Anna-Teresa Tymieniecka. As yet, few of the Pope's books have been translated into English, but happily, Dr. Tymieniecka has translated one, which is now available to American readers—*The Acting Person* (Reidel Publishing Company, 1979).

The writing style of John Paul II is complex and involved. Most of his sentences are long, averaging forty-five to fifty-five words.

Stylistically, the Pope uses many parallels and enumerations, usually in threes. As you read his prose, you can almost hear the voice of the lecturer. Like a teacher, the Pope often asks rhetorical questions, thus setting up the reason for the response.

In problematical matters, the Pope is never afraid to sound uncertain—probing, seeking, asking. Yet, in both personal letters and scholarly papers, there is the image of the teacher who leaves a lesson to be learned by all. Each sentence seems to have a hidden meaning that promises to reveal itself in time.

I found it interesting that the Pope uses a modern technique in writing—the frequent use of dashes.

On the personal side, the Pope is an active listener and an active speaker, using his hands eloquently to illustrate a point, a gesture giving added dimension to what he is trying to say. Yet his hand motions are very gentle, showing his humility and concern for people of all walks of life.

I recall when Karol Wojtyla went out to greet the people for the first time as successor to St. Peter, his hands, even before his words, started to capture the hearts of the people in the square below.

While listening, the Pope often cups his hands in front

of his face. He leans forward a lot, as if to concentrate better on the person before him.

He also maintains eye contact. Some people are made uncomfortable by his penetrating, level gaze. One man, who had met the Pope four years before, told me that John Paul's gaze had been so penetrating that "I can still feel it."

It is known to all his friends that Karol Wojtyla has a deep baritone voice. Some have joked that he can't carry a tune in a bucket, however, his voice has added a certain style to his personality.

In the old days, Wojtyla would sing all the time—alone and with people—not only in church but outdoors, at receptions, picnics—you name it. There was always singing when you were in the company of Karol Wojtyla.

When he became Pope John Paul II, he participated with youth in Poland, during his 1979 visit, singing at a music festival called "The Sacrosong," which was created and nurtured by him when he was cardinal archbishop of Krakow. Someone recorded the singing and I was sent a copy from Rome.

The Sacrosong is an ecumenical festival of song and music dedicated to the enrichment of Polish culture and religious ideals. In June 1979, three million Poles came to see and hear him sing and interact with youth. They went away, taking with them a musical message of peace, understanding, and brotherly love.

No one likes music more than the Pope, especially religious and folk music, as well as music to tap to, and he is frequently tapping something as he listens, with a little smile.

In those first few months in Rome, John Paul II did indeed suffer in his longing for Krakow. As his first Christmas in the Vatican approached, he held a reception for Polish seminarians studying in Rome. He spent several hours reminiscing with them about the old days, much, I am sure, as he had when I had dinner with him and some Polish bishops at the Vatican during the 1980 Easter season telling of his homesickness for the mountains, forests, and lakes.

The seminarians, capturing his mood, started singing the traditional song of his region:

Goralu czy ci nie zal
odchodzic od stron ojczystych . . .

He sat listening to the whole song, which, translated,
says:

Oh highlander, why do you leave your mountains?
Aren't you going to miss the pine trees and the
silvery streams?
The mountaineer looks at his beloved mountains,
wipes away his tears and says, "I must leave them
to earn my daily bread."

They were just about to start a new chorus when the
Pope raised his hand and asked them not to sing this song
any more. "I get very sentimental for Poland when I hear
that, and I shall start crying." And he already was.

When the seminarians left, he extended his arms and
embraced each of them as if they were his own sons. Tears
fell from his eyes, and he said, "Please pray for me that I may
be worthy of this important responsibility that I have accepted, and *please* come to see me often."

Some people are puzzled by the Pope's intense feeling
for Poland—after all, didn't he and his churchmen suffer
enough there, and didn't he almost lose his life there in World
War II?

Remembering those days of hunger and hiding from
the Nazis, the cardinal once said to a group of us on the bus
to Baltimore, "To die for one's country is an art, but a still
greater art is knowing how to live for her."

Concerning his own love for Poland, in spite of its regime and his problems with it, he said, "One must love one's
own country more than all other countries, for this is required
by the order of love."

10

The Black Madonna

*I*t would have been the thrill of a lifetime, watching the investiture mass for John Paul II held outdoors on the steps of St. Peter's Basilica. Even leaders of several non-Catholic churches attended, including the Archbishop of Canterbury.

Royal spectators for the occasion included Prince Rainier and Princess Grace of Monaco, and King Carlos and Queen Sophia of Spain. But the royalty I would have enjoyed seeing on that occasion even more were our American figures of "royalty"—National Security Adviser to the President Zbigniew Brzezinski and Speaker of the House of Representatives Thomas "Tip" O'Neill, Jr. As a Knight of Malta, I would have been seated among them.

However, I soon was embroiled in defending the Pope and scotching the rumor that the Pope had once been married.

I had to cancel plans to go to Rome for the installation of my friend because that very friendship precluded such a trip. How could I go, knowing that such a rumor could get out of hand? I had to clear this up and be on hand to answer other reporters' questions.

It all began the day after Cardinal Wojtyla became Pope John Paul II. CBS-TV correspondent Richard Threlkeld mentioned that a rumor of the Pope's having been married was getting some attention.

I have the foreign-language newspaper published in New York, which headlined the story on its front page, *Nowy Dziennik*—Polish Daily News.

Obviously, the Polish Marxist regime was trying to discredit the new Pope as part of its anti-church propaganda.

That portion of the story, which appeared above a five-column picture of the new Pope, began, *Karol Wojtyla jest wdowcem*—"Karol Wojtyla is a widower."

The gist of the story was that, before he became a priest in war-torn Poland, Wojtyla was married and that his wife was killed by the Nazis during World War II, and it was after that he decided to become a priest. The rumor went further to say that the two had met and married when Wojtyla had worked in a stone quarry and in a chemical factory before and during the war.

I had known that one of the actresses who had helped fight the Nazis in the underground had been assumed killed by the Nazis—while involved in helping certain Poles to a safe place—Poles who were wanted by the Nazis and probably were Jews.

I checked the Vatican press section and was assured that the story was without basis, and I reported to White House correspondents who were asking me about this, assuring them that my own friendship with the man had yielded no conversation which would indicate a marriage or romantic interest in a woman.

As I explained, there had been a girl who had been part of their underground theater, and she was murdered by the Nazis, which had saddened Wojtyla and the others in the underground Polish army, but this was a long way from marriage. He had also been grieved by the deaths of several other freedom fighters—males.

Later, in Rome, I learned that the rumor had also been circulated there, probably planted by the Polish Communists.

That version said his wife had died after a long, lingering illness, and ever since he had been especially concerned with ministering to the sick. The wife's name was supposed to have been Hedwig.

It is clear to me that the woman with the lingering illness was his own mother, Emilia, who suffered a serious kidney ailment for years before dying in childbirth.

I talked with the National Conference of Catholic Bishops and they investigated further and gave me this statement:

> Rumor has suggested that Karol Wojtyla married at this time, a report which the Vatican has emphatically denied. Similarly, a report that Karol had "at least one steady girlfriend" has yet to be substantiated.
>
> The very sensitivity of the problems of love and marriage in Karol Wojtyla's later writings, especially *Love and Responsibility* (1960), has been cited to explain the persistence of the rumors that he had been married to a girl killed by the Nazis.

I believe that I did help keep the matter from becoming a *cause célèbre* in this country. Only the Lord knows what would have occurred if I had not stayed around.

As it was, I was able to tell the true story to White House correspondents and others who phoned me from all parts of the country to check the rumor. I explained exactly what His Holiness had told me about a certain girl when we had spent time together in 1976. And I quoted, to the very best of my recollection, the story of his connection with that girl, as he had told it to me. I am putting it down now for the benefit of history.

It was one of those mornings in Philadelphia, after breakfast, that we sat talking of the old days of his life in Poland and my father's life there, and Cardinal Wojtyla said, as I remember it:

> The situation in Poland during the Second World War was beyond words, tragic. It was

the duty of everyone to survive and to help others to survive as well as to preserve Poland's history and culture. As for myself, I finished the *gymnasium* when war came to Poland. In order to stay alive and avoid deportation, one had to have an *arbeit karte* ["work card"]. I also performed in the underground repertory theater, since all cultural activities were forbidden by the German authorities.

We tried to save others in our underground efforts. Several of my friends in the theater were killed by the Gestapo or sent off to Auschwitz concentration camp. One person that I remember was a young girl who was new to our group. She was an actress but she was also in the underground—but more active than I was. She was caught by the Gestapo and executed.

The Germans would make unannounced spot roundups of people on the street. Those without a work card were deported to Germany or the concentration camp and many were killed in reprisal for the killing of Germans.

It was not uncommon to learn that 100 Poles were executed for one German soldier. We did all we could to help the suffering Jewish population of Krakow by hiding them in homes, churches, and barns, and then getting them out of the country under new identities with baptismal certificates. Soon thereafter, I was on the Gestapo list and had to suspend my full-time activities.

Incidentally, the author of the Polish newspaper article claimed that the story had come from reliable sources in Argentina. Further investigation on my part showed that members of the Polish community in Argentina were also outraged at this rumor.

I have a postscript to that story. For some mysterious reason, the Polish newspaper cancelled my subscription, and I had to continue reading it through a friend.

I was pleased to see that the nasty rumor did not inhibit the Pope when he made his first trip back to Poland. In fact, His Holiness himself made a teasingly oblique reference to the matter when he abruptly curtailed a reminiscence about his family, saying, "Well, that's enough of the past. I'm not going into details. There are a lot of reporters around, ready to investigate. Matters of the heart and youth should be left to God, who calls human beings at different stages of their lives."

From everything I know or have heard of Karol Wojtyla, his contacts with girls were definitely not romantic. In fact, as a youth, according to one story, he seemed to feel guilty if he even had a romantic thought.

The story is told that once, when his father took him to see a romantic Polish movie, Karol spent the rest of the evening singing, over and over, a song from the film, a love song to a girl, with the refrain, "You are the only girl for me."

The next morning, as if to atone for his thoughts, he rushed to mass before breakfast.

One friend who did go to Rome to witness the investiture later had an audience with Pope John Paul II and came back to tell me that the Pope had asked about me, hoping I would visit Rome. When my friend told him that I was working back at home in his behalf, the Pope jokingly replied, "I am glad that *someone* is working." His Holiness gave my friend a few mementos to deliver to my family and me.

Meanwhile, like millions of other people around the world, I watched the investiture on television. However, I enjoyed it even more by sitting in the same armchair in which John Paul II sat in 1976 when he was the little-known cardinal from Krakow.

And in my hand I held a letter that helped give reality to the scene, so unbelievable was it to realize that I actually knew a Pope and could call him a friend.

The last parts of the letter said:

I pray for you daily in every Mass,

because I want you to become a very successful person some day.

He then continued, writing in flawless Polish, urging me to take advantage of all the opportunities around me. He made it seem that they were boundless and I had only to reach out.

"You may not realize it," he said, "but I see that you can become a very influential figure in your own right because you have all the necessary ingredients for this." Wojtyla said that was why he was urging me to take advantage of all the good things in store. He added that he could see many positive forces working for me.

This time he ended the letter, "May God Bless you and Our Blessed Mother keep you in her care. With sentiments, Karol Wojtyla."

The dateline on that letter was "Krakow, April 23, 1978." By then, it was almost two years since I had met and travelled with the cardinal, and the days were numbered before he would be named Pope.

Even to this day, I still think that it is all a dream. I believe that the ways of the Lord are indeed inscrutable. As one friend remarked, "Just think, we are living in interesting times—the moment in history when, after two thousand years, a Polish Pope has been elected, fulfilling the prophecy."

John Paul II was the third Pope I had met, but the only one I could claim as a friend. The first Pope I met was Pope Paul VI in October 1965, when he came to the United States to address the United Nations.

I was presented to Pope Paul VI in a private audience in the residence of Francis Cardinal Spellman. I met him again in Rome—my first trip there—in May 1976, when I attended a reception in honor of the diplomatic corps, accredited to the Vatican. Being a Knight of Malta, an honor I received in 1967, I was invited to participate in this private audience.

I have never been so dressed up since. I was required to wear white tie and tails with all my Vatican decorations. At this meeting, Paul VI gave me a silver medal in honor of the Holy Year that had just taken place in 1975 and which takes place every twenty-five years.

Actually, I have received five decorations from the Vatican. In 1967, knighthood in the Order of Malta; in 1969, Pro-Ecclesia et Pontifice; and in the same year, the Benemerenti Medal.

In 1976, I also received two honors: Order of St. Sylvester and Order of St. Gregory.

The second Pope I was honored to meet was John Paul I, when he was Albino Cardinal Luciani. I met him also in May 1976, at the time that William Baum, archbishop of Washington, was elevated to cardinal.

The meeting took place after a solemn pontifical mass at St. Peter's Basilica. When I met him, the future Pope was all smiles, so much so that I could see the gold fillings in his teeth.

I remember him holding my hands and saying, "So you are an American journalist. I welcome you to the Eternal City. I hope it meets your expectations."

We talked about journalism for a while, comparing the American and Italian approaches to stories, and I found him warm and easy to talk to. When his term as Pope was cut short by death after only thirty-three days, I was shocked and saddened. He had seemed to enjoy life so much and had been the first Pope in centuries to refuse to wear the beehive-shaped papal tiara, with its three crowns, at his elevation to the throne of St. Peter.

John Paul II had followed the lead of his predecessor wearing only a miter at his investiture, as a sign to the world that the *spiritual* mission would be the important thing with him rather than worldly or political power.

I was glad that whenever the Pope needed the comfort of familiar things, he had only to go to the Polish Chapel in the Vatican, with its familiar image of the Black Madonna, a reproduction of the icon, Our Lady of Czestochowa. There, in the little chapel, he could feel again that he was back in Poland at the monastery in Jasna Gora—the place where he had gone so many times when his spirit was troubled.

When Poland was invaded by the Nazis in 1939, almost daily Pope Pius XII went down into the crypt of the Vatican where the Polish Chapel of Our Lady of Czestochowa is located to pray for the suffering people of Poland. Little did anyone know that, years later, out of the ashes of Poland's ruins, there would arise a great leader of the church—a Slavic Pope.

Some now believe that the prayers of Pius XII may have saved the life of Karol Wojtyla—underground resistance member and fugitive from the Nazis—for the task that awaited him exactly thirty-nine years later.

To be born a Pole is to grow up with the mystique of the Black Madonna. For almost two thousands years, the Black Madonna has cast a spell over the minds of Poles, and today's generation of Poles is no different.

There are many legends about the Madonna. The one that I grew up with, as did Karol Wojtyla, is that it actually was painted by St. Luke on a table in the home of the Virgin Mother, Mary. It may have been because of this painting that, hundreds of years later, in the thirteenth century, St. Luke was designated the patron saint of artists.

The way the Polish legend goes, after the death of Christ, His mother lived in Jerusalem as part of a colony of Christians. Luke, who became a disciple of Christ after Christ's death on the cross, came to Mary's home to gather material for the gospel that he was writing.

On one of his visits, he wanted to paint his vision of Mary as a young woman with the Infant Jesus. The table that he used, so the account goes, had been made by Jesus, himself, when he had been a carpenter. Mary had kept the table after the death of her husband, Joseph.

The haunting icon painting that resulted, on linden wood, showing a sad-faced Madonna in contemplation, holding a thoughtful baby Jesus with blond curly hair, is said to be the first painting ever of Mary with the Holy Infant.

As for how the painting made its way to the hill called *Jasna Gora*—"Bright Mountain", about fifty-five or sixty miles from Krakow, is another fantastic story, half-hidden in the turbulence of Poland's history. The way devoted Poles tell it, the icon left Jerusalem with Saint Helena, the mother of Constantine the Great, who had gone there on a pilgrimage in A.D. 326. When she returned to Constantinople, she took with her the charismatic icon of Mary and Child.

Constantine, who had converted to Christianity, built

a church in honor of Mother Mary in the city named for him, and that is where the icon was installed as the major feature. Many came just to look upon it.

The painting gained devotees immediately, and it was believed that it protected those around it from wars and riots that raged through the city. There is a long, involved story about what is supposed to have happened next in the travels of the Madonna, but the important thing is that the exact date is known of her arrival at Czestochowa on "Bright Mountain."

It was on August 26, 1382, that Prince Wladyslaw of Opole, whose homeland had been attacked by Tartars, was taking the icon from a church to his own home in Upper Silesia for safekeeping, after an arrow from the invaders had pierced the Virgin's neck.

As the story goes, an enemy arrow struck the Black Madonna and a strange darkness fell on the whole region, causing the enemy to lose their way and be annihilated by the Poles.

As his horse and wagon arrived at Jasna Gora, the horses stopped suddenly and refused to move. He could not understand it. And after hours had gone by and the horses still would not move, he prayed for guidance.

The Divine answer that came to his mind was that it was the Will of God for the painting to remain at Jasna Gora. By Divine Providence, Pauline Fathers escaping the Tartars also arrived at the little town of Czestochowa on Jasna Gora, and they built a shrine to house the icon, as well as a monastery for their home.

Even today, as it was in the time of my father's childhood and the Pope's childhood, the day the horses refused to move is celebrated in Poland, with pilgrims arriving from all over to worship at the shrine of Our Lady of Czestochowa.

Just as the Madonna was believed to have protected the people at Constantinople, so is it believed that she has protected people of faith in Poland. Because of this, many pilgrims brought gifts of precious stones and gold to the Madonna. And these were eventually made into a precious metal and gem-encrusted gown.

Now the plot thickens. Hussites attacked in 1430 and

on Easter morning of that year—April 16—they sacked the monastery and tried to snatch the bejeweled icon. They found that it could not be moved. When one soldier used his sword to strike the icon, it fell to earth and broke into three pieces— seeming to be rendered worthless as a painting.

But they chopped away at the jeweled gown of the icon, ripping it off and taking it with them. To show his contempt, a barbaric swordsman twice thrust his sword into the cheek of the Madonna, leaving two deep scars.

Later, the pieces of the Madonna were carefully gathered, and the Madonna was tenderly restored to her former self. But the scars on her cheek and neck were too deep and had to remain, endearing her still more to the hearts of the Poles.

Queen Jadwiga, the wife of King Jagiello, for whom the university the Pope attended is named, personally helped to fashion a new gown for the Madonna made from gold and more precious stones brought by an adoring nation, eager to bring the Madonna back to her former glory.

The restoration was completed in 1434, and all went well until 1655, when the monastery was again under attack, this time by Swedish invaders. The Madonna was credited with inspiring the bravery of the monks, who threw back the invaders after a brutal forty-day siege.

In honor of the victory, which was considered a miracle, King Jan Casimir, in 1656, proclaimed the Madonna "Queen of Poland." Pope Clement XI went a step further in 1717 and donated a crown for the Black Madonna to wear.

Now a bit of American Revolutionary history gets involved in the background of this miraculous painting. The monastery was again attacked—this time by Cossacks—and the hero of the defense, General Casimir Pulaski, went on to give his life in the American Revolution.

One would think that the Madonna had had adversity enough, but again in 1909 the Black Madonna suffered the indignity of having her gown and crown stolen. Now it was Pope Pius X who re-crowned her, while faithful worshipers again heaped gifts of jewels upon her until there were enough for still another gown, the one she wears today.

As my gift to the Madonna, in 1966 I sent my most precious worldly possession, a sapphire ring, in gratitude for her many graces in my life and that of my family.

In 1962, when I got involved in obtaining restitution for the family of Polish-born Father Joseph Szarek of upstate New York for crimes against his family by the Nazis in World War II, Father Szarek gave me a most precious gift. It was a little shred of the original veil that had been attached to the painting of the Black Madonna. I carry it in my billfold with a little copy of Our Lady of Czestochowa.

No one knows why the Black Madonna is black. It is part of the mystique. Her features seem Caucasian—in fact, elongated—but that is not the important thing. What is important is her mystical effect on the spirit of Poland.

The Poles felt, and still do, that the Black Madonna is their patron saint and must never leave the country.

Even as a cardinal, Wojtyla would ride his bicycle from Krakow to Czestochowa to visit the revered shrine, protected behind the gates of the centuries-old Pauline Monastery, set high on Jasna Gora.

Sometimes he would arrive late at night with a crowd of his students and would stand ringing the night bell until a monk came and let them all in.

The greatest pilgrimage to Our Lady of Czestochowa saw a million Polish youth gathered to hear both Karol Wojtyla of Krakow and Cardinal Stefan Wyszynski, the primate of Poland, Wojtyla's superior.

They came by bus and train and horse-driven cart. And many came on foot, walking for days, just to gaze upon the Black Madonna and hear the sermons of both holy men.

No wonder Pope John Paul II chose to keep the symbol of the Black Madonna always before him in the form of the letter "M" in the largest segment of his shield—the "M" standing for Mary or Madonna. He had used the same letter when he was archbishop and cardinal.

Other Popes had chosen other emblems with which to identify themselves for all time. Pope John Paul I had featured the lion of Venice to show his origin, and the shield of Paul VI had pictured the mountains of northern Italy to signify his origin. But John Paul II had wanted to express his strong devotion to Mary and his tie with the archdiocese of Krakow, with its world-famous shrine to the Black Madonna.

It is almost by the hand of God that my particular interest in painting and other forms of art had been directed to ecclesiastical subjects in the reproduction of religious icons. And most especially, with my Polish background and interest in the religious history of Poland, I have for years been involved in the making of reproductions of the famous Black Madonna, which is enshrined at the monastery of Jasna Gora in Poland.

How could I have foretold, as a fledgling young artist, in Washington, D.C., obsessed by this mysterious icon, that in Poland, a young churchman, from the time he had been a child, had made pilgrimages to this shrine, and that it would have special meaning for him even when he grew up to become Pope.

When we met eventually—he as a Polish cardinal and I as an American journalist—the Black Madonna was just one of many things that brought us together in friendship.

Studying the icon, Our Lady of Czestochowa, from various photographs and reproductions I had collected, I worked for years in making reproductions of the icon, with the jewels—in collage fashion, using imitation stones, of course.

In all, I made five reproductions of the Black Madonna of Czestochowa, leaving the fifth half-finished.

One of my reproductions played an important part at the National Shrine of Our Lady of Czestochowa, in Doylestown, Pennsylvania, in 1966, right above the altar. President Lyndon Johnson came for the dedication ceremonies on the afternoon of October 16, flying in by helicopter with the First Lady and their daughter Lynda.

A crowd estimated at 135,000 had come to see the dedication and celebrate an outdoor mass presided over by Archbishop John Krol of Philadelphia. My painting was on full view for all to see, gleaming in the bright outdoor light.

After his speech, the President was taken for a grand tour of the shrine and seemed to take a special interest in my reproduction of the Black Madonna, sparkling with particles of jewels, just like the original, except of course that mine were imitations.

Reverend Michael Zembrzuski, director of the shrine, told him, "This painting of the Madonna was done by one of your former employees at the White House, Mr. John Szostak, who is now working for Senator Edward Kennedy."

President Johnson was very impressed and stood there for a long time studying the details. Though I was one of the honored guests, I did not feel it would be my place to go up to the president and push myself on him. If he had been asking for me, I could have been found very easily, hovering nearby.

But my turn came later. When President Johnson returned from his Vietnam trip, he had a meeting with Senator Kennedy at the White House and there he told Kennedy about me and the painting. My boss, the senator, was much surprised and told me about it.

He told me that the President had expressed an interest in having such a work of art for the first Polish church that had been built in Texas in the early 1800s—Panna Maria, meaning "Our Lady"—in a town with the same name. I was happy to take the hint, and I donated one of my reproductions to him for that purpose, which pleased him very much.

A third reproduction was presented to Pope Paul VI when His Holiness visited the United Nations on October 4, 1965. He gave it to his host, Francis Cardinal Spellman of New York, who gave it to Richard Cardinal Cushing, who had admired it and said it would be perfect for a particular church in his archdiocese. I have yet to find out where it is, because he died soon afterward, and I cannot remember the name of the church he mentioned.

A fourth reproduction of Our Lady of Czestochowa hangs in the Sisters of Resurrection Convent in Albany, New York, near my hometown of Schenectady.

I did not finish that fifth icon until Karol Wojtyla became Pope, and then I knew I must have been saving it for him. Now I had a reason to finish it.

It was just before Pope John Paul's trip to Poland, which was scheduled for June 2 to June 10, 1979, that I received a mysterious caller at my office. After some verbal sparring, he let me know that he was in possession of some important information concerning the safety of the Pope, while he would be on his nine-day visit to Poland.

He said that he had confirmed that I was, indeed, someone who had a pipeline to the Vatican and that was why he was choosing me to transfer an important message. He would not give his name, but said that he had been in the Polish intelligence service, but that the brutal assassination of a friend of his had disillusioned him, and he had become a double agent, now working against communism. The visitor advised me that he would be in touch with me again.

All my reporter's instincts advised caution, but the man seemed authentic to me, and if this was a hoax, why would some stranger go to all this trouble? Would I cooperate to help save the Pope's life, he wanted to know.

I answered, that of course I would, but again questioned why I was being singled out. After all, many people knew the Pope, and what about the American authorities?

The mysterious visitor told me that the message was being given to several people, but that in such matters one never knew who would dismiss it, thinking it was the ramblings of some crackpot.

Also, he said, highly placed individuals are often the ones who do nothing and just sit. As a final explanation, he said he wanted the information to be leaked to Poland so that those who were part of the plot would reconsider now that even a reporter knew about it.

It was a fantastic situation, and yet I believed him. I knew the Polish Communist government was against religion, but why would they want the Pope dead? What difference did it make at this point?

As the visitor explained it, it was a matter of control over the people, most of whom were Catholic, and over whom the Pope would have great control. "They're not afraid of him," he said. "They just don't want to put up with his meddling for the next umpteen years."

That, according to Mr. X, was the rationale. So, the game plan was to arrange some kind of accident. If there was an assassination, the world would mourn a great loss, and in

Poland, the Pope would be hailed as a martyr. The plotters did not want this, which could conceivably even cause an upheaval, maybe even inspire people to revolt and try to change their government. But an accident would be met with more acceptance. The people would remain docile. And another Pope would soon be in his place—one outside of the Communist sphere of influence.

Now I could hardly wait to hear what kind of fatal action had been planned. At this point, he seemed to be as convinced of my desire to help as I was of his authenticity. The accident, he said, was simply that the helicopter would have engine failure. After all, he said, accidents do happen, and helicopters are prone to certain kinds of accidents.

I suddenly remembered that a secretary general of the United Nations—Dag Hammarskjöld—was rumored to have lost his life in such a planned plane accident while on a mission to the Congo in 1961.

Once having learned that the alleged plot would be by means of a helicopter accident, I went to work on blowing the cover. My informant left, telling me he was leaving the matter in my hands to figure out how it was to be done, and that he would return for the final arrangements.

And so it happened that on May 23, 1979, at 3 A.M. I transmitted messages two ways—one, by ordinary cable, and the other by secret contact in code. Any spies or informants would have no trouble picking up the message one way or another. The text read as follows:

> RELIABLE INTELLIGENCE SOURCES HAVE INFORMED ME
> THAT THE LIFE OF POPE JOHN PAUL II WILL BE IN
> DANGER, WHILE IN POLAND. A HELICOPTER ACCIDENT
> OR OTHER PLOT IS CONTEMPLATED. PLEASE
> INVESTIGATE THIS MATTER. PROPER SECURITY
> MEASURES FOR HIS SAFETY MUST BE TAKEN. IT IS
> IMPERATIVE.

Copies of this cable were sent to the various church authorities in Poland and to the Vatican via code and normal channels. That meant that if all went well, each designated individual would get two copies of the same text.

Those who were behind the plot would surely think twice and perhaps abort the entire operation, since every letter and cable in Poland is subject to inspection.

Several months later, after the Pope was safely back in the Vatican, I received an overseas call from a Vatican source thanking me, in a guarded way, for "certain information" and for being on top of an interesting situation that was of help to everyone.

I may never find out what actually did happen, just as the Secret Service at the White House never gives out their follow-up on tips they have received. However, I am glad that my efforts may have helped prevent the unthinkable.

I did see my mysterious visitor again, and he added a few interesting tidbits—that Moscow had been more concerned with getting rid of the meddling Polish Pope than the Polish Communists. The Russians had wanted the Poles to do their dirty work, which would, incidentally, also prove their loyalty to their Russian comrades.

He said the Soviet KGB soon found out that blood runs thicker than water and that even the top Communist officials in Poland considered themselves Poles first and Communists second. In other words, they were reluctant to carry out such a cynical operation.

I don't know where the truth lies, but I do know that during the nine days that John Paul II toured Poland, I sweated from afar, especially watching for helicopter scenes on TV. I did not feel at ease until the Pope returned to the Vatican.

Naturally, I was fascinated, as was the world, to watch on TV and read the details of the new Pope's return to his native land. Having my own private sources in Poland helped me to get additional details about the emotional, history-making trip.

Clearly, the regime would have preferred that the Pope had stayed in Rome. They had prevented a previous pontiff, Pope Paul VI, from making the trip, but to have done the same to a Polish Pope would have strained the delicate relations between the government and the church to the breaking point.

Upward of eighty percent of Poland's inhabitants, who

are Catholic, would have kicked up a tremendous fuss. Consequently, the regime had little choice but to make the best of it, trying to paint a rosy picture of religious tolerance while maximizing their hard currency earnings from foreign visitors.

At the same time, the regime tried to minimize the political impact of the visit. "Nothing is going to change," official spokesmen announced.

For the benefit of indolent reporters, the Polish press agency passed out stories of each day's events so that the foreign press could file an account pleasing to the Polish government via telex without having to take the trouble to put ink to paper.

To show the attitude of the Polish government toward its people's interest in the new Pope, in January 1980, well after the Pope's triumphant visit home, an actress was forbidden permission to recite the Pope's poetry.

What happened is that Polish actress Halina Mikolajska was scheduled to recite the poems of the Pope, written when he was still a bishop and published under two pen names—Stanislaw Gruda and Andrzej Jawien.

They were to have been recited in the city of Wroclaw on January 15. However, upon her arrival there she was taken to police headquarters, informed that she would not be able to "recite the Pope's poetry or any poetry," and put on a train to return her to Warsaw.

How differently things were done in the United States. I am thinking of just one little incident. It happened in New York, in the Brooklyn diocese, where a little ten-year-old girl had been chosen to represent her orphanage, Angel Guardian Home, for a great honor.

She was to march out on a special carpet at Flushing Meadows and hand a bouquet to the arriving Pope. Through a comedy of errors, the "little Angel" got lost in the crowds and did not arrive on time with her flowers. It was a tragedy almost greater than she could bear.

Then, a few phone calls by the guardian angels of the Angel Guardian Home, Palma and Jerry Dallesandro, fixed everything. The little blue-eyed, blonde-haired child was invited to bring her flowers to Washington and to present them to the Pope at the White House itself.

She was flown there and was lifted up in the arms of

the kindly man in flowing robes, who kissed her tenderly and took her flowers.

From the moment that John Paul II emerged from the jet which brought him home to his native soil, Poland was his and his alone. Vast crowds of Poles came to see and hear the former cardinal of Krakow who, less than one year before was elevated to the See of St. Peter.

Never before had so many turned out for a visiting dignitary, not even for Charles de Gaulle. Nikita Khrushchev, who held the record among Soviet leaders as a drawer of crowds in Poland, did not come close even with the help of the party machine.

During his visit, the Pope placed a wreath at the Auschwitz concentration camp. He also placed flowers at the graves of his mother and father in his beloved Krakow—at the Rakowski Cemetery. Years before, he had moved his mother's body from Wadowice to be near him and to be buried with his father.

And then, as he had done so many times before, he made a pilgrimage to Jasna Gora to see his beloved shrine, the Black Madonna, Our Lady of Czestochowa.

I know that the Polish authorities were aware of my involvement in the Pope's safety, because, when I was planning this book and had gone to the Polish Embassy for my visa, I had another visit from Mr. X. He informed me straight and simple that I had better give up any idea of visiting Poland, because I would not be welcome there.

I said that all I wanted to do was take pictures of the Pope's childhood home in Wadowice and talk to those who had known him in childhood. I added that I had already gathered a great deal of material from Poland in a roundabout way—sent to a mail drop in another country and then remailed to me.

My strange friend strongly advised that I stick with the information I had already received from Poland, since any photographs I took while there would be unlikely to get out of the country in one piece. Moreover, my friendship would not do anybody in Poland any good.

What will be the effect on Poland now that the people

have their own man in one of the most powerful posts in the world? A friend of the Pope, who at one time was a member of the underground during World War II, said that John Paul II had, in effect, invested the last thirty years struggling with Poland's communist regimes.

John Paul II, he said, knows what Marxism really means. But, he is inflexible when it comes to church matters and human rights. In his new office, the Pope is expected to demonstrate his previous talent in his dealings with Communist governments.

Yet, he must also tread a careful path so as not to embolden his countrymen to the point of armed rebellion against the Communist system that could see them crushed under the heels of the Soviet military might.

One Pole said it very well: "It is a new era for us Poles. It is also a period of joy, because the new Pope is a Pole. But it is also a period of great anxiety. Where do we as a Polish nation go from here?" The same question is being asked by everyone in the Communist bloc nations. Where do we go from here?

His last words to me on the subject of church and state relations in Poland back in 1976, when he was cardinal, were, "Genuine political change in Poland—and in the entire Soviet bloc—is a possible reality, only to be achieved not by revolution, but by evolution." He also said, "We look to America and its church for inspiration to the people of Poland."

11

USA Revisited

The Pope is coming! The Pope is coming!

Such excitement! Cities were fighting for the honor of having the Pope visit them on his projected trip to the United States. It was reminiscent of early British history when the coronation of a king was to take place and the cathedrals of Canterbury, York, and London each vied for the honor of having the ceremony held there.

The same rivalry came about in August among the U.S. cities which have large Catholic populations. It should be explained that a Pope just doesn't invite himself. He doesn't say, "I'm dropping in to see you." For reasons of diplomacy, he must have an invitation.

Pope John Paul II had made it known that he would like to visit the United States and then had sat back and waited for the invitations to pour in—which they did.

Orchard Lake's Polish Seminary near Detroit thought

that Pope John Paul II should visit their new library named in his honor. Miami's Catholics argued that Florida had the first Catholic congregation and the oldest Catholic church—in St. Augustine; and Savannah, Georgia, wanted the Polish Pope to help honor Polish-American Revolutionary War hero Casimir Pulaski, who died there. Meanwhile, Baltimore was making a strong case as the location of the primatial see and the first American Catholic diocese. This is just a sampling of invitations that the Vatican received.

The final choice was made by the Pope, himself. Having travelled with the Pope and listened to his reasoning in the past when he was a cardinal, I predicted he would retrace his steps.

Sure enough, the only addition to his 1976 itinerary was his trip to Iowa to see rural America. On August 25, the cities that he would visit were finally announced. They included Boston, New York, Philadelphia, Des Moines, Chicago, and Washington. He was to arrive October 2 in Boston and depart October 7 from Washington, D.C.

It was to be his third visit to Boston. Again, his old friend Thaddeus Buczko, auditor of the State of Massachusetts, was the star for having visited the Pope in Rome and convincing him to come to the city that had loved him when he was cardinal.

I did not fare so well, I am sorry to say. Competition extends even into church circles, and so does jealousy, as you will see.

My overseas church contacts had informed me in late spring 1979 that John Paul II would be arriving in the U.S. in the fall—probably in September or October.

In June, a full month before the formal announcement was made, I learned confidentially that the Pope would be arriving October 2. On July 21, 1979, the announcement was made public in a brief communiqué by Vatican press spokesman Father Romeo Panciroli:

> In response to the invitation given him by
> the Irish Bishops' Conference, the Holy
> Father will go to Ireland from September 29 to
> October 1 for a visit of a pastoral nature. On

On official business and at all public
ceremonies, the Pope carries a staff with
a cross at the top—technically known
as a crozier. The hat that he is wearing is
called a miter.

Wherever he goes the charismatic Pope, John Paul II, has drawn multitudes of people in a two-way outpouring of love. He is the first Pope to use an auto to get around St. Peter's Square in order to touch and be touched. Here, with St. Peter's behind him, he is standing in the white jeep that wheels him around.

The Pope does not sit on the throne of St. Peter as the average person supposes. That throne is part of the treasures of St. Peter's Basilica, on view above and behind the high altar. He sits on this portable white velvet throne that is even carried to outdoor audiences in St. Peter's Square, as shown here.

The Pope is reading the Gospel during the Midnight Vigil Easter Mass.

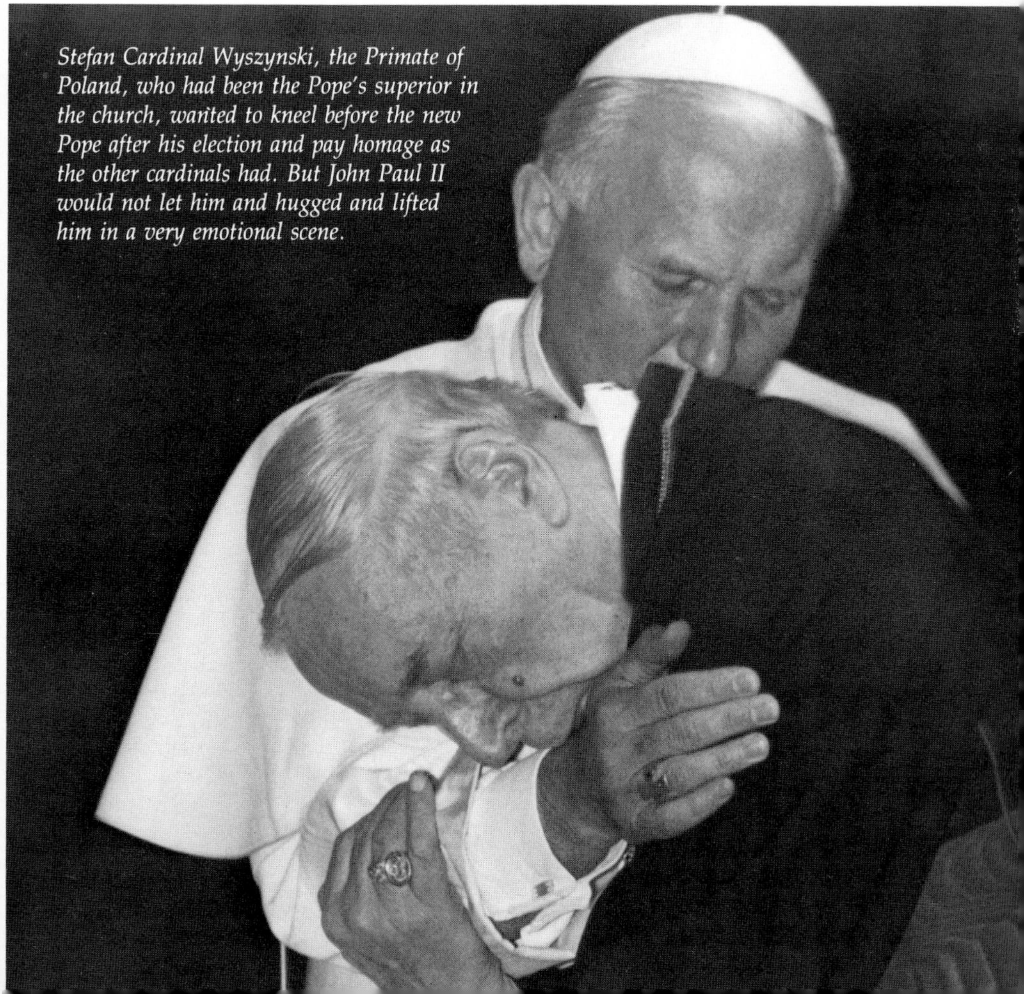

Stefan Cardinal Wyszynski, the Primate of
Poland, who had been the Pope's superior in
the church, wanted to kneel before the new
Pope after his election and pay homage as
the other cardinals had. But John Paul II
would not let him and hugged and lifted
him in a very emotional scene.

The Pope stood on this balcony after the message was delivered to the crowds in St. Peter's Square that the world had a new Pope—Habemus Papam. The Pope uses the balcony only on very special occasions, including Christmas and Easter.

During his first trip back to Poland in 1979, the Pope lays a wreath at Auschwitz concentration camp in sad memory of those millions of Poles—Jewish and non-Jewish—who died there.

The Pope takes care of a matter for a nun in his office. As you can see, he has file cabinets just as any businessperson would have.

The Pope is curious about all things. Here he chats with the pilots in the cockpit of an airplane.

Much of his trip to the United States as Pope in 1979 was a retracing of his steps in 1976, when he was a cardinal. Here he is speaking at the United Nations.

The Pope is the most relaxed man in the room as he meets with the immediate family of President and Mrs. Carter in the private quarters of the White House in the second floor yellow sitting room.

▶

John Paul II looking out from the balcony of the Episcopate Palace in Krakow, where he lived as Archbishop and Cardinal. His first trip back to Poland in 1979 was a triumphant return for Karol Wojtyla, who, as a member of the Polish underground and secret seminarian during World War II, had lived hidden in the basement of the palace. John Paul II's personal coat of arms as Pope hangs from the balcony. It features the "M" standing for the Virgin Mary, especially as she is portrayed in the Shrine of Our Lady of Czestochowa, to which he made pilgrimages. With him is the man he chose to succeed him—Franciszek Cardinal Macharski.

The Pope sports an Italian boy scout's hat that has just been given him in St. Peter's Square.

John Paul II plants a little fir tree at the North American College in Rome. Above his head to the right is a new member of the Vatican curia, William Cardinal Baum, former Archbishop of Washington, D.C.

One of the first acts of the new Pope was to visit Bishop Andrzej Deskur at a hospital in Rome. The Bishop, who is in charge of all press and communications from the Vatican, was thought to be on his death bed. However, after the Pope's surprise visit, he made a miraculous recovery and is back at work at the Vatican, where I visited with him briefly in spring 1980. This picture, which shows us together, was taken in his apartment in 1976, during my first visit to Rome.

The Pope pays honor to the memory of martyred early Christians who were thrown to the lions in the Colosseum.

The Pope always pays special attention to children wherever he finds himself. Here the Pope hugs a Mexican lad during his visit in 1979 and is hugged in return.

John Paul II became the first Pope in the memory of the Vatican to hear confessions, just as any parish priest, at St. Peter's. To do this, he donned a black coat over his white robes and slipped into the confessional through a back entrance to hear confessions in Polish. By coincidence, I chose to give my confession to a Polish confessor and was startled to learn afterwards that I had been talking to the Pope through the screen which hides the priest and confessor from each other.

Here I am, posed with the icon I made, a copy of Our Lady of Czestochowa, which helped decorate the Pope's parade route from St. Matthew's Cathedral to the White House. By the time he arrived at this spot and had the limousine pause for a moment while he looked at it, I was already at the White House covering the event of his arrival, in my capacity as White House correspondent. I was lucky to have a neighbor stationed at the spot to tell me the Pope's reaction. Also shown is a detail of the icon itself, showing the scratches.

This was two days after I had had dinner with the Pope in his private quarters, and he was surprised to find me here. I was in St. Peter's Square with a group of Polish professors from the Catholic University of Lublin, where he was once a fellow teacher. He raised an eyebrow and said, "When did you become a member of the Lublin faculty?" I said, "This morning, Your Holiness." Just after this picture was taken, he gave me a bear hug. Incidentally, the white-haired man behind the Pope is his personal physician. The Pope, I learned, like the president of the United States, must always have his physician with him.

Candid shot of a garden party in the backyard of the Episcopate Palace in Krakow in the summer of 1978. Tea and cakes were served. But the highlight was Cardinal Wojtyla reading his poetry aloud. Seated to the right of Wojtyla is Cardinal Wyszynski. To the left is Monsignor Zdzislaw Peszkowski, an old friend of mine, now a professor at Orchard Lake Seminary in Michigan, the only Polish seminary in the United States. To the far right is the secretary to the Polish Catholic Episcopate, Alojzy Orszulik.

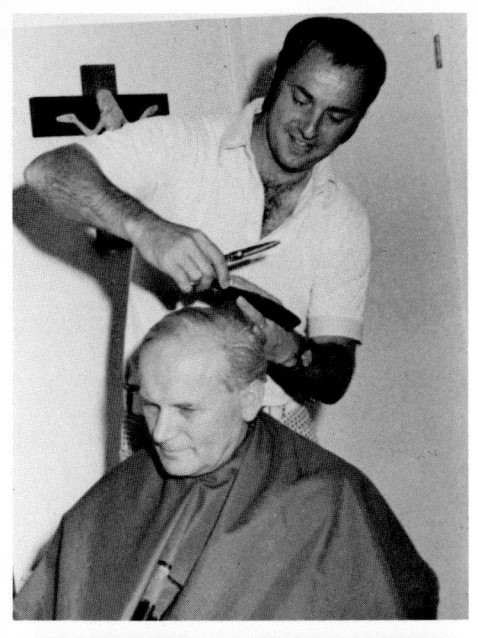

A future Pope gets a haircut. This photo was taken at Orchard Lake Seminary in August 1976 by my friend, Monsignor Zdzislaw Peszkowski. Cardinal Wojtyla was there to attend and give a week-long seminar on theology and ethics.

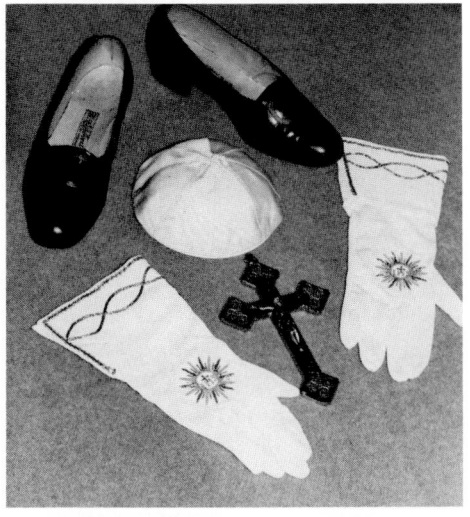

These are the shoes of the Fisherman—John Paul II, 263rd successor to the original Fisherman, St. Peter. They are red, and in the form of slippers, the traditional papal shoes. Also shown here are the gloves the Pope wears on special liturgical occasions and his white skullcap, which he rarely removes in public. The cross was a gift to my family from John Paul II, when I visited him in Rome in spring 1980.

This is the cobbler who works in a tiny shop outside the Vatican walls—at 10 Borgo Santo Spirito—making shoes for the Vatican. Cobbler Telesforo Carboni was sure that a non-Italian Pope was to be named because he suddenly got an emergency message, during the conclave, to make immediately a pair of papal shoes in a large size—size 11. Italian men wear shoes that are rarely larger than size 8 or 9.

October 2, in response to the invitation
given him by Kurt Waldheim, Secretary
General of the United Nations, His Holiness
will visit the headquarters of the U.N. in New
York and will speak to the General Assembly.
Afterwards, in response to the desire
manifested to him by the Bishops Conference
of the United States of America for a visit of
a pastoral nature, and in response moreover to
the invitation expressed to him by President
Jimmy Carter, the Holy Father will stay several
days in that country.

In the first two weeks after the announcement that Karol Wojtyla had metamorphosed into Pope John Paul II, I was giving briefings to my fellow scribes about the Pope's background and my relationship with him while he was in America in 1969 and 1976 and helping with anything that needed clarification.

Everyone, from the TV media on down to weekly newspapers and newsletter reporters, was seeking information from me. I even got calls from as far away as Australia, England, and Canada. Word travels fast—there were many more calls from around the United States at all hours of the day and night. I hardly had time to write my own news column, but I finally came out of the clouds, sat down, and wrote:

MY FRIEND THE POPE
John M. Szostak
White House Correspondent

We are living in interesting times. Little
did I realize when, in 1976, I first met Cardinal
Wojtyla, the Archbishop of Krakow, that he
would become Pope John Paul II, the first
Polish Pope.

To meet a Pope is a rare honor, but to
know a Pope—corresponding with him,
working with him, and having him come to
your home—is a gift from God. With this rare

gift I feel there comes an obligation to be
more Christlike in one's daily life. Those who
share this rare privilege of knowing the
Pope are in a way an extension of him.

This memorable experience can be traced
back to 1962 when I became involved in
Polish-American activities concerning the
Catholic Church in Poland. . . .

And speaking of "tracing back," everyone was asking
me to explain the comment from the Vatican that the new
Pope was "the youngest" since such and such and "the first
non-Italian Pope" for centuries.

I explained that John Paul II, at age fifty-eight, had become the youngest Pope since Pope Pius IX reigned from 1846
to 1878. It was during Pius IX's pontificate that the dogma of
the Immaculate Conception (*Ineffalilis Deus*) was proclaimed.
It was also in his time that the Virgin Mary appeared to St.
Bernadette at Lourdes, France (1858), now a world-famous
shrine for incurables.

John Paul II, in becoming the 264th Pope, also became
the first Pope in history from any Slavic country.

As for the last non-Italian Pope—that had been the
Dutchman, Hadrian VI of Holland, Pope only for a year—
1522–23. Even so, the Dutch pontiff was known as a saintly
man. All the other Popes who followed him in the next 455
years were Italian.

It's interesting to see the ancestries or countries of origin of the approximately fifty non-Italian Popes who preceded
John Paul II. History during first millennium of Christianity is
murky and the exact number remains unclear. Twelve Popes
in the last 2,000 years are believed to have been French, 11
Greek, and six Syrian.

Two were Jewish—St. Peter, of Galilee, the first Pope,
and his third successor, St. Clement, who, however, was
listed as a Roman. The rest of the non-Italians were Germans,
Africans, Spanish, English, Dutch, and Portugese.

John Paul II is also the first to be called the "Travelling
Pope," and the "International Pope" for the fact that he trav-

elled all over the world before and after his elevation to the papacy.

Not only did he come to the United States twice before mounting the throne of St. Peter, but through the years he spent considerable time in Rome, even before being assigned his first parish. In 1973, en route to the Eucharistic Congress in Sydney, Australia, he took the opportunity to stop off in Asia to have a look around, and in 1974, 1977, and again the following year, he went to West Germany in a concerted effort to reconcile the Polish people with their former conquerors, who now had established a small democratic government.

In 1969 and 1976, he visited Polish communities in Canada and Latin-American countries.

News of the election of Karol Wojtyla as Pope had certainly thrown my life into high gear. Everyone was leaning on me.

It seemed that everyone was desperate for information about the Pope's two previous U.S. visits, and I was the only one they knew of who had this material stored away in my archives. The White House needed information. The church press and the church administration in Washington needed material. I had suddenly become invaluable.

I put together a packet of information that contained over one hundred pages. It gave the names of people, places, schedules, and his lifestyle and needs in 1976. It even included copies of his speeches. The 1979 visit turned out to be about the same but was expanded in light of his position as Pope.

The first to receive my information packet was the U.S. Secret Service. They were most appreciative and almost ecstatic about the amount of data it contained. I was told that this saved them weeks of work. I had provided them with information that they never would have been able to get otherwise.

The second and third groups to receive the material were the White House staff, who were involved in the trip, and the Office of Protocol of the State Department. I had received a communication from the Vatican, from one of the Pope's aides, suggesting that since I was known to the President and his staff, I could be of "considerable help" by advising the White House staff on arrangements.

I did give suggestions on what the Pope would enjoy and some suggestions on how the White House might handle certain angles of the visit that the church officials might have left out. Later, I saw that many of my suggestions were followed, even in the matter of music to be played at the White House.

I knew that Pope John Paul II did not want much fanfare. However, it was to be dignified and in good taste. He would want to go out among the people on the White House lawns, and it would be fine if there could be little children among the adults.

I explained to the White House and in my report that the Pope would not be interested in discussing politics, but only matters involving religion and ethics.

That particular suggestion bore fruit even before the Pope arrived, as was seen in the way President Jimmy Carter replied to a reporter's question about the purpose of his upcoming visit with the Pope. The president answered, "I expect to meet with him in the White House in a private fashion. My belief is that it is his desire to come to our country not on a political mission but on one involving religion, morals, and ethics."

This was almost exactly what I had suggested to the White House. And I was delighted with the results.

Finally, I gave the same packet of material to Father Robert N. Lynch and Bishop Thomas C. Kelly of the U.S. Catholic Conference of Bishops, the coordinators of this visit. They needed it because they were putting together background notes for the press. I was gratified to see they used much of my material for their press kits.

Once I had helped others all I could, I proceeded to get my own press accreditation to cover the trip. Even as a White House correspondent who already had Secret Service clearance, I still had to apply for the special passes. Some events were pool assignments—a few reporters were selected to cover for the group and then shared with the whole press corps who hadn't attended—so being a pool reporter required still another pass.

With all the multicolored passes around my neck, I soon looked like some well-decorated war hero. Most of the Secret Servicemen knew me already, and this made my coverage of the White House event much easier—especially since I continued to provide them with valuable background information.

As a matter of fact, the Washington office of the Secret Service had photocopied my material and distributed it to field offices where the Pope would be visiting.

In view of the fact that there had been a possible plot on the Pope's life in Poland, I was not about to take any chances in the United States.

I also reported to the Secret Service each time I received a threatening letter or crank call. The stories about me in the press, as a friend of the Pope, had touched off some hate groups and religious fanatics. I was never told what happened on the followup of these letters and calls, except that I knew they were being investigated.

All was joy, and I thought my cup runneth over. I was the man of the hour around the press, the White House, and the local Catholic clergy. Everyone was leaning on me. My only concern and desire was to help the visit of my friend in his new high office be the great event it deserved to be.

I gave so freely of my time that I sometimes saw my material used before I could get to it. While the preparations for the trip were in progress, I was often interviewed by the TV networks and the print media, both local and national.

The greatest moment of all in this media coverage was when a plaque was placed at my home commemorating Pope John Paul II's visit in 1976, while still a cardinal. The dedication took place on September 19, 1979, at 10:30 A.M. The plaque reads:

CARDINAL KAROL WOJTYLA NOW POPE JOHN
PAUL II BLESSED THIS HOME ON HIS U.S. VISIT
JULY 29, 1976

And this was the turning point. Possibly because of all the press and TV coverage I got, the local lower-echelon churchmen—priests, monsignors—suddenly turned against me.

Part of it was not their fault, because the stories about me had simply gone too far. One reporter in particular had gone overboard in making it seem as though I was trying to be something I was not. But let me back up a minute and take it from the top.

I am looking now at the letter I received from a member of the papal staff, telling me that it was the Holy Father's wish that I and a particular local Washington-area priest, who had accompanied him part of the time in 1976, help with the new visit.

It would not be proper to reproduce the whole letter or make public the name of the parish priest, but I see no harm in sharing the opening of the letter:

> Dear Mr. Szostak:
> His Holiness Pope John Paul II has asked
> me to designate you and the Reverend . . .
> to be the unofficial advisors to the church and
> civil authorities who will be responsible for
> the arrangements of the Pope's visit to
> the United States this Fall. . . .

The letter, on stationery bearing the papal seal and the words *Secretaria Statvs* and *Ex Aedibvs Vaticanis*, was dated July 12, 1979.

The letter goes on to explain that the "request comes as a result of your past association with His Holiness when he was a cardinal. As press liaison to then Cardinal Wojtyla in 1976 at the Eucharistic Congress in Philadelphia, your experience and that of Father . . . will prove to be of great value to the authorities who are making these arrangements."

I was pleased, of course, but I was certainly not surprised to receive this letter, because it was true that that priest and I had helped not only Cardinal Wojtyla, but many other churchmen coming to the U.S. for years before 1979.

144

As a correspondent for several Polish-American news-papers, and with my close involvement in Vatican and church affairs, Karol Wojtyla himself had arranged for me to be the media liaison and personal photographer for the cardinal and nineteen Polish bishops at the 1976 Eucharistic Congress. And as I mentioned earlier, because of specializing in Eastern European affairs, I had been corresponding with the Polish curia—or administration—for more than a dozen years prior to the cardinal's visit.

The letter also told who would be arriving from the Vatican to work out the visit's details, but suggested that since I was a White House correspondent, I might be able to help in the interim by advising the presidential staff. And that was what I did.

The letter ended, "His Holiness Pope John Paul II bestows upon you and Father . . . His Apostolic Blessings. Sincerely yours in Christ . . ."

I study that letter now and have to smile as I see that the writer of the letter, in his last paragraph, says, "We have every hope that you will do well in that the authorities in charge will be pleased by this contribution on your part."

The truth of the matter was that while the secular world of White House and Secret Service very much appreciated the help, the church officials in Washington responded with almost fury that I, a layman of no particular importance, was suddenly acting officious and making suggestions.

They labeled the letter a fraud and told me they would take care of everything themselves. Naturally, they did not wire the Pope himself to ask for the truth.

Embarrassing as it was, I simply notified everyone I had started working with that I was no longer working on arrangements and everything would be handled through official channels in Washington—the United States Catholic Conference and the National Conference of Catholic Bishops.

At that point, I was too stunned to even question their judgment. That would come later. When I related the incident to a State Department official in the protocol office, to whom I had supplied material, and told her that I was no longer authorized to answer questions, she could not believe her ears, but said, "Letter or no letter, this does not diminish in any way your experience in knowing the Pope and the value your material has proven to be to us."

She was sorry that I would not be helping her any more, or be a member of the official party. She had been counting on me, she said. Some of my press friends also expressed dismay when I told them I was no longer authorized to answer their questions for them and directed them to the authorities responsible for the Pope's U.S. visit.

After the stunned feeling had worn off a bit, I pressed local church authorities to get verification, at least through the local office of the Vatican—the Apostolic Delegation. I kept pressing and eventually, in a few weeks, was told that they had checked with the Vatican and the signer had no knowledge of the letter.

The point was that the letter should have been sent via diplomatic pouch to the Vatican delegation in Washington and then forwarded to me. I realized that was proper procedure but was not concerned because since I was a friend of the Pope, when he was Cardinal, all the letters I had received from him had gone through the mail. And hadn't he appointed me helper in 1976? And even as Pope, I have heard that he has sometimes sent letters and messages to friends in Krakow right through the mail.

There was no reason for me to question the letter—it sounded so much like other messages I had received from him, or from others delivering a message from him. Nor did I feel it would be proper for me to send him a letter demanding to know what was going on or burdening him with my problems.

Anyway, I did not have to communicate with him directly on the matter because at this point I was sending weekly confidential reports to one of the Pope's personal assistants and, among other things, I did fill him in on this.

The Pope also knew what jealousy was like, having faced it long ago when he was just made bishop at an early age and older men of greater sophistication and cultural backgrounds were passed over. Some of the clergy had looked down on him. They were used to taking their directions from a man who had been born a prince, Adam Sapieha, whom he had succeeded in the archdiocese of Krakow.

Wojtyla had borne up as best he could under this air of condescension, and even with humility and resignation, saying to those who expressed concern, "I can understand, but there is nothing I can do. They look at me as a former laborer and they looked at him as a prince, which was his birthright."

This took care of the case of my friend, and I hoped that time would be on my side, too.

Then I remembered and took comfort from something my friend had said in a letter several years before: "God will never let you down even though for some unknown reason things may be dark. He sees fit to try his faithful servant. But trust him all the more: don't give up praying."

I knew that the Pope would not want me to return the treatment in kind or be vindictive, for hadn't he said when still a cardinal, "There is no injury that cannot be forgiven." I determined to rise above my hurt and still smile and be helpful.

Even those who looked at me with cold, unfriendly, even hostile eyes, trying to shut me out, I determined would not get to me. For hadn't Wojtyla said, "When unfriendly eyes turn their gaze upon us, we must do all we can to make our gaze a friendly one."

At this point, it really didn't matter that the local churchmen wanted me to cease helping them with the Pope's imminent visit, because I had already rendered all the help I possibly could and had handed them freely the material from my files.

Then an amusing thing happened that showed they still needed me in spite of themselves.

I received several calls from the U.S. Catholic Conference asking if I could use my influence to have the Pope write an article for *Woman's Day* magazine. I could not resist saying that I was amazed by this phone call asking for my help and suggested they might prefer to ask someone who knew the Pope better—after all, why ask me, under the circumstances?

They admitted they were asking me because speed

was of the essence, since the article they had in mind was for the Christmas issue. I swallowed my pride and said, "We shall see what can be done."

Immediately, I sent a letter and a sample copy of the magazine to my contacts in the Vatican, explaining the situation.

With all my work in preparing for covering the papal visit for my newspaper clients, I forgot about the matter until my wife picked up the magazine at the neighborhood supermarket—not at Christmas, but in April 1980—and there it was.

By then, the Pope had come and gone. But the article was of lasting value—his words on love and marriage as taken from his works when still a cardinal.

Eventually, I was told by Vatican friends both in New York and Rome that the letter I had received had not been a hoax but had been perfectly sincere.

In Rome, additional details were given as to how the confusion had come about. I was told that hundreds of letters go through that particular office—the office of the Vatican Secretariat of State—in the course of the day, and they are simply signed by one of several people who are on duty at the time.

The particular person whose name was on the letter sent to me had been asked by someone from Washington about it and had replied that he had no recollection of such a letter. But I'm getting ahead of the story.

Now the press gossip columns jumped at the chance to tell this good joke about a bogus letter concerning someone's friendship with the Pope. As one columnist put it on September 6, 1979, "Someone's idea of a joke brought embarrassment to a Washington newspaperman and a Virginia priest."

The little item, high in the column, went on to tell how "Szostak, a White House correspondent for several ethnic newspapers," had received a letter making him and the priest unofficial advisors for the upcoming papal visit.

The columnist added, "Church officials in the United States, however, knew nothing of the appointment."

On looking back, I realize how unfortunate it was that

the letter had not been sent through official channels, or that a carbon copy or Xerox of it had not been sent by the Vatican to the church officials in the Washington area.

After the incident was over, and after the Pope was gone, I did see at least one item saying the effort to make me an unofficial adviser had not lacked veracity. Sarah Mc-Clendon wrote in her column in *Washington Weekly*, October 16, 1979:

> Polish Journalist John Szostak was vindicated. Vatican aides traveling with the Pope knew of the "cross you have had to bear," from those who said his letter about helping with arrangements for the Pope's visit was a fraud. . . . He had a visit with the Pope who posed for pictures with him. . . .
>
> Then the Pope stopped his motorcade on Connecticut Avenue to look at a picture Szostak had painted of the Polish saint which was on display in Raleigh's window. . . . Some day in Rome, Szostak will give that picture to the Holy Father. . . .

At least this helped repair the damage her previous stories had done.

Earlier, Sarah McClendon had been the one to break the news in her column of August 16 that I was one of two persons who were authorized to help on the Pope's trip. Unfortunately, she had not used the proper phrase of "unofficial advisers" and that is probably what had caused the violent reaction. It did sound a bit outrageous. Her item of that date had flatly stated, "The Pope has designated young Szostak and Father . . . to make arrangements for his visit here . . ." It was an unfortunate choice of words.

I'm afraid her story that day also had the effect of giving a few other false impressions as well. She had interviewed me and perhaps I had not made things clear enough in my conversation.

At any rate, I may as well set the record straight and have done with this once and for all. The column for the day was headlined "The Pope's Man in the Washington Press Corps" and the item starts out, "Only one American layman can boast of having entertained the Pope in his home. John M. Szostak . . ."

I don't know how many homes the Pope was in when he visited the United States in 1969 and 1976, but I am sure there were many more than just mine. Mine may have been the only one in the Washington area in 1976 but I'm not even sure of that. Also, the word "entertained" is a big one for just a short visit.

In fact, the item says the Pope was "honored at a reception there," and I am quoted on what the cardinal ate. The reception was at Gadsby's Tavern, which I thought I had made clear, and the menu pertained to Gadsby's. In the column Sarah McClendon adds that, as an afterthought "John also took the Pope to Gadsby's Tavern and to the K. C. (Ed Note: Knights of Columbus) Hall in Alexandria to meet the Polish community."

I'm sure that Sarah meant well, but her column did succeed in raising the hackles of certain churchmen, who in turn overreacted.

She continued to be my friend, and when I was cut off abruptly by the Washington church groups, I continued to answer whatever questions she asked.

On September 27, she announced in her column that according to a Catholic University publication, a public relations firm had been hired to handle publicity for the upcoming visit of the Pope. Her column goes on to say:

> . . . Meanwhile at least one totally inexperienced person, Stephen Ackerman, has been hired to do research and put out background material on the Pope and to travel with him across the country. Needing guidance, the inexperienced one had the benefit of background material on the Pope, prepared earlier by John Szostak, Polish journalist here, who knows the Holy Father personally. . . . But the Bishops are dodging John Szostak like he had the plague of the

Dark Ages. . . . They do not want him to get
near the Pope. . . . Hope the Pope finds
out about all this. . . .

All in all, I viewed Sarah's stories as a mixed blessing.
Fortunately, I could prove that I made no claim that
mine was the only home the Pope visited. In a newsletter circulated at Parkfairfax, Alexandria, Virginia, where I live, I had
been interviewed for the May 1979 issue. The Association of
Condominium Owners of Parkfairfax were proud of two
things—the national figures who had lived there—namely
Presidents Gerald Ford and Richard Nixon and Secretary of
State Dean Rusk—and the fact that a Pope had blessed my
home.

So I had been interviewed in regard to the placing of
a plaque at my home, and my comments were accurately reported in the newsletter:

> What His Holiness thought of Parkfairfax
> is not known, although he remarked to John
> that the apartment reminded him of his
> own in Krakow. John told us that although
> this visitation may be unique for Parkfairfax,
> Pope John Paul II has stayed in many
> homes in the United States on his two visits
> prior to assuming the Papacy. John found that
> his visitor likes to ski, canoe, play ping
> pong, that he sings and is a former amateur
> actor. But perhaps best, John found that
> deeply rooted gentleness given to only the
> truly wise occupants of our moment in eternal
> time.

It was hard to know how to handle myself. As I re-
gained my sense of humor, I realized that though this whole
incident might be a tempest in a teapot, still it was causing
some slight injury to my reputation as a responsible journalist.

I was determined somehow—I hadn't figured it out
yet—to let the Pope know eventually what had happened and
find out the truth about that letter.

When the Pope arrived, I was still in Siberia as far as the church welcoming committees were concerned.

I wondered whether I was the only one. Had those who had previous contact with the Pope, especially those who knew him far better than I, been asked to serve on advisory committees on making the arrangements? Would they be able to visit with their old friend?

I soon learned to my dismay that the answer would be a flat no. Absolutely not. I further learned that once again modern "inn keepers"—even some who had snubbed him in 1976, when he was an unknown visiting cardinal—were now trying to keep him for themselves and making sure others were kept away—especially close friends and associates who would take his time.

Instead, there was a whole new list of more prominent names who were involved in the history-making visit—the event of the century. And that's how it turned out. The Pope was not able to meet many of his old friends in America, not even his dear friend Ted Buczko, a Pole and high-ranking official in Massachusettes, who was not even invited to be part of the welcoming ceremony at the airport in Boston.

What makes this especially ironic is that Buczko was the very man who, in a trip to Rome, had influenced the Pope to include Boston on his U.S. itinerary, when, originally, I was told the plan was to arrive at New York and skip Boston.

Not that Buczko complained. He was too well-mannered for that. But it was a sad commentary that the Pope saw only the lucky few who stood very high in the church's hierarchy pecking order. This was the sorrow that was brought about by the 1979 visit—the lack of attention to old friends. The excuse the American churchmen gave was that there was not enough time, and, to be blunt about it, I was told that "after all, he is not coming just to visit the Polish communities in America."

As a journalist, I was one of the fortunate ones who, by hook and by crook and by the hand of God, was able to see him. There were many others who knew the Pope far better than I, but who were too refined or timid to resort to trickery—as I did—or begging, and so priests who had worked with him in Poland, college professors, people dear to him, with whom he corresponded—all these close friends were not even allowed a chance to say hello.

Later, after the Pope had left, some of the people who were callously left out suggested that an "Exile Club of John Paul II Friends" be formed.

Why hadn't the Pope spoken up? For one thing, I'm sure he didn't know how widespread the shutout was until later. Also, he was a diplomatic guest. It was not his way to make waves, knowing that God would provide a second chance and somehow there would be other meetings with his friends.

In my case, he had become aware of efforts to keep me from being a part of his entourage, but he knew that somehow I would work it out. And, by golly, I did. From start to finish, it was a battle of wits to get some time with my friend. I had no problem with the Secret Service, for they knew me well. The problem was at places other than the White House—getting through the wall of petty clergy officials.

For obvious reasons, I cannot reveal who guided me, but I can tell how I achieved my goals. Let's take how I got to the side of the Pope at the United Nations—our first quick meeting and my first encounter with him as Pope. I arrived wearing a complete bishop's costume, stepping out of a rented limousine. When security officials met my limo, I gave them holy cards and my blessing, in broken English, with a Polish accent.

Months later, I got a kick out of reading that Hamilton Jordan, top White House aide, had also resorted to wearing a disguise on a special mission for the president—a fake mustache and gray wig. I'm sure he had his correct identification papers along, if anyone should challenge him.

And, of course, so did I have my credentials along, had they been needed. The most important thing was that I did have proper security clearance—without which this would have been impossible to do. My disguise was only a means to get through the clerical officials.

After I had removed my bishop's robes, I became a reporter again and milled around with over five thousand correspondents accredited for this visit. In another place, Philadelphia, my role became that of a Polish correspondent assisting a Polish bishop by carrying the bishop's garments over my arm. Again, I made sure that I had plenty of holy cards to go around, the same cards that others were giving with the likeness of the Pope—and which had been sent to me from Rome.

Without going into detail for security reasons, I was able to meet with one of the Pope's assistants and, before the Pope finished his address to the U.N. General Assembly, I left for the residence of the Vatican Observer to the United Nations with personal arrangements made.

It was there that I had my first meeting with the Pope—a brief but exciting ten minute reunion. I said, "We'll have to stop meeting this way." He laughed at my creativity in overcoming every hardship to get to him, but said he knew that somehow I would make it.

I reminded him, he said, of his own early days when he had survived by his wits in World War II, slipping in and out of windows to escape the Nazi authorities.

The Pope looked tired, and I could see he had a lot on his mind. Otherwise, he looked the same as he did in 1976. The warmth was there as much as ever. I got that old bear hug of his and was told to "keep up the good work for the church and the people of Poland." He even remembered to send his wishes to "The Little Cardinal," and my "philosopher wife, Constance."

We had enough time to have a photo taken and to exchange a few mementos. He gave me several little things he had brought for me. I gave him a photo of the family and a letter written by my elder son, Eric. He put it in his pocket to read at his leisure. I had taken the precaution of saving a Xerox copy and can tell you what it said in large, childish scrawl with fanciful margin.

> Dear Pope:
> I'm sorry I can't see you in person now.
> But I'm Lucky I'm a alterboy.
> You are a great Man!
> I am going to see you later
> "Niech zyje Nam sto lat"
> Love
> Eric Szostak
> 9 years old

Most comforting to me was the Pope's assurance that he understood how some had been trying to keep me away from him.

As long as he knew it, it didn't matter what the others were saying or thinking. I remembered his words when he was a cardinal about not expecting things to be easy. "Every great thing must be expensive and difficult," he had said. "Only small and worthless things are easy." To me, helping behind the scenes to make the Pope's trip a success had been perhaps the greatest thing in my life, and so I could not complain that it had not been easy. Others had tried to make me look foolish by discrediting my connection with the Pope and by saying it could not be real, but it did not matter because the Holy Father had known all along.

And something else came to mind that he had said and that assured me in the long run I would be vindicated. "Truth," he said, "has in it a quality of endurance, but falsehood dies a quick death."

By a small miracle, the only person who recognized my disguise was a wire service photographer who, as a friend, understood and kept my secret. However, he still teases me by saying, "How is Your Eminence today?" to which I reply, "Just fine. Bless you, my son."

It was at the United Nations that the Pope expressed the theme that I had heard so often. But this time, he said it with even greater force: "I again proclaim the dignity of every human person." And it was here he said that the poor of the world are the brothers and sisters of the rich and well-fed.

And then he spoke the words that would be quoted over and over and which will take their place in history: "You must never be content to leave them just the crumbs from the feast. . . . You must treat them like guests at your family table."

At Yankee Stadium, he was still hitting away at inequality, materialism, and overconsumption of both nations and individuals. "We must find a simple way of living," he said. "For it is not right that the standard of living of the rich countries should seek to maintain itself by drawing off a great part of the reserves of energy and raw materials that are meant to serve the whole of humanity."

He went on to explain that "Nowhere does Christ condemn the mere possession of earthly goods," but rather that, "He pronounces very harsh words against those who use their possessions in a selfish way without paying attention to the needs of others."

The Pope warned, "We cannot stand idly by when thousands of human beings are dying of hunger. Nor can we remain indifferent when the rights of the human spirit are trampled upon. . . . "

He called this unequal distribution of wealth and the violation of individual human rights the two great threats to world peace.

That same day, at St. Patrick's Cathedral, a priest who was conducting the choir was suffering terribly from nerves at the tense situation, as well as heat prostration. Suddenly, he felt a touch. It was the Pope himself who had reacted with sympathy and come over to wipe the sweat from a brother's face.

The Pope's picturesque humility appeared again in Harlem, where a young monsignor knelt to kiss the ring of the Pope. Instead, the Pope quickly pulled him to his feet and kissed him on both cheeks.

It was most appropriate. The choir was chanting the words, "Speak boastfully no longer, let no arrogance issue from your mouths."

In Harlem, he lifted a black child into his arms and kissed him with the same tenderness he had kissed other children. This is important to mention because it gives the lie to some mutterings I have heard that he only kissed white children and had been too isolated in all white Poland to feel close to blacks.

Wherever he went, he responded to children, often following their lead. In Brooklyn, when one little boy held up a hand to be shaken, the Pope shook it gravely, then blessed all the children around him.

Youth of America of all denominations were spellbound by the Pope. They met him with the fervor that they had once reserved for John F. Kennedy. When the Pope was having lunch with the Vatican's U.N. observer, for example, they kept up a steady chant until he came out to greet them, yelling, "Who do we want? John Paul! When do we want him? Now!"

The next day, on Wednesday, October 3, Pope John Paul II was met by twenty thousand youths at Madison Square Garden in a great outpouring of love. For long minutes, they had a nonsensical but enthusiastic exchange—he and the young ones—which brought them together.

The Pope rocked back and forth in his chair and happily shouted "Whoo, whoo" into the microphone.

The young ones responded in kind, "Whoo, whoo," and back and forth it went.

Then the Pope changed to "Whoo, hee, whoo," and the youngsters responded with "Whoo, hee, whoo."

The only person who seemed upset by this display was Terence Cardinal Cooke, the host in New York. Worried about timing and the Pope's schedule, he spoke into the Pope's ear and the Pope calmed his audience, raising his hands for silence and explaining, "We shall destroy the program."

At first, the Pope had not even wanted to sit on the platform but down among the teenagers. He seemed to feel a part of them, and they responded with gifts. One gave him a tape recording of a teenage singing group and another gave him a guitar to share the symbol dear to youth. It will not be wasted. I am told he knows how to play it to accompany himself.

I remember that it was raining that day, especially afterwards, when the Pope went to Battery Park for his speech. At one point, the Pope noticed some children playing on the swings in a playground. Suddenly, he deviated from the schedule by going over to greet them in the rain, again much to the consternation of Cardinal Cooke. It was understandable—at that point, they were running about an hour late.

The man I had known as Karol Wojtyla had not changed. He loved children. He felt that he had all the time in the world for children, just like Jesus had, when He said, "Suffer the little children to come unto Me."

At Battery Park, the Pope had a special greeting for Jewish leaders who had come, saying, "I greet you with a word taken from the Hebrew language, '*Shalom!* Peace be with you.' "

He told them their presence honored him greatly and of a recent meeting he had had with an international group of

Jewish spokesmen in Rome and restated what he had told them:

"Our two communities are connected and closely related at the very level of their respective religious identities. . . . We recognize with utmost clarity that the path along which we should proceed is one of fraternal dialogue and fruitful collaboration."

He said he was glad to find in the United States "a common determination to reject all forms of anti-Semitism and discrimination," and affirmed, "Various forms of collaboration for the human advancement, inspired by our common biblical heritage, have created deep and permanent links between Jews and Catholics."

From Battery Park, I flew with the papal backup press plane to Philadelphia. There, again, I had to skip a few more stops in order to be on time at the airport. We arrived in Philadelphia at about 3 P.M., still on the same day, Wednesday, October 3.

Immediately, John Paul II took a brief tour of the Cathedral of St. Peter and Paul and from there he went to Logan Circle, where he said mass as a guest of John Cardinal Krol.

There was one touching moment at St. Peter and Paul that still haunts me. A little five-year-old crippled boy with very poor vision was there to meet the Pope, and he clutched a slim bouquet of red and white carnations as a gift for the Pontiff.

The Pope noticed him and sent word that he wanted to meet with the little boy and receive his gift. But after the mass was over and the Pope had passed right by without stopping, the mother was leaving with her son, thinking His Holiness had forgotten them. But he had not. A Secret Serviceman went hurrying after her to tell the mother that the Pope would meet them in the rectory.

Later, the mother told how the Pope had placed his hand over the child's eyes and then on his head, and had blessed him.

The mother was very moved. But the child, little George Bannar, took it in stride and put up his arms to be lifted. The Pope gathered him up and kissed his cheek, and the little boy kissed the Pope's cheek. Boy and man could not let go of each other. As the little boy hugged the Pontiff, the

Holy Father reached in his pocket and put a rosary in the little boy's hand.

At about 6 P.M., the Pope had dinner at Cardinal Krol's residence, located near St. Charles Borromeo Seminary. At 9 P.M., helped by my contacts, I was happy to be at the seminary where the Pope came to visit with the young seminarians. There I was again able to meet with him briefly in the crowd. But how different it was from when we had stayed there together in 1976.

I told him that this trip should bring back memories of the old days when we stayed there together. The Pope smiled and said, "Yes, I remember well." Then, as an afterthought, he jokingly chided me, "When did you become a seminarian?"

I replied, "Just now—ten minutes ago."

He chuckled and went to greet the other people.

Covering the Pope's visit was not at all easy in that it was just impossible to be at one event after the other. The logistics made it difficult. I found out that in order to go from point A to see the Pope's arrival at point B, one would have to leave point A half through the event and then rush to point B. This was the only way some pool reporters were able to cover every step of his tour.

Thursday, October 4, was going to be another long, drawn out day—waking up in Philadelphia, then flying to Illinois and Iowa before returning to Washington that same day. At 8 A.M. in Philadelphia, I went to the Ukranian Cathedral of the Immaculate Conception to see the Pope's meeting with the church leaders of the Eastern Rite. There, the Pope gave a brief talk and led the assemblage in prayer. Then, at 9 A.M. he attended mass for the representatives of the clergy at the Philadelphia Civic Center.

Here, again, I got to see him at close range and exchanged a few words. I expected him to ask me, "When did you become a priest?" But all he said to me was, "I see you are finally working," and smiled.

As usual, we arrived late in Des Moines, Iowa, over an hour late. John Paul II stopped first at St. Patrick's Church in nearby Cummings. There, again, my bishop act had to be utilized in order to get in closer. Speaking Polish and English with a broken accent was my ticket.

Everyone thought I was direct from Poland. The holy

cards that I gave out went like hotcakes. I was well-prepared.

In St. Patrick's, the Pope felt most at home. He led the people in prayer and was even able to joke with the congregation.

It was unbelievable. People were in a state of shock. Just imagine, a Pope coming to a remote farming community's church. However, he put them at ease before it was all over. Everyone was relaxed and able to enjoy the visit.

At one point in the brief service, several Italian news photographers got into the church. The *paparazzi* were very insistent to the point of yelling to the Pope, *"Prego, prego,"* in order to get his attention for their cameras.

The Pope, seeing all this unfold, got up and mildly mocked them, not in Italian, but in English, "You are also parishioners? How did you get here?" At that moment, everyone laughed good-naturedly.

The *paparazzi* left shortly thereafter. After his benign air about my little prank, he could not be too severe with them.

From St. Patrick's Church, the Pope's motorcade drove to the Living History Farm Museum, where he offered an outdoor mass. It was an impressive event, to say the least. There, again, I was at a close range, able to observe his emotions and facial expressions. One could clearly see the joy he had in being with these farm people.

At one point, I could see him rub his eyes and knew that the trip to the rural community of Des Moines was a sentimental journey for him. When a journalist asked him in Polish, "What is your reaction to this rural visit?" the Pope replied, "It brings back memories of my youth as a parish priest."

The outdoor mass was also in keeping with John Paul II's final act in Krakow, on his triumphant return to Poland as a visitor, after becoming Pope. He had said mass in an open field of Krakow. And it had been a mutually emotional outpouring between the Polish Pope and his flock.

With the sentimental journey to Des Moines at an end, the Pope departed for Chicago. I went along on the press plane to that city, and from there took a flight back to Washington, where I could rest up a bit and prepare my special greeting to him that was already nicely placed along the parade route in the window of Raleigh's department store.

It was, of course, my fifth reproduction of the Black Madonna, Our Lady of Czestochowa. I had already talked with the Pope about this in New York, and his aides had been briefed on where along the parade route to draw his attention to it.

Not only had I told him about it, but it had already been noticed by the media and had made news. In fact, UPI had sent out a story on the wire about it.

12

A Pope at the White House

No one had any idea of the size of the crowds the Pope would attract way back in July and August of 1979 when the planning for the trip was in the infant stage.

It was as if John Paul II was an idea that snowballed.

To show the sheer hugeness of the event, in New York, alone, the city had to sweep up one hundred tons of tickertape and confetti after the Pope's parade—a cost of $43,000. It had taken one hundred fifty men to clean the area the Pope had travelled by motorcade from Madison Square Garden to downtown Manhattan and Battery Park.

To compare with another blockbuster day, the event of the Yankee's winning the World Series had topped this display, with one hundred fifty tons of paper. Pretty good for one man against a whole team.

All through this trip, the Pope was greeted with a surprising lack of hostility, considering how large the crowd had been—literally millions of people. However, there were a few threats to kill the Pope, which the FBI investigated.

In one case, before the New York visit, a cache of guns and four boxes of ammunition were seized in Elizabeth, New Jersey.

And as I well knew, the Pope had faced greater security problems in Poland.

Even greater security than in Poland was thrown up around the Pope in Turkey, where he later visited for three days to encourage the reunification of the Roman and Eastern Orthodox branches of Catholicism—a union that would unite hundreds of millions of Catholics around the world.

Security guards cleared all the streets John Paul II was driven through in Ankara. And even the airport was deserted except for the officials who greeted him. I heard afterwards that a reporter who had been part of the press travelling with him had asked just before the plane's doors opened whether the Pope felt he was in danger in making this trip.

The Pope had looked at him and answered, "Love is stronger than danger."

So tight was security that even the press were excluded from viewing the Pope as he made various visits, such as at the Presidential palace and at the home of the Vatican's emissary in Ankara.

I have the inscription John Paul II wrote in a guest book after laying a wreath at a national shrine, and it gives one much to think about. Translated from French, it says:

> The government of the peoples is in the hands
> of God. He creates at the right moment the
> leader who suits them because love of liberty
> and respect of the law makes a nation
> great, but it is God who secures its future.

The Pope's trip to the U.S. had many good effects, not the least of which was the first step in a coming together in ecumenical spirit of various denominations of Christian faith.

Two things happened. First, the Pope met with members of eight denominations to pray together at Trinity College Chapel in Washington. And second, in Boston, the Pope was given a silver pectoral cross as a gift from leaders of the Protestant, Anglican, Orthodox, and Roman Catholic faiths. Inscribed were the words: "That We Might Be One."

The Pope was going directly to the White House after his parade down Connecticut Avenue from St. Matthew's Cathedral. My ego nudged me to be standing on the parade route beside my icon of the Black Madonna—Our Lady of Czestochowa—that had such great meaning for the Pope.

But, as much as I wanted to be there when the Holy Father passed by, I could not, because I had to get through the crowds and arrive at the White House early enough to position myself in a good spot. Being a veteran of many state visits, which I covered from the vantage point of the White House, I knew from experience where I would get the best view of the honored guest and get the best pictures.

The day before it had rained, but like a miracle, Saturday morning dawned clear and beautiful for the event. On hand was a military honor guard and a marching band.

How beautifully the whole store window had been arranged—my icon reproduction high above and a sketch of the Pope by another artist below it. As I went by, I noticed a cluster of Secret Servicemen near it, which made me happy. Everywhere the Pope planned to stop or even pause had extra Secret Service coverage.

When the Pope entered the grounds of the White House that Saturday, October 6, 1979, it healed an estrangement between the Vatican and official Washington that had lasted for more than two hundred years.

Not only was John Paul II the first Pope in history to visit the White House, but as he himself told President Jimmy Carter at their greeting on its front steps, he came as a "messenger of peace and brotherhood."

A little while later, in a prepared welcoming statement, the President said that God had blessed the United States by sending the Pope and added, "Welcome to our country, our new friend."

The Pope, deeply moved, embraced the President and bestowed a papal kiss.

What a difference this was from the attitude that prevailed in the United States in the last century, when Catholics were sometimes even kept from getting good jobs. I had long heard how, when the Washington Monument was being built on the mall behind the White House back in the early nineteenth century, world rulers had sent stones to be set inside the monument with the name of the donor carved on it for all posterity. A beautiful Italian marble slab had been sent by Pope Pius IX, but the equivalent of a "lynching party" had hijacked the stone in the dead of night and thrown it away— some believe into the Potomac River.

This portion of the White House visit was attended by high government officials: the cabinet, agency heads, members of the Supreme Court and of the U.S. Congress. President Carter introduced Pope John Paul II with his remarks, and then the Pope spoke.

But first, he gave a compliment to President Carter for his "good Polish" in the welcoming introduction. Everyone laughed. Afterward, someone asked me to say the phrase correctly, "Niech bedzie Bog pochwalony"—"May God be praised."

After the talks, both President Carter and Pope John Paul II went to shake the hands of the visiting dignitaries. All this took about an hour, followed by a picture-taking ceremony in the Oval Office.

Then the American President took the honored guest to the family quarters on the second floor for him to have a quiet, private visit with many members of the Carter family— including the First Lady, Rosalynn; little Amy; mother, Miz Lillian; and son Chip. Within months, the Pope would be taking the Carter family to his own private quarters for a visit in Rome. It was interesting to see the exchange of gifts between the President and the Pope. The Pope brought with him a sculpture—a piece of polished petrified wood mounted with silver plate and decorated with an olive branch. The message read *Pax Tibi*, meaning "Peace to you."

He also brought a silver medallion bearing his likeness and a papal seal on the reverse side, contained in a lovely white leather presentation box.

In return, the President presented His Holiness with a

brown leather photo album stamped with a gold presidential seal and containing photographs of unmanned space flight—Voyager I's encounter with the planet Jupiter.

The president explained that the photos were chosen from among 19,000 which had returned to earth showing its closest approach to Jupiter and the Galilean satellites in March 1979. The Voyager I, he said, had been launched several years before, September 5, 1977.

At about 3:30 P.M., the scene switched to the South Lawn, the backyard so to speak, of the White House. We reporters hurried outside from the press room to a scene that was much more relaxed. In fact, a picnic-atmosphere prevailed among the seven thousand guests.

Most of them were Carter supporters and friends. They stood now talking happily and looking up expectantly until President Carter and John Paul II suddenly appeared on the balcony, waved, and stood a few moments until pictures had been taken.

Then they came down to the lawn and stepped up on a small platform to say a few words. The 104-piece National Symphony Orchestra, under Maestro Mstislav Rostropovich, played music by American composers and then turned to religious music, which had been one of my suggestions.

However, where I suggested the playing of "Ave Maria," they opted for "Our Father."

The selections with an American flavor were William Schuman's "American Festival Overture" and Dvořák's "New World Symphony."

I was pleased that at the end of the reception the orchestra followed the suggestion I had given to the White House and played the emotional Chopin piece, "The Polonaise." I had felt it would be perfect for a Polish Pope to hear a Polonaise since the word means a stately Polish dance, in triple time.

And even above that, there was another reason.

As I'd mentioned to the White House, Chopin's "Polonaise" has special meaning to every Pole living today. In 1939, when Poland capitulated to the Nazis during the early days of World War II, this memorable piece was the last thing that the sorrowing station managers sent over the Polish radio airwaves from Warsaw.

And as the strains of "The Polonaise" ended and before the station clicked off, a voice said, "Poland is not lost. Poland will again be free."

One of the moving moments of the afternoon had occurred when the president asked the Pope to give his Apostolic Blessing to everyone on the South Lawn. It was a clear reminder to all of us that Christ is not only in the Vatican, but at the White House, and everywhere on this globe.

After their talks and the Pope's blessing, both President Carter and John Paul II went out to the crowd to shake hands. Again, I got to talk with His Holiness briefly, although the crowd pushed in around him. The Pope said with a smile, "I see you are working and looking well."

Among the guests at the White House on that red letter day were prominent American Poles from all over the country. Just to mention one state, Michigan, there was the mayor of predominantly Polish Hamtramck—William Kozerski—as well as Anthony Derezinski, Public Affairs Director of the Michigan Catholic Conference, from Lansing, and Stanley Krajewski, editor of *The Polish Daily News*, a guest from Detroit.

There was Zbigniew Brzezinski, of course, Carter's top adviser on world affairs.

There was Edmund Muskie, soon to become secretary of state.

There were Congressmen Clement Zablocki of Wisconsin, Edward Derwinski of Illinois, Barbara Mikulski of Maryland, and Lucien Nedzi of Michigan.

There was former Ambassador to Poland, John Gronouski of Wisconsin.

There was philanthropist Edward Piszek, president of Mrs. Paul's Kitchen.

There was famed baseball player Stan Musial.

And finally there was the president of the largest Polish fraternal organization in the U.S.—the Polish National Alliance—Aloysius Mazewski.

After all the hand-shaking and the final strains of "The

Polonaise," some people began to leave. At that moment President Carter and the Pope went back up to the Truman Balcony to wave good-bye.

Since I was close to the balcony and standing with several guests who were Polish, I started to get up on a chair and sing to him the familiar "Sto Lat, Sto Lat," which brought back the days of 1976—"May you live to be a hundred." The Pope and President Carter, hearing this, motioned me to come closer—both waving their signal from the balcony.

I continued singing as I walked, the others joining in. Then, we sang a religious song in Polish, with the Pope joining in, singing along with us, "My Chcemy Boga," which means "We Want God." The Pope then waved to say "Well done" and departed by the North Portico.

Among the many notables standing there that day, I met the NBC *Saturday Night Live* star known as "Father Guido Sarducci." The Vatican gossip columnist was none other than Don Novello. He was there too, covering the Pope's visit as a contributing journalist for *Rolling Stone* magazine. He said that in spite of his being a TV comedian, he had great respect for the man, John Paul II, and intended to write a serious story. I had a photo taken with Don Novello.

A reporter told me afterward that, as he was leaving the White House, John Paul II stood up in his open-topped car, stopped the car a moment, and blessed the White House.

I almost thought I was back in 1976, when John Paul II was cardinal and I was travelling with him. Again people were saying, "How can he be so human—a holy man, a Pope, kissing babies and talking and laughing?"

Again, as I had done three years before, I quoted that old Polish proverb that explained it all, "*Kto do Tanieca, ten do rozanca*"—"A man who can dance can also say the rosary."

Later, I attended a White House press conference at which we asked the President his feelings about the Pope's visit. President Carter admitted that he had been "thrilled" to meet the Pope and felt it was one of the most beneficial visits from a world leader that the nation had ever had.

He admitted too that he had been surprised at the degree of warmth and enthusiasm with which the American people had received the Pope. "I expected the welcome to be warm and friendly, but I had no idea that it would be that enthusiastic and that large a number of people—and neither did he," Carter said, referring to the Pope's own modest expectations.

As for why there had been such a response—about seven thousand people at the White House, including almost every member of Congress, the cabinet, and the Supreme Court, and some two hundred thousand on the Mall, President Carter said, "I think there's an innate hunger in our country for moral and ethical and religious principles—things that do not change during a time of rapid change brought about by a technological revolution throughout the world.

"I believe there's a hunger for things that are decent and honest, for principles of which we can be proud. I think the Pope, as a religious leader, accurately mirrors, for many people, those aspirations and hopes.

"I think it shows that this hemisphere is the most deeply religious, perhaps in the world—certainly the most deeply religious Christian population in the world."

As for the subjects they had discussed, one important topic was atheism as a state policy. "We had long discussions," said Carter, "about what this meant to other nations— the threat of atheism as espoused and enforced by the state against the inherent desire of people for religious belief."

I do not recall when I last saw the President in such good spirits—perhaps at his inauguration. It was obvious that both men hit if off well that day. There was something spiritual about them. Although coming from different faiths, they were very much alike, because they are both men of deep faith and that aspect of their spirituality showed throughout the White House visit.

Later, after the Pope had left the country, I had a personal interview with President Carter and learned a little about what had transpired and his reactions to the high church visitor.

For me, Sunday, October 7, was another long, busy journalistic day. And for Pope John Paul II, this would be his last day in the United States. At 8 P.M., he would depart for Rome. At nine o'clock that morning, I went over to the Shrine of the Immaculate Conception at Catholic University, arriving at the conclusion of his service, just in time to catch the Pope going to the side chapel of Our Lady of Czestochowa to pray to Poland's patron saint.

It was just what he had done when he was a visitor to the Shrine in 1969 and 1976. From there, I went to the press center to watch on TV a rerun of the Pope's activities and to hear his address to the faculty at the Catholic University gymnasium. From the press center, I left for Trinity College, bypassing the ecumenical prayer meeting that was going on inside the college chapel.

I went directly to the area where the Pope would meet later on with the handicapped. This was a small gathering of the press and participants, different from the huge crowds elsewhere. It was perhaps the most moving occasion of the Pope's visit. One could see the heartfelt concern he had for these people. Several times, I could see him rubbing his eyes to wipe away the tears.

The Pope was especially moved to see very young children disabled. He took time to greet almost every one of them. He touched. He looked deep into the eyes of the sufferers. He showed he cared. Watching this great fatherly figure, I could not keep the tears from my own eyes, especially at what happened next.

A handicapped little girl said, "Bless me, Pope John Paul." He leaned over, eyes brimming, and said to the little girl, "First you bless me."

The little girl blessed the Pope in a tremulous voice. Then John Paul blessed her, embraced her, and shed more tears.

From Trinity College, the Pope went to the Apostolic Delegation for a reception with reporters. I was not invited, although I was a reporter.

When I called the delegation, they said that it was only for reporters who came with the Pope from Rome. However, I knew many others who did not travel with him and who were invited. The delegation members did not know I had already seen the Pope privately in New York, circumventing their pettiness, and already had my invitation to visit the Pope in Rome.

While the Pope was meeting with reporters at the Apostolic Delegation, I was at the press center, relaxing and getting myself prepared for the outdoor mass on the Mall which would climax his U.S. visit.

The gigantic mass was starting a bit late—at about 3:45 P.M. Before ascending the special platform for members of the press, I had to find a restroom. I asked a Secret Serviceman where the restroom was. When he saw my clearance passes, he pointed for me to go to the Smithsonian Castle Building, which was located directly behind the altar where the Pope would hold mass.

I was on my way back out of the Castle when I heard sirens getting louder and closer. A Secret Serviceman motioned for me to wait.

Moments later, Pope John Paul II and several cardinals and bishops arrived. It was a rest stop for His Holiness to put on his vestments. Also, at the Castle, before mass, the Pope was presented with the prestigious Smithsonian Award by Supreme Court Chief Justice Warren Burger. The last recipient of the award had been Queen Elizabeth II.

It almost seemed like the hand of God was guiding me. The petty-minded had tried to keep me away from the Pope at the reception, and now the Pope was brought to me. It was again a joyful reunion, which startled the Secret Servicemen. The Pope embraced me.

I stood by while he put on his robes for the celebration of mass. He suddenly pulled out a stack of holy cards commemorating his visit to the United States and gave them to me for my friends and family. There must have been at least fifty.

He said, "I hope you are doing a good job."

I replied, "The work is not easy."

He nodded his head, understanding my unspoken pain at how we were being kept apart.

"But one does not lose one's sense of humor," I said, pulling out a bumper sticker someone had given me and which I had been saving to show him. In large white letters against a solid background was written: "Pope Paul II in '80."

John Paul II looked and smiled at this political joke, and then, on his way out, said in jest, "You behave yourself." These were to be the last words he said to me on this trip.

After mass, he walked past the press section, and I yelled out to him in Polish, *"Niech zyje nam sto lat!"*—"May you live to be a hundred!" He looked into the crowd, saw me, and smiled and waved good-bye.

As he spoke, facing the multitudes on the Mall, I felt thrilled and comforted at his words on the continuity of life: "Human life is precious because it is the gift of a God whose love is infinite—and when God gives life, it is forever."

It had been a fantastic adventure, watching preparations for the outdoor mass that would take place on the Mall, near the Washington Monument. A huge and rugged altar was built of solid beams of red oak ten feet long and sixteen inches thick. They were hand-planed and bolted together.

It took three weeks to build and when it was through it weighed five thousand pounds. All work had been a service of love—the modern design by Robert C. Smith of Smith, Segretti and Temper, and the execution by the Arlington Woodworks and Lumber Company.

Afterwards, many churches vied for the honor of having the Pope's special altar installed in their churches. But finally a whole new church was designed around the style of the altar, because it was much too big to look at home in an ordinary size church.

The new church, to be called St. Bernadette's, will be built in Springfield, Virginia, and will seat 1,300, making it one of the largest churches in the Washington area.

The platform on which the altar stood was ten feet above the ground and the Pope's chair was fifteen feet above the ground to make him visible to the multitude who made up the congregation that day. I will never forget the sight of John Paul II in his gleaming white robes and green vestments, the one thousand choir singers from every Catholic church for miles around whose voices were augmented by six hundred loud speakers, and the two thousand priests and assistants passing out communion wafers.

But nothing in life is perfect and even as 200,000 people rejoiced at the Mall that their Pontiff was there among them, a few blocks away demonstrators were picketing the Pope and demonstrating in support of gay rights, legalization of marijuana, and abortion on demand.

A Yippie organization pie thrower had been imported from New York City. But he had not managed to get near the Pope during the mass. Later, he would have another chance.

The Pope had been perfectly at home, perfectly comfortable. I will never forget the moment when, somewhere along the line, he saw a long-haired youth and called out in English from his car, "You need a haircut."

The youth replied, without a moment's hesitation, "*You* need hair."

It had been a good-natured exchange on both sides.

From a distance, I watched John Paul II being escorted to his limousine that was parked in front of the Castle building. From there, he went directly to the Apostolic Delegation to get ready for his departure for Rome.

I started for the military airport, hoping to hear him say a few more words before boarding. I learned that his final act before he left was a fifteen-minute meeting with Vice President Mondale at the vice-presidential home on the Naval Observatory grounds, directly across the street from the Apostolic Delegation.

The vice president was so impressed that he asked the Pope to bless the official residence for his family and for all those who would live there in the future.

Fortunately, there is a helipad on the Observatory grounds, and the Pope flew directly to the airport at Andrews Air Force Base by helicopter.

For me, the departure had an edge of sadness as I realized that what had been in 1976 could never be again because a Pope has no more freedom and privacy than a President. How true the words of that old Polish song we had sung together, of how time races by "and soon we will not be together again."

The Pope gave a farewell talk just as he had done at a different airport—a commercial one—when he was in Washington in 1976. But now security was intense. Even so, a nasty incident that could have marred this solemn occasion was stopped just in time. A Secret Serviceman caught a man with a pie ready to throw into the Pope's face. It was the Yippie's last chance, and he was foiled again!

The Pope seemed unaware of it.

Then the Pope was gone, and his departure left a great void. I milled around, not wanting to leave the airport yet, and reviewed the whole visit in my mind. There had been such a mob that I had not even gotten close enough for a personal farewell.

Though I mourned our closeness of 1976 when we had been able to really talk with no rush and no barrier of flanks of officials, I still felt spiritually enriched. As I stood alone, I could visualize that luminous face—so gentle, so expressive, so much a compendium of a life of hardship, scholarship, and inner sanctity.

His face alone was a benediction. Its mobility reflected the quick adjustment to each occasion—from serious discussion with the President or an ambassador to delighted chuckles as he held up infants to cuddle and caress. Each he did in full measure. In Rome, they have a saying, *Festina lante,"*—"Make haste slowly."

While others were fretting about his schedule, he was wandering around refusing to be bothered by the ticking watch. If there was a child to comfort or a broken body to touch, John Paul II took all the time needed to bring a smile of hope to that face. And it was not done with an elitist condescension, but rather in the profound humility of a servant of the Lord.

It was the same whether he was alone or surrounded by people. He seemed to move surrounded by his own little center of quiet. One night, long after midnight, the security guards had become concerned about a light in the chapel of the Apostolic Delegation, where the Pope was staying in Washington. Was there a break-in? They hurried to investigate and found Pope John Paul II alone and deep in prayer.

Why had he come to America? To bring the message that without love there is no living. And that the human heart is the common denominator of the human race. And, taking it a step further, he wanted to reiterate the Vatican's support of the United Nations in its support of human rights.

The Pope had certainly not lost the light touch I remembered so well. While in Chicago, he had kidded a group of seminarians. "See how important you are? The Pope has come to see you."

When it came to stating what he believed, even if he knew it meant losing some friends and fans the Pope had the courage to tell it as he saw it and mince no words. And, indeed, he did this suddenly and with spirit, half way through his visit which had been, up to then, simply a love fest.

Many liberals within the church and even some conservatives were shocked, but I would have been surprised had the man I knew been anything but the traditionalist he is. The Pope declared himself against abortion, contraception, women being ordained priests, and priests marrying.

That was his message spoken in the United States and flashed around the world. It did not make him less charismatic as a speaker or less of a warm friend to the world. It just meant that he was standing by the traditions of the church as they had been upheld by previous Popes.

Sometime after it was all over and my plans had been worked out, I told President Carter that I would be going to Rome to see Pope John Paul II for the writing of a book. He asked me to deliver his kindest regards to His Holiness.

I was gone for several weeks from my old White House haunts, but as soon as I had returned President Carter noticed I was back. At the first White House press conference I attended after my return from Rome, the President spotted me as he was leaving the East Room and said, "I'm glad to see you back from the trip."

I said, "Mr. President, I bring you a greeting from His Holiness, John Paul II. And by the way, may I congratulate you on your choice of Senator Muskie for secretary of state—all the Poles will vote for you." I was chuckling.

The President smiled and said, "I did it just for you."

I replied, "You are too kind, Mr. President."

He was chuckling and about to say more, but we were being separated and he was being pushed along by Secret Servicemen and reporters as he left to go upstairs to his private living quarters.

13

Dining with Pope John Paul II

*I*t is said by his friends that the Pope will eat anything put before him, but that he prefers coffee to tea and often asks for buttermilk. He does not smoke and usually likes beer with his meals, even as you and I—and especially I.

He truly loves Polish cuisine above all others. Clerical help around the Vatican comment on the different odors that now emanate from the Vatican kitchen. Instead of the garlic and tomatoes and other ingredients for the sauces for the pastas, there is the unfamiliar heady odor of sauerkraut and kielbasa (Polish sausage).

But food is not the first thing that His Holiness turns to when he arises at 5:30 A.M. in his apartment in the Vatican. First, he celebrates mass in his private chapel, a few feet from his bedroom. He prays and meditates until breakfast is served.

John Paul II has his breakfast in his sitting room–

audience room. The Pontiff does not like to have breakfast all alone, and he doesn't have to. Joining him every morning is his pet cat, who was brought from Poland by one of the nuns. Just the two of them sit in silent companionship for the morning meal.

The Pope has not succumbed to the Italian breakfast—*colazione*—rolls and coffee, or crescents and jam, the French continental breakfast. But he has made a slight bow to the Italian way by switching to a glass of wine occasionally before lunch, instead of sticking with the beer that he once preferred.

The typical breakfast runs like this—espresso coffee with milk, scrambled eggs, ham, sausage, black bread, and soft rolls. During the breakfast, the Vicar of Rome reads several newspapers in six languages. One of the Swiss guards purchases them for him every morning at a newsstand located under the Apostolic Palace, where he lives. (While I was in Rome, I also bought my U.S. papers there.)

There is an interesting story about those scrambled eggs. It goes back to shortly after John Paul II's installation, when he had company from the United States—William Cardinal Baum, the former Archbishop of Washington, and Baum's assistant, Monsignor Gillen.

They were invited for breakfast at the Vatican one morning but instead of sitting down at the table immediately, the Pontiff turned to Monsignor Gillen and said, "Can you fix me scrambled eggs the American way as you did for me in Krakow?" After the Pope's visit to the United States in 1976, Baum and Gillen had visited him in Poland the following year.

The monsignor was amazed and somewhat stunned at this request from a Pope, but he quickly answered, "I will be delighted to do so, Your Holiness."

They all went to the kitchen, and the Pope watched every step of the procedure. Then they all sat down and enjoyed scrambled eggs, the American way.

When I traveled with the future Pope, in 1976, he would lecture me, and the bishops who joined us for breakfast, about a good morning meal. He placed great value on matters of health and felt that this was the most important meal of the day. He loved fruit for breakfast, especially blueberries, and said he even enjoyed gooseberries when they were in season.

I remember running around and getting him extra blueberries. Then, after a hard morning of paper work and audiences, the Pope has a light lunch at about 2:30 P.M., generally consisting of soup and sandwich or salad.

When the Pope was elected, he sent for the elderly Polish nuns who had taken care of his kitchen and knew what he liked to eat in the Episcopate Palace in Krakow. However, they found they could not keep pace with the demands of the life at the Vatican and the difficulties in preparing meals for unexpected guests.

They never knew how many people the Pope would invite to dinner any given evening—the Pope hates to eat alone. And in the Vatican, away from his beloved Poland, he needed more company than ever. Sometimes he would even invite people he had run into in the course of the day.

The problem was complicated by the fact that the cooked food at the Vatican is brought to the Pope's private dining room via elevator from the kitchens. The stoves are gas ranges. The kitchen is not particularly modern, but is very efficient and meets the needs of the Pontiff.

Also, the menu is now either Polish cuisine or Italian, depending on his guests. The nuns were used to Polish cuisine. (For Italian dishes, incidentally, the Pope leans toward veal.)

When the Pope visited Poland in 1979, his first trip back—he asked the Mother Superior of his household staff to send him some younger nuns who could cope with the rigors of the difficult schedule and special problems.

Two new nuns, both from Poland, are responsible for the cooking, and meals are planned by the very efficient Sister Teodata of Poland, who is in charge of the household help. She is said to be a wizard of flexible menus to accommodate whatever number of guests arrive for lunch or dinner.

When I visited the Pope in the spring of 1980, I was gratified and happy to be invited to have dinner with him. I will give you the menu and directions for making most of the things we ate, but first let me tell you other things about how the Pope eats now and favorite dishes he remembers from his childhood.

And let me tell you of my eating adventures with John Paul II, when he visited the United States in 1976, and I spent more than a week traveling with him. But for this story, we have to go back further to his first visit to the U.S.

Karol Cardinal Wojtyla developed a great appreciation for seafood during that visit in 1969, especially lobster. It happened when he was the guest of Thaddeus "Ted" Buczko, in Boston, a man you've already met several times on these pages.

Ted, a good friend of mine and a dedicated layman of Polish extraction, had taken the cardinal and his official party to place a wreath on the statue of Revolutionary War Polish hero, General Tadeusz Kosciusko, at the Boston Gardens. And then they had proceeded to Jimmy's Harborside Restaurant.

As a memento of the occasion, Ted presented the cardinal with a Paul Revere bowl, representing America's fight for freedom. Not only did the future Pope enjoy the beauty of the inspiring gift, but he discovered lobster. Ted Buczko filed this away in his mind and seven years later, when the cardinal returned to Boston, he again hosted a dinner for him and again served lobster.

I was not surprised that Ted asked me to do him a favor when I told him I was going to Italy to do research for this book. "John," he said, "I asked His Holiness what he would like, and it was just one thing—lobster. So will you please take him three large lobsters—about six pounders—if I send them to you frozen?"

I was already carrying camera equipment, a lead box to protect the film from airport X-ray machines, and a heavy wooden carved head of the Pope, a gift from a Polish sculptor who had immigrated from Krakow. I had promised to present this exquisite artwork for the artist. Then, of course, I was also carrying an artwork of my own to present to His Holiness—the Black Madonna. That was not light either.

But thinking of how Karol Wojtyla had relished those lobsters, I could not say no.

However, I couldn't resist protesting, "Ted, are you sure he wasn't kidding?" He insisted that when he had visited Rome in June 1979, the Pope was indeed still talking nostalgically about his lobster experience.

"Ted," I said, "what in the world did the Pope eat with that lobster at Jimmy's Harborside back there in 1969?"

The menu, according to the state auditor, included Boston clam chowder and crackers, salad, lobster, baked potato, green mixed vegetables, and rum buns.

So I carried the heavy sea monsters with me and proudly delivered them to one of the nuns who supervises the Vatican kitchen—mission accomplished.

She opened the package, and the dry ice was gone. The lobsters were no longer frozen, and she explained that they could not take any chances with the Pope's health. It was thanks, but no thanks. She said that she would explain all of this to His Holiness.

On one of my meetings with the Pope, he commented on the sad ending to the wonderful gift from Ted Buczko, saying, "It is sad that I could not enjoy this treat which is considered to be a rare delicacy this side of the ocean."

He asked me to assure Buczko that his generosity had not gone unnoticed or unappreciated, and he sent his warm thanks to him.

The Pope also enjoyed shrimp. In 1976, when I accompanied him to Philadelphia, he was honored at a neighborhood banquet hosted by Monsignor Jaworowski, pastor of St. Adelbert Church.

The buffet menu had been a combination of American and Polish delicacies: stuffed shrimp, filet mignon, golabki, pierogi, and kielbasa.

The kielbasa is available at stores, but you'll find the recipes for golabki—stuffed cabbage—and pierogi in this chapter.

Though Karol Wojtyla developed a fondness for lobster and a few other American delicacies, he really loved Polish food best, and missed his sauerkraut when travelling abroad. One of the things that was hardest for him to get used to in travelling, he said, were the banquets in his honor.

Not only did they keep him from important work, but there was the unfamiliar food.

However, he had learned that the banquet route was the best way to meet people whom he could later call upon to get to know in greater depth.

One day, the future Pope, on urging, revealed his favorite Polish meal, but protested that food was not the important thing in life—there were more important things, such as food for the soul. The meal he mentioned was borscht, pork shank in aspic, mushroom and cabbage pierogi, and babka. If you would like to prepare this meal, the recipes are all in this chapter.

The Pope is not always a hearty eater. As a matter of fact, all through the years in Poland he was known for going on very sparse rations to be in tune with the poor.

He also did this during his visit to Philadelphia in 1976. One day, he visited the parish of St. Adelbert and celebrated mass for the community. Then he ate a "poor man's supper" to share the hunger of many people in far-flung lands.

A Pope can be as curious about how food is prepared as anyone else. In Philadelphia, in 1976, he and the accompanying bishops were treated to feast at a restaurant called The Casbah. The meal was a mishmash of American and Polish delights—stuffed shrimp and filet mignon taking their places among golabki, pierogi, and kielbasa.

Before the night was over, the cardinal had marched into the kitchen, praising the cooks and soliciting some of their culinary secrets, much to the amazement and delight of the restaurant's owner, John Cikota.

Not only did Cardinal Wojtyla talk to the kitchen workers, but he laid his hands upon them and brought them a feeling of joy. "Whenever you saw him," Cikota recalled, "he was smiling. And if he wasn't shaking someone's hand, he had his hand on someone's shoulder. He was very warm, open, and happy."

Looking back at those days in 1976, as Philadelphia and the nation prepared for the new visit in 1979, Cikota predicted, "Once the people of Philadelphia and all over the country come in contact with the Pope, they will know that they have met the kind of leader the like of which they have never witnessed before."

Echoing his thought, Marie Hartney, another Philadelphian, said, "He is allowing himself to be known by us all in a very special way."

Not only did the Pope want Americans to know him in a special way but *he* wanted to know Americans in a very special way, even to their food habits. In fact, when he was coming to the United States as Pope, he had his office instruct TWA, which was in charge of feeding the Pontiff during his flying visit of over 5,000 miles, that the Polish food bit should not be stressed. Some Polish specialties, yes, but he had no food restrictions and preferred to try all kinds of foods.

Even so, Trans World Airways wanted to do something special for their illustrious guest and one day of the trip suggested they serve him a different meal from the other passengers who made up his entourage. The Secret Service immediately put its foot down, saying the Pope must eat what everyone else eats to avoid the danger of anyone sabotaging his food.

What evolved was a delightful mix of Polish and American foods at the same meal. For example, a breakfast of cheddar cheese omelette and *kolache*, a Polish pastry filled with nuts, apples, and raisins.

The Pope was treated to an orange flavored dessert molded in the shape of a Liberty Bell and had his first taste of an American two-fisted drink, favorite of blue-collar workers, a screwdriver. And, as a gift from TWA, the Pope took back to the Vatican with him a beautiful cake sculpted and decorated in the shape of a Bible.

How would you like to have the same Christmas dinner that Pope John Paul II enjoyed with friends on his first Christmas as Pontiff? I was elated to talk with a friend in the Vatican who was there and partook of the festive meal and to hear the menu firsthand.

It was Polish fare, of course, start to finish, and a complete change from the typical American holiday dinner. So it might be a complete change of pace for Americans, and of course there is the added thrill of partaking of something that has historic significance.

I'll give you the menu now, but further along in this chapter there will be recipes for the Polish delicacies and more hearty dishes:

POPE JOHN PAUL II'S CHRISTMAS DINNER, 1978
Borscht
Pierogi (small stuffed dumplings)
Roast Pork
Kielbasa (Polish sausage)
Plum Knedle

The desserts the Pope enjoyed as a child are still on his list—plum knedle, ponchki, a Polish kind of doughnut, and something every Pole including my parents called "Grandma's Cake" or "Old Lady's Cake." I am including the recipes for all three at the back of this chapter.

Sunday night suppers are very special with the Pope. These are the times the Pontiff invites a parish priest as his guest, giving several days' notice so the priest will be able to fit the dinner into his schedule.

One priest—Father Ugo Peressin—made a bit of history at the Vatican by being more nervous than all the rest. When his turn came, he presented himself at the Vatican gate with a package under his arm which looked suspiciously like it might contain a strong beverage, and he was trembling so badly from stage fright that the Swiss guards barred his entrance and were waving him away.

Fortunately, Cardinal Poletti of the Vatican, who is the Pope's vicar, recognized the good Father from a distance and came running out to rescue him.

Father Peressin had special significance for Pope John Paul II because the priest was the rector of Our Lady of Czestochowa at Rome's La Rustica parish, representing the patron saint whom the Pope has even made a part of his papal emblem.

So His Holiness was more than anxious to see the Father and, hearing the story of how he had almost been barred at the door, gave him a big hug.

They hurried into the dining room, where other guests had already gathered, among them a bishop and the cardinal who had rescued him.

Realizing that he was still carrying the disreputable-looking package in these elegant surroundings, Father Peressin attempted to hide it under his chair. But the Pope, himself, demanded to know what was in the mystery package.

Looking uncomfortably at the filled wine glasses, the parish priest humbly admitted that he had taken the liberty of bringing along some homemade wine that his parishioners had made—"but it's only rough stuff."

"No, no," said the Pope, "that would be much better!" He ordered the fine French wine taken away, and the glasses were filled with the home stock.

The meal proceeded with the Holy Father turning waiter and tossing the salad. He served it himself, topping each plate with Parmesan cheese.

The informality and good fellowship had Father Peressin much relieved and relaxed until His Holiness had another idea, asking his guest of honor to sing a particular hymn about the Black Madonna. Overcome with emotion at having to "sing for his supper," Father Peressin gave it a try, but it was hard going. Suddenly, he was not alone. The Pope was singing with him, enjoying every moment of it and even leading an imaginary chorus with his hands.

Not only did he enjoy taking part, but the Pope also joined the applause when they finished.

It was a thrilling adventure for me to be invited to have dinner with the Pope in his private quarters in the Vatican. The date set was March 31, 1980, six o'clock. It was a long way to go for dinner—close to four thousand miles and across a big pond—but I would have gone another thousand miles for the rare privilege.

March 31 was a Monday, following Palm Sunday. In fact, I had stood in St. Peter's Square and watched him in the ceremony of the blessing of the palms. He himself carried a long array of dried palms, woven into an ornate shape. It was all most unusual, and I am happy to have pictures of this event.

I presented myself to the Swiss guards at the Vatican gate nearest the Pope's apartment, and my name was on the guest list. But before going to the papal apartments, some other guests and I were first ushered to a reception room for cocktails.

Several guests were already there, sipping drinks and talking against a background of classical music, and before we were ushered into the presence of His Holiness there were ten of us. I was the only lay person. But all of us had one thing in common—we were Polish.

I drank sherry, but others had mixed drinks. One of the Pope's assistants introduced us to each other, and we chatted about local Roman news as well as the American presidential campaign, with everyone asking me if Carter was going to win.

Somewhere along the line, the aide quietly cautioned me not to pull out any reporter's notebook or take any pictures. He explained that at the evening meal John Paul II ceases being a Pope and becomes a Pole. His Holiness, he explained, feels that dinner is the time he can relax, and he likes to relax with his friends—in private.

I assured him that it would be only a social occasion.

At about seven, we were ushered into the library, where the Pope awaited us, shaking hands and embracing this one and that. He was dressed in his white robes with the long sash and gold embroidery and fringe. The sash was embroidered just above the fringe, with his coat of arms.

He had a friendly word for everyone and was in a wonderful mood. Soon he said, jokingly, "Why is everyone standing around? Please come and sit with me." He was beckoning to the table which was under a large chandelier in the center of the room.

But before anyone sat, the Pope said grace. It was in Polish, but it was still the same blessing he had probably heard his father say in his own home and that is said at tables across the world. The only difference was that we stood instead of sitting to hear it, His Holiness at the head of the table, with his guests on either side:

> Bless us, O Lord, and these Thy gifts, which
> we are about to receive from Thy bounty.
> Through Christ our Lord. Amen.

We sat then and I was interested to see that no one sits across from the Pontiff. We were merely ranged on either side. Everyone hung on all the things the Pontiff said and enjoyed his little jokes and kidding remarks while the meal was served by a butler dressed in a black suit. He was not a priest.

I was impressed by the table linens and silverware. The crystal glasses sparkled and the dinner plates had the Vatican crest in the center, of tiara and crossed keys, and a band of gold ran around the outer edge. Under our feet was an oriental rug, and I noticed that the walls were covered with damask instead of wallpaper.

It was an all-Polish meal, and the conversation, too, was all in Polish, filled with nostalgic anecdotes about Poland and many messages of regards were given from friends the Pope had left behind in Krakow. The menu was:

Borscht
Polish duck with veal dressing
Kielbasa   Applesauce
Parsley potatoes   Red cabbage
Polish black bread   Hard rolls
Mixed salad
Poppyseed torte   Fresh whole fruit
Espresso

While we were eating, a nun would come in now and then with a fresh platter of hot food to replenish the table, but the single butler, dressed in dinner jacket, did all the serving.

With the meal, we had a choice of wine or Polish Pilsener beer. I chose the beer, as did John Paul II. After the meal, we had Polish vodka, which packed a wallop, being famous the world over for its strength.

I was delighted and surprised to see that the dessert

was the same as he had eaten in Washington four years ago—
poppyseed torte. It turned out to be one of his favorites.

Fruit was served in a large bowl, but neither the Pope
nor I took any. A few others peeled an apple or orange or nib-
bled a few grapes.

After dinner was over, I thought perhaps we were expected to leave immediately, but His Holiness asked that we
stay for a while. He left the table first, and we slowly followed
him in a few minutes. I was happy to have a nice private chat
with him before saying goodnight.

First, let me reconstruct the meal that I so enjoyed at
the Vatican, starting with the borscht. At the end of the recipe, you will learn how the beet soup was served that night.
But there are several other things you should know.

The Pope has had many versions of borscht and loves
them all. However, this is the more typical way it would be
served him through the years in Poland.

BORSCHT

If you have some meat, such as short ribs of beef, use
it, but the addition of meat is considered a really luxurious
borscht in impoverished Poland—especially in the days when
the Pope was growing up. In Eastern Europe, duck meat is
also used in making a borscht that becomes a one-dish meal.

Salt pork is also optional. A quarter of a pound of salt
pork gives flavor to the borscht and can be used as the only
meat in it or along with beef or duck.

In Poland, a housewife would save her meat stock to
make her porridge if she had none of the meats listed above.
And the very poor, who, at times, included Karol Wojtyla,
frequently had vegetarian borscht with a dollop of sour
cream.

(1 lb. duck meat, chuck, or short ribs of beef, or
    other meat, optional)
(¼ lb. cubed salt pork, optional)
(3 tbsp. butter, optional)
1 large onion, coarsely chopped

5 large beets, peeled and sliced, along with the
   stems and leaves
3 carrots, cleaned and diced
1 clove garlic, chopped
2 cups cabbage, coarsely chopped
¼ cup fresh parsley, chopped
1 stalk celery, chopped
2 tsp. salt (or less if you are using salt pork)
2 quarts water and/or soup stock (boiled med.
   whole potatoes, optional)
2 cups sour cream
(1 cucumber, chopped, optional)
1 tsp. pepper

First, sauté the salt pork until the fat has been rendered, and brown the meat in it if you are using meat.

Otherwise, brown the chopped onion in butter, and then add the beets, carrots, garlic, cabbage, parsley, celery, salt, and pepper in a large heavy pot and cover with water or soup stock, or a combination of the two.

Cook everything until the beets are tender. If you are using meat such as short ribs, cook it first with the onions and garlic until the meat is very tender. Then use the stock for cooking the vegetables and cut up the meat to put back in when the vegetables are done.

Serve the borscht in big bowls, topping generously with sour cream, to which you may add chopped cucumber, if so desired.

You may also enjoy adding one boiled potato to the borscht just before topping with sour cream.

The borscht that I was served at the Vatican was the same as in the recipe above, except that the duck meat and beef were missing.

However, it was served with a topping of sour cream, to which the chopped cucumber had been added. Also, in each bowl, under the sour cream, were two halves of a medium-sized potato.

And, surprisingly, the borscht was served cold.

POLSKA KACZKA Z CIELECE NADZIEWANA
(Polish Duck with Veal Dressing)

½ cup chopped salt pork
½ cup chopped onions
1 lb. chopped veal
2½ cups bread crumbs
1 egg, beaten
½ cup milk
1 tsp. dry mustard
4–5 lb. duck
1 tbsp. salt
1 tsp. pepper
(sage and thyme, optional)
½ cup butter
2 cups dry white wine

Render the fat from the salt pork, and sauté the onions in it. Then, also slightly brown the veal adding half the salt and pepper. Now combine with the bread crumbs, egg, milk, mustard, and sage and thyme, if desired to make a stuffing. Stuff the duck and tie it closed with a string. Place the duck in a roasting pan, rub with the rest of the salt and pepper, and bake in a preheated 375° oven for 1½ hours, or until the duck is very tender.

Baste the duck with melted butter and wine every half hour. A delicious gravy can be made from the juices in the roasting pan by cooking them a bit longer with the rest of the white wine.

The applesauce was served at the same time as the kielbasa. And it was not out of the can, but freshly cooked and liberally sprinkled with cinnamon. It was made from tart apples.

The parsley potatoes were simply boiled, buttered, cut in fourths, and sprinkled with parsley. Those who wanted to added a little of the gravy made from the duck.

KAPUSTA CZERWONA ZASMAZANA Z WINEM
(Red Cabbage Sautéed in Wine)

>   1 medium red cabbage
>   4 tbsp. shortening, lard, or butter
>   3 tbsp. flour
>   2 tsp. salt
>   3 tbsp. sugar
>   1½ cups red wine
>   ½ cup lemon or vinegar

First, slice the cabbage into strips about ½ inch by 3 inches, and parboil in water to cover for about 5 minutes. Drain the liquid, place cabbage in frying pan with the shortening, and let brown for a few minutes over high heat.

Now add the rest of the ingredients and continue cooking until most of the liquid is absorbed and the cabbage is soft.

The mixed salad had a base of lettuce with slices of tomatoes, cucumbers, and onion. The dressing was vinegar and oil, with a dash of lemon juice.

I was so pleased to be eating poppyseed torte at the pontifical table that I made a mental note to tell my mother. She had baked this for me all through childhood because it was my favorite dessert. I would tell her it was a papal favorite, too.

The slice of cake was a beautiful oval with concentric circles of poppyseed filling inside.

TORT MAKOWY
(Poppyseed Torte)

>   1 cup milk
>   4 egg yolks
>   1 tsp. salt

½ cup butter
¾ cup sugar
1 tsp. vanilla extract
½ tsp. almond extract
¼ cup lukewarm water
2 cakes yeast
4 cups flour

First, scald the milk, then let it cool to room temperature. Meanwhile, beat the egg yolks with salt until the mixture thickens. Cream the butter and sugar together and add the almond and vanilla extracts and beaten egg yolks.

Dissolve the yeast in the lukewarm water and add it to the above. Finally, add the sifted flour and cooled milk. Mix them, place the dough on your board and knead it until it does not stick to your fingers.

Cover the kneaded dough with a slightly damp cloth and let it rise until it doubles in size. Punch it down with your fist, and again let it rise until it doubles in size.

Now divide the dough into two equal parts. Roll each half into a rectangular shape—about the thickness of a finger. Spread with the poppyseed filling given below, making sure to keep the edge clear of the filling.

The dough should be rolled lengthwise, to make two long narrow rolls. To keep the filling from seeping out, carefully pinch the dough together along the edges, sealing it shut.

Place each long roll in a greased pan about 13×4×3. Cover the pans and again let the dough rise until it fills the pans. Bake in a 350° oven for about 45 minutes.

POPPYSEED FILLING

2 cups ground poppyseed
1½ cups milk
2 eggs
1 tsp. vanilla extract
½ tsp. almond extract

Scald the milk first and add the poppyseed. Cook until milk is absorbed into the seeds by stirring constantly for about

5 minutes. Then add sugar and cook a bit more. Beat the eggs slightly then stir a *little* of the hot poppyseed mixture into the eggs—about 2 or 3 tablespoons. Next add the remainder of the poppyseeds until mixture becomes thick. Do not boil. Remove from heat. As mixture is cooling, add extracts. Let it all cool and spread over the dough.

Now, let's look at the Pope's first Christmas dinner after his installation.

The recipe for borscht is found earlier in this chapter.

PIECZEN MIESO WIEPRZOWE
(Roast Pork)

    5–6 lb. loin of pork
    1 onion, coarsely chopped
    3 cloves garlic, chopped
    2 tsp. salt
    1 tsp. pepper
    2 cups port wine, dry
    ½ cup brown sugar
    parsley for garnish

Marinate pork overnight, using all the ingredients except parsley. Turn the meat over at least twice. Save the marinade. Bake the loin in a 375° oven for 1 hour, basting occasionally with the marinade, and then reduce heat to 325° and bake until brown and well done (about another hour and a half), continuing to baste.

When pork is done, make gravy using the drippings at the bottom and adding a little flour and water, if necessary.

Pierogi or stuffed dumplings are an elegant way to eat vegetables. The Pope's Christmas pierogi were filled with cheese and potatoes, however, in Poland, they are frequently filled with sauerkraut or cabbage. Pierogi can also be filled with a mixture of fruit, such as prunes, and topped with whipped cream and cinnamon to make a lovely dessert.

PIEROGI
(Filled with Cheese and Potatoes)

    2 egg yolks
    1 egg white, beaten
    2 cups flour
    ½ tsp. salt
    2 tsp. butter
    2 tbsp. sour cream
    boiling, salted water—enough to cover dumplings
        well
    additional 2 tbsp. melted butter for topping

Combine the eggs, flour, salt, butter, and sour cream, and knead with your hands until soft and pliable. Empty onto a floured board and roll with a rolling pin until the dough is almost as thin as a pie crust.

Using a knife, make squares about 2 to 2½ inches wide. In one corner of a square place a spoonful of filling. Then fold the opposite corner up over the filling to make a triangle and pinch the edges tightly together.

Lower the pierogi into boiling, salted water and let boil briskly for 5 or 6 minutes. Carefully remove from the water, brush with melted butter, and serve hot.

FILLING FOR PIEROGI

    2 cups mashed potatoes
    1½ cups dry cottage cheese
    ¼ cup melted butter
    1 med. onion, chopped fine
    1 tsp. salt
    ½ tsp. pepper

Combine all ingredients and you are ready to fill the pierogi.

Now for the Pope's Christmas plum knedle. The Pope

prefers fruits of a purple color—plums, blueberries, prunes. So I was not surprised that he chose this dessert:

KNEDLE Z SLIWKAMI
(Plum Knedle)

> 1 tsp. salt
> 2 cups flour
> 2 tbsp. butter
> 4 cups warm mashed potatoes
> 3 eggs, well beaten
> ½ cup sour cream
> 12 to 15 fresh uncooked plums (small to medium size)
> sugar cubes
> boiling water to nicely cover
> 2 tsp. salt
> buttered bread crumbs
> brown sugar

Don't be afraid of this recipe just because you see mashed potatoes. When you eat this delicious dessert, you will hardly be aware of their presence.

Add the salt to the sifted flour, cut in the butter as for pie crust, and set aside. Now combine the mashed potatoes, eggs, and sour cream, and stir into the flour mixture.

Empty the bowl onto a floured board and roll into a long roll, 2 inches in diameter. Cut into 1½ to 2 inch segments. Pit the plums, placing a sugar cube in each as the stone is removed. Pull the dough up to cover the plum completely.

Drop the knedle into briskly boiling water, to which you have added 2 tsp. salt, and cook for about 8 to 10 minutes. Remove the knedle from the water, top with bread crumbs that have been browned in butter and brown sugar, and serve.

Now you might like to try making the Pope's favorite meal, which features a different kind of pierogi—mushroom.

But, first, here is the cold meat dish he enjoys.

WIEPRZOWE NOZKI W GALARECIE
(Pork Shank in Aspic)

    4 lbs. pork shank
    4 pigs' feet, cut in segments
    1 large onion, cut up
    water to cover
    2 cloves garlic, coarsely chopped
    2 bay leaves
    2 stalks celery, chopped up
    3 tbsp. vinegar
    1 tsp. salt
    2 tsp. pepper
    1 carrot, sliced
    1 hard-boiled egg, sliced
    1 lemon, sliced

The pigs' feet are needed for their gelatin content. Clean them very well. Put them in a large kettle with the cut-up pork shanks and add the onion, stirring occasionally until the onion is slightly browned. Now cover with water, and bring to a boil.

Skim off the first fat that forms on top. Reduce heat and add the garlic, bay leaves, celery, vinegar, salt, and pepper. Simmer until the meat comes off the bones when you test it with a fork.

Toward the end of the cooking, boil the sliced carrot in water in a separate little saucepan. The slices are only for decoration, so make them thin. Also prepare the egg and the lemon slices.

Remove the pot with the meat from stove, allow to cool a bit before taking out the meat and straining the liquid.

Then, cut up the meat into little cubes, and add to the clear strained stock, reserving a scant cup of strained stock for later use.

Pour mixture into loaf pans, and cool until it gels. Skim off fat which has formed on top. Lay the carrot, lemon, and egg slices over the mixture in a decorative pattern, and glaze it with the rest of the broth that has been set aside.

Slice and serve. A little additional lemon juice or vinegar is dribbled across the top to give it a bit of a tart taste.

The recipe for pierogi dough is found elsewhere in this chapter, with the Pope's Christmas dinner. But, here is the pierogi filling for his favorite Polish meal:

GRZYBY I PIEROGI Z KAPUSTOM
(Mushroom and Cabbage Filling for Pierogi)

> 1 cup coarsely chopped cabbage
> water to cover
> 1 med. onion, chopped
> ½ cup butter
> 3 cups mushrooms, coarsely chopped
> ½ tsp. salt
> ½ tsp. pepper

Parboil cabbage a few minutes in salted water and drain, set aside.

Start to fry onion in butter, and as soon as it starts to soften, add chopped mushrooms and cabbage. Add seasonings. Fry until tender and nicely browned. Now you are ready to fill pierogi squares (see pierogi recipe).

At Easter time, when he was growing up, Pope John Paul II would have the traditional Easter cake which translates from the Polish as Grandma's or Old Lady's Easter Cake. Nothing about tennis shoes.

BABKA WIELKANOCNA
(Grandma's or Old Lady's Easter Cake)

> 1 cup milk
> 3½ cups flour
> 2 cakes yeast
> ½ cup sugar
> 3 tbsp. warm water
> 2 tsp. salt
> 10 egg yolks

1 tsp. almond extract
½ cup melted butter
1½ cups chopped blanched almonds
1½ cups chopped candied peels—a mixture of
citron, lemon, and orange

Additional butter, bread crumbs, and brown sugar
for topping

Scald the milk and slowly beat in ½ cup of the flour, continuing to beat until you have a smooth mixture. Set aside to cool. Now break up the yeast and cover it with warm water to which you have added 1 tbsp. sugar. After 5 minutes, combine the yeast and milk mixtures and let sit until yeast mixture has doubled in size.

At this point, toss the salt into the eggs and beat the eggs for several minutes, gradually adding the rest of the sugar as you beat. Now combine this with the yeast mixture, and add the almond extract and the remainder of the flour.

Using your hands, knead the dough for 8 or 9 minutes. When it has a fine consistency, pour the melted butter into a little indentation that you make on top and continue kneading for another 8 or 9 minutes.

Finally, pour the chopped almonds and candied peels into a new cavity on top and knead just long enough to mix them through. Let the dough rest until it has doubled in size again. Using your fist, punch the dough to press it down and let it rest until it rises once again.

Grease a loaf pan and place the cake in it uniformly. To give a crisp, glossy finish, sprinkle top with mixture of brown sugar and melted butter to which you have added some bread crumbs. Place in a 350° oven and bake for about 1 hour.

As a little footnote, when I was working for Senator Ted Kennedy in the mid '60s, my mother made a babka for his family and by happy circumstances, they served it to Princess Margaret at a reception.

The Pope grew up eating a Polish version of our doughnuts. You might like it very much. I do.

PONCHKI, *or* PACZKI
(Polish Doughnuts)

3 cups flour
1 cup milk, scalded
2 cakes yeast
6 egg yolks
1 tsp. salt
¾ cup sugar
1 tsp. vanilla extract
½ cup melted butter
blueberry jam or preserves, or orange marmalade
  (extra thick)
granulated sugar and cinnamon mixture

Combine a half cup flour and the scalded milk, beating until smooth. After the mixture has cooled, crumble the yeast and mix it in. Let sit until its size has doubled.

Now beat the egg yolks adding the salt, sugar, and vanilla and combine with yeast mixture. Then continue beating as you add the rest of the flour. Now pour the melted butter into a little hollow in the top and, using your hands, knead the dough until the butter is completely integrated. Again, let the dough rest until it has doubled. Then, using your fist, punch the dough until it is flattened and let it start to rise again.

Now place the dough on a floured board and roll to about a half-inch thickness. Spread the jam, preserves, or marmalade on half the dough and fold the other half over it.

Using a small cookie cutter—about 2 inches—cut small circles and let them rest 25 or 30 minutes until they have risen again into nice plump balls. Drop into deep fat and fry as you would doughnuts, 3 or 4 minutes until brown.

Remove and place on paper towels to drain off some grease, then roll in granulated sugar which has been dusted with cinnamon.

Mushrooms are a great treat in Poland and one of the ways His Holiness likes them best is creamed.

GRZYBY DUSZONE
(Creamed Mushrooms)

1 med. size onion, chopped fine
3 tbsp. butter
½ lb. mushrooms, sliced
1 tsp. salt
½ tsp. pepper
2 tbsp. bread crumbs
½ cup cream

Sauté the onion in the butter until onions become transparent. Then add the mushrooms, salt, and pepper and continue to fry, stirring until most of the liquid is gone. Then toss in the bread crumbs and let them brown a bit, gradually stir in the cream, and simmer for a moment or two.

To brighten a meal, how would you like to serve potato pancakes fit for a Pope?

KARTOFLANE PLACKI
(Potato Pancakes)

2 cups raw potatoes, finely grated
2 tbsp. flour
1 tsp. salt
½ tsp. pepper
2 eggs, well beaten
2 tsp. onion, finely grated

Combine all the ingredients and beat for 1 or 2 minutes with a wooden spoon. Heat lard, chicken fat, or vegetable oil in a heavy skillet, and drop the potato batter into the sizzling fat from the end of a large wooden spoon or tablespoon. When the patties start to brown, turn them over with a spatula.

It is good to know how the Pope ate his cabbage—a favorite vegetable—all through the years in Poland.

KAPUSTA Z GRZYBAMI
(Cabbage with Mushrooms)

1 med. onion, chopped
1 cup fresh mushrooms, sliced
½ stick butter
1 med. head cabbage, shredded (about 5 or 6 cups)
1 tsp. salt
1 tsp. pepper
2 tbsp. vinegar
3 or 4 tbsp. water

Sauté the onion and mushrooms in butter and then toss in the shredded cabbage, frying it for a few minutes to lock in the flavor and coat with butter.

Now add the seasonings and vinegar and a few table-spoons of water. Cover the pot and steam for a few minutes until the cabbage starts to become tender.

In Poland, mushrooms are not always available and so Karol Wojtyla was accustomed to eating this recipe minus the mushrooms.

Now let me tell you how to make the stuffed cabbage that the Pope enjoys.

GOLABKI
(Stuffed Cabbage)

1 med. head cabbage
boiling water to cover cabbage
2 tbsp. vinegar
1 tbsp. salt
3 tbsp. butter
1½ lbs. ground beef
½ cup rice, partially cooked (do not use precooked rice)
1 egg, slightly beaten
¼ tsp. celery salt
½ tsp. marjoram
½ tsp. pepper
salt to taste

1 large onion, chopped
1 clove garlic, minced
2 cups tomato sauce and 1 cup water
1 cup sauerkraut, optional

First, soften the cabbage leaves by scalding in boiling water with vinegar and salt. Pour out hot water, pour in cold water, and remove leaves, drying each carefully and cutting out the heavy veins at the base.

Sauté onion in butter until soft, and put aside. Mix meat, garlic, rice, egg, seasonings, and the onions. Place 2 tbsp. meat mixture in the center of the leaf and fold the two sides over it. Now roll the top and bottom ends of the leaf into a tight roll. It will look somewhat like a Chinese eggroll.

Lay the cabbage rolls in a greased roasting pan and almost cover with a mixture of 1 part hot water to 2 parts tomato sauce. To give a nippy flavor add sauerkraut to the pot. Bake covered at 350° for 1½ to 2 hours. If too much liquid evaporates, add more water or tomato sauce.

This is a favorite soup of the pontiff:

KURZY ZUPA Z KLUSKAMI
(Chicken Soup with Egg Drops)

Chicken soup is chicken soup the world over. Simply gather together all leftover bits and pieces of chicken—wings, neck, gizzards, hearts, backs—and cook with one chopped onion, a sprig of fresh parsley, 2 bay leaves, 1 chopped garlic clove, and salt and pepper to taste until the chicken is tender. Take out the parts and strain, and cut up the meat into tiny pieces for gravy. But for this recipe, make egg drops to add to the clear soup. (Taste the soup and add additional seasonings.)

KLUSKI LANE (Egg Drops)

2 eggs, well beaten
½ tsp. salt
½ cup flour
1 tbsp. water

Be sure your soup is still boiling.

Combine eggs, salt, and flour and beat until there are no lumps. Thin with the tablespoon of water. Now simply drop spoonsful of the egg mixture into the boiling soup and continue boiling until done.

This is one of the Pope's favorite salads:

MIZERIA
(Cucumber Sour Cream Salad)

> 3 med. cucumbers, peeled
> boiling water to cover
> 1½ cups sour cream
> 1 tbsp. chopped dill
> 1 tbsp. sugar
> vinegar to taste (about 2 or 3 tbsp.)
> ½ tsp. pepper
> 1½ tsp. salt

First slice the peeled cucumbers very thin and soften by pouring boiling water over them. After they have stood for 15 or 20 minutes, pour out hot water and pour in icy refrigerated water. Let stand a few minutes and drain.

Let cucumbers rest 15 or 20 minutes in refrigerator.

Now make sauce of the sour cream, dill, sugar, vinegar, and pepper. When ready to serve, sprinkle the salt over the cucumbers and then pour in sour cream mixture, stirring lightly. You may want to add a little more vinegar if you like a tart flavor.

This chapter would not be complete without a favorite chicken recipe, which I am told the Pope enjoyed throughout his years in Poland.

KURA PO KROLEWSKU
(Chicken, Royal Fashion)

> 3-lb. chicken, cut up
> 1 stick butter
> 1 large onion, chopped

2 cloves garlic, minced
1 tsp. salt
½ tsp. pepper
1½ cups hot water
1 pt. sour cream
2 tsps. paprika

Brown chicken in the butter for a few minutes before adding onion. Then sauté until onion softens. Now add the garlic, salt, pepper, and hot water and cook slowly, covered, until tender.

Just before you are ready to serve the Royal Chicken that the Pope enjoys, gradually add the sour cream to the sauce at the bottom of the pot, add the paprika, and reheat. Serve the chicken smothered in the rich sour cream sauce.

———————————

The Pope also enjoys roast lamb.

BARANJNE SKOPOWA DUSZONA ZE SMIETANA (Roast Lamb with Cream)

rolled lamb shoulder (approximately 5 lbs.)
1 stick butter
1 large onion, cut up
3 or 4 parsley sprigs
handful of celery tops
¼ cup vinegar
½ cup flour
1 cup heavy cream
½ cup mushrooms, sliced

Sauté meat in butter until it starts to brown. Add onion and sauté a few more minutes, until it starts to brown. Add parsley, celery, and vinegar and bake, covered, in moderate oven until almost finished.

Remove roaster from oven. Make a roux of flour and heavy cream, and gradually add to the juice in the bottom of the pot. Add mushrooms, and bake another 10 or 15 minutes.

The Pope loves to catch fish on camping trips. Here is one of his favorite fish recipes.

RYBA SMAZONA
(Polish-style Fish Fry)

> 2 eggs
> ½ cup flour
> 2–3 tsp. water
> 6 fillets of pike or crappies or other fish (fresh
>   water)
> 1 tsp. salt
> bread crumbs
> butter for frying
> horseradish sauce

Make a batter of eggs, flour, and water, keeping a thick consistency. Salt the fish fillets and dip each into the batter and then into bread crumbs. Fry in butter. Serve with horseradish sauce.

While I was writing this chapter on food, my editor, Oscar Collier, at Prentice-Hall, told me with some excitement that he had just had dinner with a Polish friend and had been served a most unusual dish called bigos, or Hunter's Stew. "By any chance, does the Pope like bigos?" he asked.

"Is a red rose red?" I replied. "That is one of the first recipes I got for this book."

Not only does the Pope like bigos, but so do I. And since my wife is not versed in Polish cuisine, I am the one who had to learn to make it.

Actually, in olden days bigos might be made with squirrel or any animal the hunter happened to bag. But the way it is now made traditionally is with rabbit, which is easily available in meat markets and even some super markets, combined with more traditional meats and a generous portion of sauerkraut to tie it all together.

BIGOS
(Hunter's Stew)

¼ lb. salt pork, cubed (bacon may be substituted)
2 rabbits (1½ lbs. each) cut into small pieces
2 lb. pork roast, cut into stewing pieces
1 lb. kielbasa (Polish sausage), cut up
4 large onions, coarsely cut up
3 garlic cloves, finely chopped
3 tbsp. flour
1 cup dry or fresh mushrooms
3 cups water
3 or 4 bay leaves
salt and pepper to taste (use whole black
    peppercorns, at least 1 tsp.)
8 cups sauerkraut
1 cup red wine
(1 cup sour cream, optional)

Sauté the salt pork until done, remove the meat, and use the fat to brown all the rest of the meat and the onion. Add garlic and flour for the last few minutes. If you are using smoked kielbasa, put it aside now and place it in the stew for the last half hour of cooking.

Now place meats, onions, and mushrooms in a large iron pot in boiling water—just covering the meat. Add the bay leaves, salt, and pepper. In about 20 minutes, add the sauerkraut. After the first hour of cooking of the meats, add the wine and kielbasa and simmer for a half hour, tasting, now and then, to see if additional salt and pepper are needed.

If desired, stir in sour cream at last minute.

This makes a hearty meal for 8 to 10 hungry outdoorsmen.

This is a simple pastry to make. The Pope might have it at tea time. It is a simple dainty sweet that looks like a ribbon twisted into a bow. It's name is chrust.

CHRUST

4 egg yolks, well beaten
¼ cup sugar
½ teaspoon salt
1 tsp. vanilla extract
2 cups flour
½ cup sour cream
powdered sugar

Combine the egg yolks, sugar, salt, and vanilla and beat until mixture has a smooth consistency. Now add a little flour as you beat, then 1 tbsp. sour cream, and again flour, alternating sour cream and flour until all ingredients are well blended.

Make a ball of the dough and place it on a floured board, letting it rest for 10 or 15 minutes, with a cloth over it to keep the moisture in. Now knead the dough until blisters begin to form—on the dough, not you.

Now roll the dough to pie-crust thinness and, using a knife, cut the dough into strips about 1¼ inch wide. Then cut ribbons about 4½ inches long. Cut a slit lengthwise in the center of each ribbon and pull one of the ends through it. This gives it somewhat the appearance of a bow.

Drop the bows into deep fat and fry a few minutes until the dough starts to turn golden. Remove. Place on paper towels and sprinkle with powdered sugar. Delicious.

And now, let me wish you a good appetite in the way Poles often do and as it was done when the future Pope and his delegation of Polish bishops were visiting the U.S. in 1976:

Za krola sasa jesc i popuszczac pasa.

It is a saying that looks back to the days of King Sas, famous for his gluttonous banquets—"Remember King Sas. Eat and loosen your belt!"

14

Retracing His Footsteps

Retracing the steps of John Paul II, Christ's vicar on earth, I went on my own pilgrimage to the places where he had walked and I talked with people he met at various stages of his life.

I went to Rome. And I retraced the steps of his visit to the United States in 1976. In Baltimore, at the Holy Rosary Church, where I had been with Pope John Paul II when he was Karol Cardinal Wojtyla, I talked again with Reverend Chester J. Mieczkowski.

The pastor, remembering how Wojtyla had looked and acted and sounded as a cardinal, said, "He looked strong, carrying himself like a boxer—like a boxer seeing if anyone is going to throw a punch." He recalled that Wojtyla had said, "I want to see and experience the country where freedom lives." He said the Polish cardinal realized that Americans had no idea of what life was like on a day-to-day basis in a country where freedom does not exist.

To get fresh material, I also went to places I had gone as a reporter to cover the Pope during his 1979 visit. But now I was reaching for more personal reactions from people he had met along the way—in Boston, Philadelphia, New York.

And, of course, I had the greatest sources right under my nose in Washington, D.C.

I retraced his steps to the Polish seminary—the only one in the United States—at Orchard Lake, Michigan, where Reverend Leonard Chrobot remembered the cardinal checking on how young men are trained to the priesthood in America and becoming like one of them, experiencing what they experienced.

Father Walter Ziemba, chancellor of the seminary, recalled how Cardinal Wojtyla reacted when shown a schedule that had been worked out for him during his visit. Even as cardinal, John Paul II had watched his health. "What are you trying to do, kill me?" he had said half-humorously.

Then, after he had sat in conferences long enough, he jumped up and said, "No. That's it. I have to get some exercise. I have to get away. I am cancelling the rest of the conferences for today, and I am going canoeing on the lake."

He borrowed a canoe and spent a good part of the afternoon alone with nature. In doing the research for my book, I borrowed the same canoe and shared something of that serene feeling.

When I went to Rome, I learned that His Holiness was still determined as ever to get his exercise. The job of Pope could be a killing one, he was aware, and I was told that he was determined from the start that the strain would not get the better of him. He made it known that he intended to run the Vatican and not the other way around.

The Pope remarked to his Polish assistant, Stanislaw Dziwisz, "They told my predecessor what he should do and when. This may have led him to his early grave. They will not tell me what to do or when. I will decide. They will not kill me."

Even though he was at the Vatican, he did stick to his vow, exercising vigorously—push-ups, jogging. He even rode a bicycle, as in the old days.

Once, when someone asked the Pope about the difficulty of his work, he replied, "I do not work any harder than I did in Krakow. The only strain I find here is working in many languages. In Krakow, I worked mainly in Polish, here I am constantly switching languages.

"I may be reading a document in Italian, then I receive people in German, followed by more paperwork in French or English, and my audiences would also be in these languages. I suppose I will get used to it after a while and find that such a strain will no longer be with me."

When John Paul II took over at the Vatican, tennis and volley ball courts were there but showed signs of disuse. Gardeners soon had them in fine working order for the energetic Pontiff, who no longer had time to search for ski slopes or go mountain climbing. There was even a bocci court on which to get a little workout.

I arrived in Rome toward the end of March and just missed some very interesting events that my Vatican friends were still talking about.

For one thing, John Paul II had planted a tree on the grounds of the U.S. Seminary in Rome on George Washington's birthday, February 22, 1980.

It was a sequoia—a California redwood—and since Washington's birthday fell on the first Friday of Lent, the Pope joined the students at the North American College in a simple Lenten meal: vegetable soup, bread, fish, and asparagus.

It was only the sixth time in the one hundred twenty-one year history of the American seminary that a Pope had visited, and the students were elated. Some had added red, white, and blue to their cassocks for a bit of patriotism, and they sang "This Land Is Your Land, This Land Is My Land."

When the happy Pope left, he did not go empty-handed. The students insisted the Pope add a touch of America to his Vatican gardens in the form of three redwood trees.

"Felici here," I quickly learned, means that the Pope's photographer is on duty. It is a long-standing custom that at all papal audiences and special events the photos of the Pope are taken only by the papal photographer—"Felici."

That is the name the photographer has been called for almost one hundred years, since there really were two brothers named Felici. The name continues to be used today as the trademark known the world over and the firm's office is located near the famous Spanish Steps in central Rome.

Only they, of all photographers, are permitted to use the papal coat of arms on their stationery, and this changes with each succeeding Pope.

It's not that other photographers are forbidden to take photographs of His Holiness, but that only the Felici photographers are allowed to take closeups. All other news photographers must work at a distance, which frequently requires use of a telephoto lens.

While I was in Rome, I could not resist going to find the man who makes the shoes of the Fisherman. I found him in a narrow street—Number 10 Borgo Santo Spirito, near St. Peter's Square.

The man who makes the shoes for John Paul II and other popes before him—papal shoes are actually soft red slippers—is Telesforo Carboni, an intense and dedicated man who insists that he knew that the world was destined to get a non-Italian Pope.

He had gotten an urgent message toward the end of the voting for the new Pope, saying that very large, red papal slippers were needed immediately—size 11. Since Italian men wear shoes that are rarely more than size 8 or 9, he knew the new Pope would be a strapping foreigner.

Everywhere I went around the Vatican neighborhood in Rome, restaurant owners and waiters alike talked of how wonderful it used to be in the old days when Karol Wojtyla would come in, and sit and talk with everyone. He was known as a *pacioccone*, which translates into "good guy," or a "regular fellow."

When he visited in 1976 as cardinal, John Paul II had talked of Monte Cassino near Rome, where the Allies and the Polish Army in Exile, under British command, had attacked and taken the mountain fortress from the Nazis. He visited the Polish cemetery on top of the mountain whenever he could.

In fact, on his fifty-ninth birthday in May 1979, the Pope had spent the day at Monte Cassino and had observed there the thirty-fifth anniversary of the end of World War II.

Looking at the field of crosses, he said sadly to the crowd, "Look at this cemetery. This land belongs to Poland, although Poland is far away from here, because freedom is measured out with crosses.

"The Polish soldiers fought here for your freedom and ours. It is difficult to say what went on in the minds and hearts of those who fought here thirty-five years ago. Whatever their thoughts, a Pope has come to pay homage to this sacred spot."

I paid my own homage in retracing his steps, even deciding to climb the stony mountain the hard way to the monastery and cemetery above, a climb that took close to three hours.

In the cemetery, I was touched to find an inscription in Polish on a memorial commemorating the heroism of the Polish soldiers. Translated, it said: WE POLISH SOLDIERS HAVE GIVEN OUR SOULS TO GOD, OUR BODIES TO THE SOIL OF ITALY AND OUR HEARTS TO POLAND.

The Vatican has not changed Pope John Paul II's insistence on simplicity for his lifestyle. Though he could have twenty-two rooms at his disposal, he chooses to use only a small suite.

The Pope's apartment is made up of three rooms of Baroque style. There is a bedroom; a library, which also serves as a dining room for private dinners; and an office, or studio, as it is called, with desk and filing cabinet, like any other office.

John Paul II reads several newspapers in several languages, including *Die Welt*, *Le Figaro*, the English-language *International Herald Tribune*, and various Polish dailies sent him by air mail. The Vatican newspaper, *L'Osservatore Romano*, is brought to him by special messenger each afternoon.

One of the innovations of the Polish Pope was to institute a Polish edition of the Vatican newspaper, and I was there when the first edition was brought out. Reverend Adam Boniecki, a Krakow priest, has come to the Vatican to be its editor, and for the first time in history ordinary people in Poland will be able to keep up with Vatican news and their old friend, Karol Wojtyla.

John Paul sleeps in an old-fashioned, iron, four-poster on the fourth floor—the top floor of the Apostolic Palace overlooking St. Peter's Square.

He sleeps in the same bed that Pope John XXIII used. The alarm clock that awakens him at 5:30 every morning is the same one that he brought from Poland.

The Pope is such a reader of books that his staff have sometimes referred to his bedroom as a library with a bed in it. The bedroom walls are decorated with religious art, and there are three special reminders of his homeland—a jar containing soil from several regions of Poland, a painting of the Madonna by a fellow member of the anti-Nazi underground, and a sweater knitted for him by a blind girl in Krakow.

What is important to His Holiness is that the private chapel is just a few steps from his bedroom. John Paul II celebrates mass there at 6 A.M. In attendance are his personal staff and his household staff, which consists of six nuns.

At 7 A.M., after breakfast, the Pope in a gym suit—a sweatsuit—jogs around the Vatican gardens. After his jog, he goes to the chapel for more meditation and works there on papers—without telephones to disturb him. This is the same routine he had in Krakow.

His workday in the office usually starts at about 8:30 A.M., when he goes to his study for about two hours of paperwork. It ranges from diplomatic correspondence to important reports from bishops. He switches languages as needed, and reads about one hundred briefs or summaries a day.

At about 10:30 A.M., he steps into the antiquated, circular bronze private elevator and descends to the third floor to start his average three hours of daily audiences.

Pope John Paul II amazes people around the Vatican with his attention to detail and his great vitality. He confers every day with one or more of the Vatican departments. He also still likes to make unannounced visits to departments and tribunals to chat with clerks and other civil servants. They say he looks and acts like a man fifteen years younger than his sixty years.

But the Pope knows how to pace himself, taking an

afternoon nap and then exercising a bit. Then he devotes an hour or more to reading, writing, and studying. He works in a study furnished with several armchairs, tall bookcases filled with dictionaries, encyclopedias, and other reference works. In the middle of the room, under a huge chandelier, sits a large executive-style desk with two white telephones.

The Pope has a television set, which he often turns on for sports such as soccer and the Olympics, and special programs recommended by his aides. There also is a stereo. He likes to listen to records of Polish folk songs as well as to the music of such composers as Johann Sebastian Bach and Henry Wieniawski, a fellow Pole. He is also much aware of what is being sent out over the Vatican Radio.

Strangely enough, the Pontiff does not like dictating. Usually he sits thoughtfully writing out what he wants in long hand, considerately making large letters so the typist will find it easier to read. The Pope usually writes in the first person "I," instead of the more formal "we." Most of the time in speaking, he also uses "I" instead of "we."

Probably the closest man to the Pope is the Reverend Stanislaw Dziwisz, his personal assistant. He also held this post when Wojtyla was first archbishop and then cardinal in Krakow. Everyone of the top Vatican brass, including the Pope, calls him Stanley, and he is considered to be the Pope's alter ego. They both not only understand one another, but also participate in various sporting events, such as camping, canoeing, skiing, and tennis.

He is the only one to go jogging with the Pope every day. Stanley, who is in his forties, is not just an athlete, but a fine scholar. I first met him in 1976, when he came as aide to the Polish cardinal and the delegation of nineteen Polish bishops. I was very much impressed with the scope of his knowledge and could see he acted as a sounding board for the cardinal's philosophical thoughts.

Stanley was slow in accepting me as part of the group, at first, but when he saw that Cardinal Wojtyla sought out my company, we became fast friends.

I again met Stanley Dziwisz in 1979 when he accompanied the Pope to the U.S., and this time he received me warmly from the start. I called him familiarly "Father Stanis-law," and he called me affectionately, in Polish, *Panie Janie*—"Mr. Johnny."

When I went to Rome in March 1980, however, though we were still friends, things had to be a little different. As Stanley sadly explained, the Vatican had special problems and he had to be very cautious. He could not fraternize with jour-nalists because this could conceivably put him in an embar-rassing situation as having possibly leaked some stories.

So we could not stop somewhere for a beer or do any of the things I had hoped. When I told Stanley that, as a White House correspondent, I could understand, and that Jody Powell and Hamilton Jordan had to be careful too, he was pleased that I was not angry with him.

I did get to see him for a moment here and there, and we had a few laughs although I missed the old days.

Pope John Paul II has a very small personal staff. He has two male assistants and a private secretary who is one of the nuns that he brought with him from Krakow. Sister Jad-wiga is her name, and she can take dictation and answer cor-respondence in English, French, and Italian as well as her na-tive Polish.

The Pope is surrounded by Poles, whom he knows and trusts. Even so, John Paul II is no stranger to jealousy and vicious rumors, even at the Vatican. When I was there during the 1980 Easter season, there was a story making the rounds and even appearing in the so-called reputable news-papers and magazines of Rome that he was very ill with leu-kemia, required blood transfusions, and was so weak he could hardly get around.

I happened to have stopped in to see the Vatican press secretary, Reverend Romeo Panciroli, and he shook his head and laughed as he commented to me and a few other report-ers in the room, "I see the journalistic profession has a great inventive talent for news. Such a pity that the Pope is so weak he is only taking off for Turin to see the shroud and then on to France and Africa."

I laughed and said, "Yes, that certainly sounds as if he's very weak."

Incidentally, while in Rome in spring 1980, I learned

from my Polish clergy friends that I was not the only journalistic personal friend of the Pope's who was given a hard time in trying to see him when he visited the U.S. in 1979.

Jerzy Turowicz, the editor of the Polish weekly in Krakow, *Tygodnik Powszechny*, was also kept from having access to the Pope. Jerzy has known the Pope for over thirty years and had traveled with him on the plane from Poland in 1976.

Even though John Paul II was expecting to see him and had mentioned it, Jerzy was kept from getting together with him until the last day when they were both at the airport ready to get on the same plane.

Among the Pope's closest advisers is a talented theologian who sees him daily—Reverend Jozef Michalik, who is also the rector of the Polish Pontifical College in Rome.

In following in the footsteps of the Pope, I met the Reverend Michalik and was delighted when he gave me a personal tour of the very rooms in the Polish Pontifical College where the Pope would stay in Rome during the time he was cardinal.

I was able to see the room where he slept, the dining room where he ate, the chapel where he said mass, and I held the chalice he had used for the mass. I took pictures of all this.

I walked out onto the patio where he used to work during the hot evenings and sat in his light blue metal lawn chair, updating my diary.

But to return to John Paul II's life at the Vatican, after his work and meditation in the private chapel, the Pope comes to his study to work and receive visitors from the curia—the administration—and hold private audiences.

In this room, he uses the same table that was used by Popes John XXIII, Pope Paul VI, and Pope John Paul I. His personal secretary, Stanley Dziwisz, prepares his official papers for inspection and signing. The Pope writes in Polish, and then it is translated into other languages—but he prefers that the originals be in Polish.

Among the persons waiting for private conferences at 11 A.M. are bishops, ambassadors, and special guests. The Pope has translators but manages to do without them, since he himself can speak twelve languages.

The audiences last until 2:45 P.M., except on Wednesdays. Wednesdays are special, because John Paul II has set this day aside for public audiences, which are usually held in St. Peter's Square. These have become a sensational success and have captivated Rome.

After lunch, he takes a nap, resting and sleeping for about an hour. After he gets up, the Pope goes to the chapel to pray and do some reading. Then he takes another jog in the Vatican gardens.

He also rides a bicycle—a ten-speed French model that he got as a gift at one of his audiences. He also plays tennis with his secretary, "Stasiu," as His Holiness likes to call him in Polish, and some of his other Polish friends. The Pope maintains that sports and exercise are essential to his health. He also has a swimming pool at his summer residence at Castel Gandolfo.

At 4 P.M., the Pope completes his sporting activities, has a cup of espresso coffee, and returns to his desk for more paperwork. He dictates some letters, studies documents, makes decisions, and at this time he also makes and takes telephone calls.

In the old days, under previous Popes, the afternoons were free during the summer months. Those who wanted to work did. This Pope has changed all this because of his strong feelings about not wasting time when there is so much to be done.

Also under previous Popes, all matters were dealt with by the Vatican Secretary of State "in the name of the Pope." John Paul II is much more involved and sees the people himself if the need is there, so the middleman has been minimized.

At 7 P.M., the Pope's official day comes to a close and then he begins to live like a Pole again. On a typical night, he has dinner with only his Polish guests and with friends and associates who came from Poland to work with him in Rome.

These moments are very private. No photos, no interviews. It is strictly a private affair. At this moment, the Pope is at ease and can relax.

No one can be more loyal to those who knew him on his way up. On one occasion, the Pope gave a dinner in honor of one of the new cardinals that he had named—his successor in Krakow, Franciszek Macharski. Even with sixty guests, the Pope noticed that an old friend Father Marian was not in attendance.

The Pontiff asked his secretary where Father Marian was, saying, "I saw him in the Sistine Chapel."

Stanislaw replied, "I do not know."

The next day found Stanley searching for Father Marian and finding him in the Vatican Museum.

"The Holy Father has been looking for you," he said. "He wants to know why you were not at dinner yesterday."

The old friend replied, "I was not invited."

And so it came about that the uninvited guest became the private dinner guest of the Pope that very evening. This is how he feels about his old friends.

I was happy to be guest at one of those private dinners at which only Polish was spoken. Of course, everyone defers to the illustrious host, but the conversation is natural and centers on current events, some happy, some sad.

One of the Pope's early dreams, I learned, had come to pass. I had missed the performance, but everyone was still talking about John Paul II's play, *The Goldsmith's Shop*, which had been presented first on Italian radio and then, as an encore, in the Vatican's Consistorial Hall on February 19, 1980.

He had written it when he had planned to be an actor, and it was a part of the repertory company of Krakow called the Rhapsodic Theater.

"So you see, my artistic future is assured," joked the Pope. But he was elated that he had finally seen performed the only play he had ever written.

"This work was never performed in Poland," he said, "and I never dreamed that one day I would see it performed in another country. I am moved, I must confess."

The play, incidentally, shows how the lives of three couples are interwoven. One act concerns a happy engagement and marriage; one deals with the tragedy of a bad marriage; and the third act shows what happens when the children of the two couples meet and marry.

A sad happening still troubling him was the crash of a Polish Airlines jet as it approached Okecie Airport in Warsaw earlier that month, on March 14. It had nosedived into a nine-teenth-century fortress, killing everyone aboard—eighty-seven people, including a twenty-two-member amateur boxing team scheduled to compete against the Polish national team.

The Pope sent a cable of condolence to Polish Cardinal and Primate Wysyznski from the Vatican, saying:

> I BEG GOD TO GIVE ETERNAL PEACE TO THOSE WHO
> DIED A TRAGIC DEATH AND CONSOLE THE FAMILIES
> STRICKEN WITH PAIN.

An 11 P.M. bedtime is early for the Pope. He often stays up until 1 A.M. if there is something special going on, or if he becomes absorbed in what he is reading. Before going to bed, he completes reading the Liturgy of the Hours from his breviary, praying and meditating.

What might keep him up late? I heard about one summer evening in 1979, when Pope John Paul II greeted several hundred youth from Poland who had made a pilgrimage to Rome. To their amazement, he invited them all to his private Vatican gardens. There, he said an evening mass in the Lourdes Grotto and then went on to build and light a bonfire and join them in singing and playing the guitar until past midnight.

How does he feel about living in the Vatican? John Paul II told some friends from Poland, "It's frightening to say that this is my home. There are many places that I have not yet seen because there is so much of it here. It is more difficult here than in Krakow, where everyone knows his corner."

About those two white telephones in the Pontiff's study, I could give you his telephone numbers, but it would do you no good. In order to get through, one must first dial 6982. The Vatican operator will answer, asking who is calling and from what telephone number.

This information is checked out, and if the call is felt to be important enough, the operator will call back and the Pope will be connected with the caller.

With a Catholic population in the world of something over half a billion persons, one can imagine how many phone

calls are received in the course of a day. Most calls are handled by Vatican staffers who speak many languages.

Now and then, the Pontiff does initiate his own calls.
I don't know who initiated it, but one evening before my trip
to Rome I received a call first from an aide to the Pope, who
spoke to me a bit and then asked me to hang on.

In another moment, it was my friend's voice on the
other end—John Paul II cheerfully booming at me, giving me
a few messages for people in Washington and saying he
would be seeing me soon in Rome.

The world has not seen such humility in a Pope or
such an effort to keep abreast of the thinking and the problems of the multitudes. I was surprised, but not too surprised,
to learn that the Pope had secreted himself behind the confessional, taking the place of an ordinary parish priest, to hear
the confessions.

By strange coincidence, I was part of this historic
event. I had gone to confession that day at St. Peter's, where
confessions are heard in several languages during the day.
Since English was not available at that moment, I went to the
Polish confession box to be heard by a Polish priest.

I could not understand what was happening. My
father confessor said things that had such great depth that a
sort of chill went through me. I had a strange mystical feeling,
as if he had known me for a long time. I did not recognize his
voice.

Eventually, I left the confessional booth in a trance.
And it was not until later that I learned that my priest had
been none other than John Paul II. He had come in the back
way, incognito, wearing a black coat.

Later, a Vatican curia friend gave me a picture he had
snapped of the Pope with his hand on the door and his head
down, leaving the confessional.

Nor was I surprised while I was in Rome and at the
Vatican over the 1980 Easter holiday to witness the humility
of Christ's vicar on earth as he washed and kissed the feet of
twelve destitute old men.

They had been found living in the home for the home-less founded by Mother Teresa of Calcutta. These were truly the poorest of the poor whom John Paul had sought. They had been brought from the Roman shelter to the Basilica of St. John Lateran, where the Pope awaited them.

Not only did he perform the same act as Christ had on the night before he died, but John Paul proceeded to join in the singing of the choir—a most un-Pope-like action.

There was much that was history-making at Pope John Paul II's outdoor Easter mass at St. Peter's Square—and I was thrilled to be there. My emotions were heightened also by the Sistine Chapel choir and sight of Michelangelo's dome.

A new portable altar was used for the first time. The massive bronze altar was sculpted by the American artist, Albert Friscia, and it is the first work of art by an American to find a place at St. Peter's.

It was used for the Easter morning outdoor service in St. Peter's Square. Now, when it is not in use, it sits in a place of honor, properly labeled for all tourists to see, under the throne of St. Peter in the Basilica.

On Sundays at noon, the Pope appears in the window of his apartment. I was there to witness his appearance. It was most dramatic to see him suddenly step before the open window, raise his hands, speak a few words, and bless the people below.

But the Pope was also making other unexpected appearances. Sometimes students would gather under his windows and serenade him to the tune of guitar music. I would often walk through St. Peter's Square in the evenings, and sometimes I would sit there for an hour or so observing the throngs of people.

During my sixteen-day stay, I saw the Pope unexpectedly come out to greet the students on five occasions, speaking to them in several languages. One time, I was part of that group.

The way it happened was that I got to talking with a priest who was chaperoning a Polish group of nuns and female students from Krakow and the Pope's birthplace of Wadowice. After we had chatted for a while, the priest said,

"Girls, you have such beautiful voices—why don't you sing for the Pope?"

For a moment, the girls hesitated shyly. Then they started to sing in Polish, and it was a moving moment as their truly angelic voices rose. In a very short time, the Pope opened his shutters and looked down at them.

"My beloved sisters in Christ," he said, "I could not help hearing those beautiful voices that have come so many miles from my beloved homeland. I rejoice with you and I shall be seeing you all in a few minutes."

Wednesday is the day everyone waits for with bated breath.

On that day, the Pope comes riding out in a white jeep, circling around the area and shaking hands. During my visit, I, too, participated to see what the excitement was all about.

Since I was treated like a VIP guest by my friends in the Polish clergy, I was given a special seat. When the Pope finished driving around in his little jeep, he came to where I was sitting, got out, and I was the first person that he greeted.

I was in the select company of some of his fellow professors from the old days at the Catholic University of Lublin. The Pope looked around at them and jokingly said to me, "When did you become a faculty member of Lublin University?"

I replied, "This morning, Your Holiness."

He smiled and said, "It is once again a great pleasure to see you." Then he chatted a bit, went to talk to other groups, and returned to talk to us at greater length.

On the Wednesday that I attended one of John Paul II's history-making outdoor public audiences in St. Peter's Square, I was amazed at the gifts both large and small that loving pilgrims brought for him.

I observed hands reaching out with flowers, bottles of wine, religious books, candy, needlecraft, and sacred vessels such as chalices for the Pope to use. I was told that the week before someone had bestowed a cage of doves and a puppy upon the Pope.

John Paul II, with his humanness, does not disappoint the giver. I watched how he accepted each gift with warmth and graciousness and then gave it to one of his aides to carry to an outdoor table, where the gifts are put on display.

In this way, not only does his flock have the joy of actually handing the gift to him, but they have the pleasure of seeing other people examining their gift amid a great display of treasures.

People who have never planned to go to Rome now find themselves drawn to the Eternal City to see the charismatic Pope and bring him gifts with special meaning, as did the three wise men following a distant star. They went to Bethlehem; these go to Rome.

I recall the talk I heard of one such man who had come from the United States. He had never been out of this country, but after Karol Wojtyla became Pope this man had found a piece of wood and had instantly known that he must carve it into a hiking staff and bring it to the Pope.

And so Les Johnson of Akron, Ohio, who was a volunteer Boy Scout leader, carved the staff with scouting symbols and showed up at one of the Wednesday outdoor audiences in St. Peter's Square.

His eyes glistened as Pope John Paul II tenderly took the staff from him and tested it out on the pavement of the square, pronouncing it very good.

"Solid," said the Pope. "Very solid." The Scout leader told him a bit about the Boy Scout movement in the United States, and the Pope blessed Johnson and American scouting.

Once it was a circus that received his blessing, after clowns had cavorted and jugglers had juggled and a female contortionist had demonstrated how she could balance a glass of wine on her forehead while smoking a cigarette held between her toes.

Again showing his great warmth, the Pope said, "May you always serve the Lord in joy and transmit to all those who see or assist in your incomparable spectacles, the traditional religious and moral values of circus people, the simple and strong faith in God, the tenacious attachment to the family, the tender love of children, the active solidarity, especially in moments of suffering and need."

The crowd murmured in awe that this was indeed a new era in which a Pope took time for a circus troupe. Some repeated the words that John Paul II had spoken: "The presence of each and every one of you is very dear to me." It was the kind of tenderness that brought tears to many eyes.

While in Rome, I lived in a religious community house during my sixteen-day stay. As a matter of fact, my window looked out on the Dome of Michelangelo and the Pope's apartment. My quarters were located in the Padri Trinitari, meaning the Trinity Fathers, a religious order connected with the Vatican.

At night, I could see when the lights went out in the Pontiff's bedroom—about midnight—and I stayed awake another hour or so writing up my experiences and interviews of the day which helped me understand how the Pope lives and how life has changed for him since Krakow.

Though I was a guest of my Polish clergy friends, I insisted on paying my own way, contributing to the Trinity Fathers. My clergy friends told me about a new project of the Pope's aimed at solving the problem of expensive housing for tourists coming to Rome from Poland and other Eastern European countries.

Actually, two goals will be fulfilled in a building complex—a center of Polish culture and a hostel to be named the John Paul II Home in Rome.

The name may seem a bit unusual to foreign ears, but the Polish clergy connected with the Vatican want to be sure that pilgrims coming to the Eternal City from the Eastern European bloc will be able to find the hostel no matter how confusing they find the hustle and bustle of Rome.

The Pope said, "I fasten great hope on these undertakings, and although I am doing this rather discreetly, nonetheless, I carry this matter close to my heart."

Any reader interested in finding out about this project can get in touch with the priest who has been designated by the Pope to head the heart-warming venture:

Reverend Dr. Kazimierz Przydatek, SJ
Secretary General of the Spiritual Center for John Paul II
Office of Corda Cordi
Piazza Pio XII, 3
00 193—Rome, ITALY

Or inquiries can be addressed to Bishop Sczepan Wesoly, who speaks English very well and heads the Office of Corda Cordi. The same address would apply. (The name means "Heart to Hearts.")

In the course of my visit, I had collected a large number of gifts and mementos to take back to the United States. Every friend and relative was waiting eagerly for something that had been blessed by the Pope. I brought them all to John Paul II at one time. He looked at my collection and just laughed.

"What do we have here," he demanded, "the Vatican treasures?"

I answered, "Only part of them, Your Holiness." Again he laughed.

In a more serious vein, the Pontiff was very complimentary of the reception he had received on his trip to the United States. He praised the President and the American people for being so warm and welcoming.

I saw the Pope the final time on April 9, 1980. It was a very emotional farewell on both sides. He embraced me so hard that I thought my glasses would break, which added a bit of humor and which kept me from breaking up in tears altogether.

His last words were, "Keep up the work, give my best to your family and my friends in America. I am sure we will see each other again."

I wanted to say, "God bless you." But I caught myself just in time, realizing that he was closer to God than I and it was beyond my meager power to bestow anything additional. I thought, as I left, that perhaps my greatest gift to him was to write a book about him that would be so clear and open that when the reader closed the book, he too would know him as a friend.

This is my gift to him.

Index

225